THE

EVERYTHING®

BUSINESS PLANNING BOOK

How to plan for success
in a new or growing business

Marlene Jensen

Adams Media Corporation
Avon, Massachusetts

This book is dedicated to Sylvia Burch and Ben Fann,
who both gave me the most precious gift you can
give a child: the rock-solid belief that there is *nothing*
I can't do if I try hard enough.
Thanks, mom and dad!

An Everything® Series Book.
Everything® is a registered trademark of Adams Media Corporation.

Published by Adams Media Corporation
57 Littlefield Street, Avon, MA 02322. U.S.A.
www.adamsmedia.com

ISBN: 1-58062-491-X
Printed in the United States of America.

J I H G F E D C B

Library of Congress Cataloging-in-Publication Data
Jensen, Marlene.
The everything business planning book / Marlene Jensen.
p.   cm.
ISBN 1-58062-491-X
1. New business enterprises—Planning. 2. New business enterprises—Management.
3. New business enterprises—Finance. 4. Marketing. I. Title.
HD62.5 .J46 2001
658.4'012—dc21   00-067651

Many of the designations used by manufacturers and sellers to distinguish their products are claimed as trade-marks. Where those designations appear in this book and Adams Media was aware of a trademark claim, the designations have been printed in initial capital letters.

This publication is designed to provide accurate and authoritative information with regard to the subject matter covered. It is sold with the understanding that the publisher is not engaged in rendering legal, accounting, or other professional advice. If legal advice or other expert assistance is required, the services of a competent professional person should be sought.

—From a *Declaration of Principles* jointly adopted by a Committee of the
American Bar Association and a Committee of Publishers and Associations

Illustrations by Barry Littmann and Kathie Kelleher.

This book is available at quantity discounts for bulk purchases.
For information, call 1-800-872-5627.

Visit the entire Everything® series at everything.com

Contents

Chapter Eight

Buying Advertising / 169

Chapter Nine

Choosing the Form for Your Business / 181

Chapter Ten

Hiring and Motivating Employees / 189

Chapter Eleven

Secrets of Financial Success / 211

Chapter Twelve

Moving Forward: Strategy and Tactics / 233

PART I

The Ins and Outs of a New Business

CHAPTER ONE

Using What You Have to Get What You Want

A Personal Inventory

Should you become an entrepreneur? Is this the right time in your life to take the risk?

It depends.

Some advisors ask you whether you're organized, decisive, street-smart, a "Type A" personality, etc. I don't believe in these analyses because I've seen too many successful entrepreneurs who don't fit the formulas you find in bestsellers or in self-help books, so I don't want to discourage someone who may not be, say, aggressive or out-wardly confident. Other qualities can work just as well for success, qualities like inner toughness and a belief that there's always a way around any obstacle.

I don't believe there is an "entrepreneur gene" that you either have or don't have. I think almost anyone who is properly *motivated* can be an entrepreneur. The question is, are you motivated enough?

That said, I'll grant you that there are some people who almost *have to be* entrepreneurs—usually because no company they didn't run themselves would put up with them! Many of these people become very successful entrepreneurs.

If you know you're motivated, you'll probably skip this chapter and move right on to the next, on what business to start. You'll find I'm not much for touchy-feely approaches. What you'll find here are checklists, guidelines, and advice that are extremely practical.

For example, if you already have a business idea, ask yourself if you can start it part-time, while you keep your current job. Can you do this? Then I recommend you investigate that business by reading the rest of this book and, if it still looks good to you, go ahead and try it. Don't worry about whether you have the "personality" for it. There's nothing that will show you better whether you should be an entrepreneur than trying to be one.

However, if you can't start a company from the safety of a job, it may be smarter to consider how likely it is that you'll be happy as an entrepreneur. You'll need to take a personal inventory, so read on!

Your Goals

What you want out of life will strongly affect your success as an entrepreneur. Think about the list of goals below. Please note that this list is not meant to cover all potential goals you could have—just those than can affect your success as an entrepreneur. Other goals, such as helping others and religious goals, can be successfully integrated into your own business or ignored—depending on their importance to you. For example, a strong desire to help others has led to some highly successful companies that design or create products that help people.

- **Money:** What do you want primarily want from money—protection or pleasure? Are you thinking about safety nets, protection in case you or your spouse loses a job? Protection in your old age in case Social Security isn't there? Or are you thinking about pleasure—a vacation in Europe? A new house? New car?
- **Time:** How important to you is your time? Are you willing to trade more time working for more money? Or do you already feel like you're working so much your life is slipping away? Do you frequently feel bored? As if you have either too much time or too much work of too little interest to fill it with?
- **Prestige:** How important is it to you to be perceived as a "success"? Somewhere deep inside is there a burning desire to show someone you're much better than they thought? Don't be embarrassed by this feeling if you have it. Many successful entrepreneurs used a desire to "show them" as their motivation.
- **Bosses:** Think about the last four bosses you've had. Do you think you could have done their job better than they did? How many of them did you have strong words with? Do you hate the very idea of someone thinking they're your boss?
- **Independence:** How independent are you? How independent would your family say you are? How independent do you want to be?

Now rank these goals on the Goals Assessment worksheet on the following page.

Your Willingness to Take Risks

While much of this book is devoted to helping you reduce the risks involved in starting your own business, it can't eliminate them.

Risks can be small or large. You can risk your vacation trip to Florida this year, or you can risk your house.

Goals Assessment

Look at the goals listed below. Think of any goals you have that are not listed here, and add them at the bottom of the list. Rank the goals in order of their importance to you.

Rank Your Goals

Goals	Goal rank
More money (for security)	
More money (for pleasure)	
More time off work	
Recognition	
Preventing boredom	
Excitement	
No boss	
Control of my own life	
Reducing stress in my life	
Other:	

There are also smart risks and stupid risks. In subsequent chapters we'll help you identify which kind you're facing.

Often, sometime in the early stages of running a business, there comes a crisis point: a serious risk. If you take the risk, you will be in big financial trouble if you fail. On the other hand, if you don't take the risk, your business may fail anyway.

You can prepare for such a decision point—but only by making sure you are as knowledgeable as possible about your business. Only your intimate knowledge can guide you at a time like this.

The Financial Picture

Starting a new business takes money. Even if it's only for printing business cards or promotional flyers. Usually a start-up takes money to launch as well as money to support you for the first several months. The worksheets in this chapter will help you to assess your current financial situation. In future chapters, you'll figure out how much money your business will need and how long it will take to start paying you a salary. You may, after seeing all the numbers in black and white, decide on a longer term plan for launching your business, giving you time to save some needed cash. Or you may find you already have the financing you need and move ahead with your launch plans.

Supporting Yourself During Start-Up

If you have plenty of money in the bank to cover your start-up costs and pay for your living expenses, or have a spouse who is earning more than enough to cover all your costs and living expenses as you launch your business, you can skip to the next chapter. If you're not in this fortunate situation, you'll need to complete the "Living Expenses" worksheet. It will help you assess your current income and living expenses, as well as tell you what you'll be facing after you've made cutbacks and changes in order to start your new business.

Money Sources

There are five sources of capital for your new business: your spouse, your savings, loans, investors, or vendors.

- **Spouse:** If you can't keep your job while launching the business, can you both live off what your spouse makes? Is your spouse willing to do this? Make sure you discuss it in enough detail to be sure your mate is really buying into this plan. A spouse who feels trapped into making such a decision can grow resentful. You don't want to be knee deep in launching a new business only to be hit with divorce papers or a separation.
- **Savings:** The financial statements you'll learn how to prepare in later chapters will indicate how long it will take for your business to reach break-even and thus how much you'll need to take from your savings to tide you over.
- **Loans:** Just remember that debt repayment on loans adds to your living and business expenses.
- **Investors:** Future chapters will discuss how to present your business in a way most likely to attract investment. Keep in mind that very few investors will invest in start-ups that aren't already past the testing stages. This wasn't the case at first for the dot-com companies, but the NASDAQ stock tumble reminded most venture capitalists of the risks in first-stage money.

  If you can interest an investor, they'll want to see a high degree of commitment from you. They'll judge your commitment by how much you have to lose if the business fails. Don't expect them to cover your country club memberships, your leased Mercedes, or your continuing vacations in the Caribbean. They'll want to see that a failure would be financially devastating for you. They'll want you living on so little that you'll be desperate to earn more by succeeding (but not so little that you lay awake nights worrying about a car payment). So if you were thinking about bringing in an investor only so your lifestyle didn't have to suffer while launching a

What Do Your Rankings Tell You?

1. If you're strong on control and want to be your own boss, you should be highly motivated as an entrepreneur.

2. If you're seeking more time for family, friends, or for personal fulfillment, ask yourself if you'll have enough time to succeed.

3. If you're seeking more money for security, entrepreneurship is a risky road to take. Never forget that most entrepreneurs have failed—at least once.

business, forget it. Any investor will *want* your lifestyle to suffer. And, they take equity (see page 11) and become de facto bosses.

- **Vendors:** While you can't normally raise a lot of money from the vendors that will service your business, you can sometimes get them to "invest" in your company by providing their services at reduced costs. If a printer's four-color machine is too idle, they might be willing to invest in your company by running your brochures for the price of the ink and a small profit—as long as they can print them whenever they have downtime.

In the "Financial Resources for Starting a Business" worksheet (page 12), fill in the amounts of the first two items—Money and Debt. Later on, once you determine how much cash you need to launch the business, you can fill in the credit item and the items you might not have thought about as resources: Barter and Services. Use of these can cut your cash needs dramatically.

> **Example:** You're setting up a tax preparation business. Everyone needs those services. You may find you can barter your services for needed equipment like computers, phones, and printing.
> **Example:** You're starting a restaurant. You may be able to barter lunches and dinners for services you need, such as cleaning services, printing, utensils, or deliveries.
> **Example:** A woman wants to launch a new magazine, but needs $1 million for it and can't find it. She gets a large publishing company to agree to provide $500,000 in *services* (which only requires time from the company's current employees, not cash) in return for a first option on buying the magazine in five years. Then, with that well-known publishing company as an "investor," she is able to interest other *cash* investors.

Risking Everything

An entrepreneur I know started a magazine, which was limping along for over a year. It was just barely breaking even—ad sales and subscriptions were just barely covering the costs of doing business.

The publishing entrepreneur did his numbers and decided that a direct mail campaign to attract subscribers would not only earn back what the campaign cost, but would also give him sufficient circulation size to make the magazine reliably profitable. So he went to a bank and tried to get them to advance him the money for 90 days. (Just long enough to get the paid subscriptions in.) The bank refused the loan. (Most banks have a hard time understanding paid-subscription publications from a financial viewpoint.)

Decision time: The entrepreneur reconsidered and found himself still very sure of his numbers. He went back to the bank and told them his printer wanted a Letter of Credit. The bank reviewed his finances and saw that he had always paid his print bills on time—so they provided it.

The entrepreneur immediately took the funds he would have used to pay his current print bill and instead applied them to the subscription campaign. When the printer didn't get paid, he didn't cut off the magazine because he had the Letter of Credit from the bank. Within 90 days, the cash received from the subscription campaign more than paid everyone back.

The entrepreneur's magazine became a financial success, and he used that success to launch another—even bigger—magazine. If he had been wrong, he could have ended up bankrupt.

By the way, don't think this example is implying you have to *like* risk. People who *really like* risk often make things riskier than they need be—for the excitement. Those are stupid risks. The best attitude toward risk is to recognize when you are willing to take one and do everything possible to minimize it.

Current and Projected Living Expenses

Look at your finances the way they are—and the way they could be. Your "revised situation" could reflect you quitting your job or you cutting back to part-time, or it could reflect no changes in income but a cutback on unessential expenses.

Remember, if you're budgeting big cutbacks, you'll have to be able to survive on the "revised" amount for at least six months.

If you have to quit your job to start your business, you may well find your Revised Situation is a loss, for example, a loss of $1,000 a month. You could still launch your new company if you have $6,000 extra cash in the bank to cover the six months of $1,000 losses. However, will you need that cash in the bank to pay for other business launch expenses?

Current Situation

Monthly	Myself	Spouse	Total	Revised Situation
Take-home pay				
Other income				
Total income				
Housing costs				
Food costs				
Insurance				
Utilities				
Telephone/Internet access				
Cable TV				
Automobile expenses				
Medical expenses				
Clothing				
Furniture/appliances				
Personal products				
Entertainment				
Eating out				
Other expenses (list)				
Total expenses				
Income after expenses				

Definition: Equity

Equity is the value of something beyond the debt connected with it. Thus your equity in your home is how much you could sell it for—say, $200,000—less the amount you owe on it—say, $175,000. In this case you have $25,000 in equity on your home.

If you launch a business by yourself, then you own 100% of the equity in that business. What is that 100% worth? Whatever you could sell the business for, minus any debts it has.

When your business needs more money, there are two ways you can get it:

1. **Loans.** If you take out a loan, you still own 100% of the equity in your business. You also have to pay back the loan.
2. **Investors:** If you have an investor, they will take part of the equity. They may want 10% of your business, which would leave you with 90%. If the business fails,

you don't have to pay them back. But if the business succeeds, they get 10% of the profits and sale price.

Investors in a brand-new business often demand 40%–80% of the equity for their investment. *If* you can find investors—because finding the first one is the hardest. Once the business is up and running, later investors typically get much less equity for their investments.

If you scored high on a need for control and to be your own boss in your Goal Assessments, do everything you can to avoid needing investors. Anyone who owns equity in your company is a partner, even if they're a minority partner (less than 50%). Partners can decide they don't like what you're doing and can even sue you to take control, claiming you're harming the company (and thus their investment).

Financial Resources for Starting a Business

	$ Amount Total
Money	
Cash in the bank	
Stocks you could sell	
Debt	
Loans from family	
Personal loans from bank	
Loans for equipment	
Loans for inventory	
Small business loans	
Credit	
30–90 day terms from major suppliers	
Letter of credit	
Unused personal credit lines	
Barter	
Value of needed services you can barter	
Services*	
Value of needed services donated	
Value of needed services traded for buyout option	
Total	

*Sometimes you can get noncompeting, larger companies to provide services you would otherwise have to pay cash for in return for a first option to buy you out, should you decide to sell.

Look at What You Know

The best businesses to start—the businesses that have the greatest chance of success—are businesses you've uncovered as part of your work experience.

Why are these businesses more likely to succeed? Because you're starting with an idea for which a need has already been demonstrated.

Say you're working in the marketing department of a large corporation. You see all the freelancers being hired by the company: graphic designers, copywriters, production managers, etc. You'll know, as part of your work experience, whether or not it is hard to get good people in any of those fields. If it's hard—you've found a potential business.

Or, say you're working in construction and you see people with particular skills—in restoration of old houses or remodeling for seniors or the handicapped—being hired for specific jobs. Ask around. Find out if there are a glut of such workers or a shortage. If there's a shortage, you've got a potential business.

Or, say you're an engineer working on a particular type of product. You see how such a product could be modified to make it even better. You tell your company, but they're not interested. It wouldn't help them that much, although it would help other companies. Bingo! A hot new business idea.

Say you're working in any kind of small office, and the boss complains about how hard it is to find a competent, reliable cleaning service. Talk to your boss. If this is a problem for other small companies as well, it represents a promising business opportunity.

The opportunities are virtually endless. Look around the place you work. What kinds of jobs are being done by nonemployees? What kinds of jobs *could* be done by nonemployees that you could supply?

What kinds of work do people in your industry *hate* to do? Wouldn't they jump at a chance to farm it out to someone else?

What kinds of specialists are in tight demand?

Examples of Success

- A smart manicurist, working in a beauty salon, got the idea of starting her own "Nail" salon.
- A smart bookkeeper, working for a local attorney, saw a specialized need and set up a "Bookkeeping for Attorneys" service.
- A smart massage therapist set up a chain of "15-Minute Back Massage" salons.
- A smart former CFO (Chief Financial Officer) set herself up as a "CFO Temp," filling in for CFOs who are on vacation or sick, and filling in where there's a long search to find a new permanent CFO to replace one who departed.

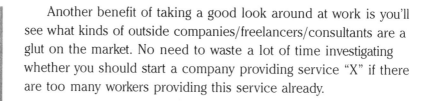

Another benefit of taking a good look around at work is you'll see what kinds of outside companies/freelancers/consultants are a glut on the market. No need to waste a lot of time investigating whether you should start a company providing service "X" if there are too many workers providing this service already.

Clarifying Your Interests and Skills

Being clear about what your interests and skills are provides invaluable information in pointing you toward potential new businesses. To help you clarify your interests, let your imagination run wild as you fill out the Interests worksheet. Don't limit yourself. Put down anything that really interests you, regardless of whether you think there's a business that could come from it. The questions are designed to pull out what is *really important* to you rather than just a mild interest.

Sometimes looking at what you fear most gives you a way to tap into a strong interest. Maybe it's a fear of becoming homeless. Maybe it's violence against women. Whatever, there may be businesses that could help protect others from what you fear. Maybe a financial counseling service. Maybe a martial arts studio. Maybe . . . well, you see how it works.

How do your skills compare to your interests? Don't be discouraged if your skills are not quite where they need to be for people to pay you for them. Sometimes what comes from evaluating your skills is a recognition of the need to polish up a skill before launching a business. Occasionally this will mean you need to complete a degree, or a certification program. But usually it means you need to work in the field—or work a little longer in it.

Pros and Cons of Following Your Interests

After you've completed the Interests and Skills worksheets, you'll probably have some ideas for potential businesses you can start. Of course, you don't know yet whether these businesses are likely to succeed. That's what you'll be exploring in the rest of the book.

But before you finalize your ideas of what businesses to investigate, take another 10 minutes to think of some possibilities you may have missed. Looking at your interests in order to find ideas yields both advantages and disadvantages.

The advantages are many. If it's a strong interest of yours already:

- You'll be eager to learn more, including acquiring any needed credentials.
- You'll be willing to work longer hours on it.
- You're more likely to dream about it, thus more likely to come up with original new ideas for it.

However, there are also a couple of real disadvantages to basing your business ideas on your interests.

- You're less likely to make big money at it. For all our diversity and special interests, people have remarkably uniform interests.

  Example: Picking anything about crafts and decorating guarantees you'll be competing against an army of others all trying to do the same thing.

  Example: Tens of thousands of people, maybe hundreds of thousands, want to write books. First novels (other than the one-in-a-million you read about that hits the jackpot) pay $5,000 to $15,000 advance on royalties. If you figure out how much that is an hour, you'll want to cry.

- You're less likely to think of "unpleasant" work. One of the biggest routes to success is to pick something nobody else wants to do and get paid handsomely for it.

  Example: Nobody likes to think about cleaning. Because of that, there can be some big opportunities in this area. One attorney in Tennessee noted that his office's cleaning service was slipshod. He talked to the office manager, who told him it was hard to find reliable help. So he started his own cleaning service, specializing (at first) in law offices.

Credentials Needed

A nephew of mine already knows at age 16 what he wants to do with his life: He wants to have his own martial arts studio. What kind of credentials will that require? A mixture of recognition credentials—(a black belt is essential and some competition trophies would be good as well)—and knowledge credentials—experience teaching in someone else's dojo and learning about small company finance. How does he get the finance expertise? By taking finance and accounting classes in school and by talking to every small business owner who will talk to him. Also, he needs to talk to dojo owners outside his local area, as local ones may not help.

Interests Assessment

Interests can help identify potential businesses to start. Here are some questions to start your creative juices flowing:

- What do you read the most about?
- What do you like to do most in your free time?
- What makes you the angriest?
- What are you most afraid of?
- If you ruled the world, what would you change?
- If you only had two—healthy—years to live, what would you do (besides spend time with your family)?
- When you were a child, what did you want to be when you grew up?

Work only in the first column. Think about your answers to the above questions, and write down in the first column only the things that interest you. Examples: cars, cats, junk bonds, politics, cooking, teaching, soccer, babies, boats, etc.

Now, for each interest, rank it in the columns on a scale of 1 to 5, where 1 is very low and 5 is very high.

Interest	How interested are you?	How knowledgeable are you already?	How much time would it take to become expert?	How likely are people to pay for it?	How likely is it that people will pay a lot?
1					
2					
3					
4					
5					
6					
7					
8					
9					
10					

Lawyers talk, soon the word spread, and he picked up a number of law offices as customers.

The best thing: He didn't have to quit his job. He just hired a good manager who ran the business for him, and he helped bring in new clients. Now he's still doing a job he loves (law), but his family's financial situation is remarkably improved.

So, think about adding to your new business idea list at least one idea that provides services other people don't want to do. It doesn't mean *you* will have to perform that service. You can hire others and manage them while *they* perform the service.

Deciding on a Type of Business

Let's look at your idea list of possible businesses and find out what type each is. The reason you have to determine the type is that some types require a lot more cash than others to launch.

Most businesses fall into one of three categories: manufacturing, service, or retailing.

Manufacturing Businesses

Manufacturing enterprises typically require the most cash, although some enable you to start smaller then grow. They also typically have fewer competitors than service businesses. They may also have the largest profit potential. After all, a mere 15 years after Microsoft was a baby start-up, not only is Bill Gates the richest man in the world, but all of his original employees are millionaires as well.

Don't think just nuts and bolts for manufacturing businesses. All the following are manufacturing businesses as well:

- Newsletters. If you launch one, you're a manufacturer.
- Cookies. Have you seen the "healthy" cookies in seemingly hand-wrapped packaging sold at health food stores? They look as if they just came from the

Definition: Subcontractor

A subcontractor is someone who does work for someone without being an employee.

Subcontractors may be more specialized than a contractor. For example, you contract with a builder to build a house. He subcontracts out plumbing work to a plumber, electrical work to an electrician, etc. You, the home buyer, never have to deal with all these subcontractors—you deal with the builder and he takes care of the rest.

Specialization is not necessary, however, to be a subcontractor. They could do exactly the same type of work as the contractor. So why would the contractor need them? Because the contractor has more work than he can handle.

Say you start the Great Muffins Company, making

(continued on next page)

oven of a nearby home kitchen. And they might have. Don't forget, Famous Amos cookies started locally and then grew.

- Clothing. Have you made a knit vest all your friends think is great? Hats? A whole clothing line?
- Fads. Think you've got the next pet rock or hula hoop?
- Greeting cards. You could just write for a commercial card company. But if you take the next step and produce your own, you're a manufacturer.

If you're looking at a manufacturing business, you're going to need more diverse skills than for any other kind of business. All three types of businesses must worry about advertising, hiring, and managing employees, but manufacturing businesses are usually more complicated in their needs in the following areas:

Sales: Although every business owner has to worry about sales, manufacturers also have to worry about *sales channels*. Do you sell to consumers? Do you instead (or also) sell to retailers? How about distributors? How are you going to get the product on the shelves?

Production: The product has to be manufactured. Even if you don't control that yourself, you still need to know (or learn) enough about the process to oversee the company that manufactures it for you.

Distribution channels: Trucks, UPS, the U.S. Post Office, boats, planes, trains, and more. In larger cities, some products are messengered to buyers.

Retail Businesses

Retail businesses are easier to understand at first, because everyone has shopped in retail stores. Retail can also require a fair amount of capital, depending on the type and amount of inventory you carry. For example, a bakery has lower inventory cash required than a computer store. Retail establishments are the only businesses that absolutely require you to spend money for the rental (or purchase) of the store itself. Most manufacturers also have a physical location, but you can start a food, craft, or apparel manufacturing business without a separate physical location. What you can't do in your home, you can get from *subcontractors* (see sidebar) in their homes.

Retail businesses require a broad range of skills, including strong people skills, and knowledge and skills in marketing, purchasing, inventory systems, and display. Many retailers underestimate what display changes can mean to their bottom line.

A high-rise condo building just outside New York City had a small grocery store on the premises. Most residents went there only if they had to or for a single item they'd forgotten to get at the stores where they did their *real* grocery shopping. Then a Korean family bought the grocery store and proceeded to change the display. They doubled the number of lights in the store, knowing that low lighting somehow is subconsciously equated with lower-quality (or older and stale) merchandise. By rearranging the layout of the store, they added a third more shelf space. They started carrying upscale impulse items, with top-name brands. The result was a store that produced five times the revenue of the former proprietor.

Service Businesses

Service businesses usually require the least amount of cash to start. Some require nothing more than printing up some business cards or flyers. Service is also the fastest growing business type in the country. What's the drawback? Exactly what the benefit is: Because they are so cheap to launch, lots of people do exactly that.

Take the consulting business. Sometimes it seems as though all executives who get fired or downsized start calling themselves consultants. At least until they land another job!

Definition: Subcontractor

(continued from previous page)

muffins for many of the local restaurants. At first, you can easily bake them all yourself. But as you start to grow, you're selling more than you can bake yourself. You can either buy another stove or subcontract out part of the baking to someone else.

Subcontractors are independent contractors, which means you do not pay them employee benefits. But it also means you cannot control the times and manner in which they work, except that you can insist upon their meeting quality standards and deadlines.

The trend is toward companies hiring fewer employees and more subcontractors—which means more opportunities for former employees to set up their own businesses.

Skills Assessment

Use this worksheet to access the skills you know you have and the skills that others say you have.

1. Enter the work skills you already have and wouldn't object to utilizing.
2. Break them down into skills, not job titles. For example, "writing," "public speaking," "analyzing numbers," "designing ads," "personal selling," "managing people," etc.
3. Now, list what other people have said you're good at. We usually know what others say, but sometimes don't pay enough attention to it.
4. Now, rank each skill on a scale of 1 to 5, where 1 is very low and 5 is very high.

Skills I know I have	How good are you at it?	How "credentialed" are you at it?	How long to become more credentialed (if you aren't already)?	How needed is this skill among employers?	What kind of pay does this skill command?
1					
2					
3					
4					
5					
6					
7					
8					
9					
10					

Skills that others say I have					
1					
2					
3					
4					
5					

CHAPTER TWO

Launching a New Business

Creating a Mission Statement

A *mission statement* is your compass for your business journey.

If you wanted to get to Los Angeles from New York, would you drive north? No, because you'd use a road map.

Trying to start a company without a mission statement is like driving without a road map, not knowing which direction you're headed. You might see some interesting sites, but the likelihood of ending up where you want to is very slim.

A mission statement is just a single sentence (although it may be a *long* sentence).

For Businesses that Sell to Businesses

For my *Ancillary Profits* newsletter, my mission statement was:

Helps publishers increase profits through spin-off businesses.

Given that mission statement, it was easy to discard article ideas that didn't meet all the criteria:

- "Helps publishers" means we didn't cover anything NOT for publishers.
- "increase profits" means we didn't cover ideas that wouldn't add profits.
- "through spin-off businesses" means we didn't cover how publishers could increase profits from ads or subscriptions, since those were already part of their *core* business, not a spin-off.

If your business company will sell primarily to businesses—a type of company known as a B2B—I recommend your mission statement at least start with this format:

Helps (your targets) *increase profits through* (how you help them).

"Increase profits" is the BENEFIT to the consumer, and your mission statement must include a benefit. This benefit is the *raison d'être*, the reason for being for your company. It's why anyone would bother to buy from you. It distinguishes you from other companies that may not offer that benefit, or may stress a different one.

Remember, profits can be increased in one of two ways:

1. More revenues
2. Lower costs (which includes saving employee time)

Let's say your business idea is an office cleaning service. Your mission statement might read: *Helps businesses save money and worry by providing a quality cleaning service with bonded employees.*

Suppose you're starting a software design service, planning to sell to companies like AltaVista and Yahoo! Your mission statement might read: *Helps Internet search engines increase profits through software that either a) attracts more Websurfers or b) handles searches quicker and better.*

If your company won't help your targets increase profits, think long and hard about why they'd have any interest. About the only thing other than profits that really attracts the interest of businesses is protection from regulators or lawsuits. For example, a company that trains managers to be sensitive to sexual harassment situations might have this mission statement: *Protects companies from sexual harassment lawsuits by training managers on how to avoid them.*

Too narrow for your company? Then you might update it to: *Protects companies from age discrimination and sexual harassment lawsuits by training managers on how to avoid them.*

For Businesses that Sell to Consumers

Mission statements directed to consumers are not as easy to write as those for a B2B, but they should never get away from proclaiming a BENEFIT to their customers.

The mission statement should focus on what your customers will get instead of what you will get. A self-interested mission statement— *To make as much money as possible*—is a *personal* goal. A *company* goal has to show *what the company will do for its customers* that will cause the customers to give them money.

Let's try some possible statements:

- Piano teaching business: *Help students learn piano as easily as possible.*

> ### Mission Statement on Display
>
> Once you have a mission statement, hang it on the wall where you and everyone else in the company can see it. It will keep you focused and save you from going off on tangents, however interesting they may be, that could destroy your company.

Why not just *"Help students learn piano"*? That might work. But if you include *"as easily as possible"* you now have something that differentiates you from other piano teachers. It's a BENEFIT to the purchaser of your service.

- Auto repair shops: Here are two different mission statements for two different types of auto repair shops:

  1. *Give car owners peace of mind by providing fast, reliable, hassle-free quality service.*
  2. *Give car owners low-cost but reliable service for their cars.*

- Dog newsletter: *Help dog owners better enjoy their dogs by 1) giving them heartwarming dog stories to enjoy, and 2) providing medical information so they can recognize dog health danger signs and act quickly.*
- Needlepoint yarn and designs retailer: *Increase customer satisfaction in needlepointing by providing attractive designs, quality materials, and a warm environment where this hobby is recognized and applauded.*
- Dog walking service: *Provide peace of mind for pet owners by looking after the needs of their pets.* This mission statement is broad enough so the business can also cover feeding and playing with pets, litter box duties for cats, cage cleanings for hamsters, etc.

Knowing Your Goals and Tactics

After you have your mission statement, you'll need to establish particular goals and tactics. However, it's better to create a business plan *before* working on your goals and tactics. Why? Because creating the business plan will make it clear what your goals need to be for the health of your company. Some of those goals will not resemble anything you might have thought up without the business plan.

Here are some examples of goals and tactics to give you an idea of what you'll want to end up with.

- **Goal:** Add two major new accounts within the next 12 months.
- **Tactics:**
  - ✔ Hire a sales rep to sell new accounts.
  - ✔ Provide new promotional materials to our distributors.

- **Goal:** Complete the new software program within 12 months.
- **Tactics:**
  - ✔ Hire freelance consultant to handle marketing, so I have more time to write software code.

- **Goal:** Add at least five accounting offices as clients to our cleaning services this year.
- **Tactics:**
  - ✔ Get written testimonials from our current clients.
  - ✔ Get accountant referrals from friends, family, and current clients.
  - ✔ Set up meetings with three accounting offices per month for next six months.

- **Goal:** Increase sales by 20%.
- **Tactics:**
  - ✔ Send out a monthly press release with info that will get us mentioned in the appropriate press.
  - ✔ Set up a store on our Web site that sells our products.
  - ✔ Start a monthly electronic newsletter that will drive repeat traffic to our site.
  - ✔ Invest $20,000 in advertising our services.

Definitions

- **Mission statement:** A short sentence that positions a company in terms of its customers, its services, and its benefits to its customers.

- **Goals**: Specific goals should take six months to two years to accomplish and be consistent with the company's mission.

- **Tactics**: Specific actions you will take in order to accomplish your goals.

Why You Need a Business Plan

Most businesses start without a business plan.

Most businesses fail.

Is this a coincidence? Probably not.

Yes, a business plan is a lot of work. For the most basic plan it will take you at least a few days; for more elaborate plans, a week or more—depending on how good a researcher and writer you are and how financially savvy.

My Mission Statement

Enter your mission statement here. Try out several versions until you have found the most concise way of expressing your target customer, your service, and the benefit you will deliver to your customer.

_____

_____

_____

_____

_____

_____

_____

_____

_____

So, why do you need a business plan? Two reasons:

1. A business plan will greatly improve your chances of success.
2. You *must* have a business plan if you need to borrow money from anyone.

Once your business is up and running, you will quickly be down in the trenches, fighting to stay alive and to win. Do you know the old adage, "You can't see the forest for the trees"? That will be you when you first start a business. The day-to-day details will consume you and you'll have no chance to see the big picture. Here's some of the questions you may never get the answers to until you start the business:

- Is your market, or your subniche of the market, growing or dying?
- Are your products what the market really wants? Or have your competitors already found more successful products and moved on to them?
- Are there enough potential customers to *ever* support you?
- Are your profit margins enough to ever create a *real profit— after* overhead?
- Is there some other product you could be providing that would be much more profitable for you?
- Is there some other way of covering any of your costs that could cut your expenses dramatically?

The biggest, best step you can take for the success of your business is to read and follow the advice in this chapter. Even if you have a simple home business, you'll be surprised by what the exercises in this chapter can teach you.

Most entrepreneurs, for instance, greatly underestimate what kind of profit margin they will need to succeed. They underprice—and sometimes fail—because they didn't run a simple cash flow statement.

Other entrepreneurs underestimate their competitive environment, not realizing that the particular business they want to start has almost no chance of success—*no matter how good they are or how hard they work.*

The Parts of a Plan

Here is a list of the components of a full-blown business plan—the kind you'll need to have if you want to attract money of any kind (from loans, investors, etc.) or top-caliber employees (who may not be willing to risk their future without seeing that you've got your act together):

Full-Blown Business Plan
- Executive summary
- Marketplace
- Competitive environment
- Product(s)
- Marketing plan
- Management team
- Financial statements
- Assumptions
- Cash flow
- P&L (Profit & Loss statement)
- Appendices

If you aren't looking for money, you can skip some of the components. In that case, you'll need just the following:

Basic Business Plan
- Marketplace
- Competitive environment
- Product(s)
- Marketing plan
- Financial assumptions
- Cash flow (monthly for two years, annual for another)

Now let's look at each of these components that make up a business plan.

Executive Summary

This one- or two-page summary of the business plan is always written last (but will appear first in the final project). It includes a paragraph from each of the sections and concludes with:

- The amount of money needed to launch the business.
- The potential return on investment.

If you are seeking money, this summary may be the only thing your potential investors really read—so it has to be clear, intelligent-sounding, intriguing, and compelling.

The Marketplace

This section of the plan comes before you write anything about the products you will be offering. Why? Because if your product is buggy whips and the automobile is becoming the vehicle of choice, it doesn't matter how good your buggy whips are or how economically they are produced. There are other—established—buggy whip companies that will be clawing each other's eyes out for a piece of the rapidly shrinking business. You don't stand a chance.

This market section should include some or all of the following.

Demographics

What are the demographics of your targeted customers? Women 18–49? Teenage boys? Adults over 60? Whatever your group is, there are government statistics available to tell you:

- How many of those people there are in the United States today
- How many there will be in five years, in 10 years, and in 15 years

You may say: What does it matter if my target group is going from 20 million to 18 million over the next six years? That's still *plenty* of people to sell to. And you're right, it is a lot of potential customers. But it does matter. It matters because it will affect your business.

Say that right now there are 20 companies selling products to the same market of teenage boys. Those companies all intend to be around six years from now and they want to be selling more product by then—to show growth. But they won't be able to. In fact, if everything stays the same, each of those companies will be selling 10% fewer products (because there will be 10% fewer people in that age group—20 million down to 18 million).

And now you want to enter that market. So if you get your share of sales, each of your competitors will be down more than 10%.

What's going to happen? What *won't* happen is everyone taking an equal cut. What will happen are things like:

- Price wars—which will hurt the profits you need to succeed.
- Big money invested in advertising by one or two of the companies to knock out some of the weaker companies.
- One company buying out or killing off the others and dictating market conditions (think Microsoft!).

Don't assume a shrinking demographic means you can't start a business for a group. It just means you're going to have to study the competitors even more than most companies and make sure you have a sustainable difference in your product that will help you succeed. We'll cover this in Chapter 4 on competition.

Geographics

Are your targets in just one geographic area? If you plan to launch a retail or local service business, there's a limited geographic area you'll be able to pull customers from.

For example, if you plan to start your own service as an electrician, you should find out how many people live within 20–30 miles of you. More important, how many homeowners are in that geographic radius? If you want to specialize, working only with businesses, how many office buildings are in your geographic range—and how many building owners do they represent? (Ten office buildings owned by one owner may represent just one potential client—assuming all repair work comes through him and not his local building managers.)

Find Good Sources

As you acquire information about your target market(s), pay special attention to information that comes from established, credible sources. You will want to quote these sources—an expert in the field, a newspaper or magazine article—directly. Maybe even include in the Appendix section a particularly good article from a quality source (but don't forget to obtain permission first) that makes the point of how good—or rapidly expanding—your market is.

If you're looking at a retail store in a particular shopping mall, how many people in your target age group come to that shopping mall each week, month, and year? How many of them stay in one of the "anchor" department stores and never even venture into the mall?

Trends and Psychographics

Your target customers may be growing, but what if the kind of product you want to sell is declining in popularity (think buggy whips, telex machines, tapes for answering machines, etc.)?

- **For product businesses**: You'll want to get some kind of trend information for what has happened to your type of product over the past decade. What were the sales 10 years ago? Five years ago? Last year? What does your industry group think the sales will be next year? In five years? In 10?

For some industries this information is easy to find. Check out any associations in your field and call them for information. If they don't track these figures, they may be able to tell you who does. Call the editors of trade magazines that deal with your market. If the numbers exist, they'll know who has them (and they've probably printed them in their magazine). If the magazine editors and association(s) in your market don't know the numbers and neither does your local librarian, the information may not be available.

Try to find information that is complementary. For example, you can't find out how many juicers are sold every year, but you can find numbers on increasing sales at health food stores, increasing vitamin sales, increasing herbal supplements, increasing "natural" products. All of these can make the case that juicer sales may also be increasing.

- **For service businesses:** In some industries, you will be able to get good trend numbers using the contacts outlined in the previous two paragraphs. For others, there will be nothing. Your worry is whether whoever normally buys your kind of service is finding other outlets for it. For instance, are individuals doing their own taxes now that there are cheap and easy software programs to help them?

Another thing to watch for is whether corporations are pulling your type of service back in-house. Have problems with outsourcing your service been mentioned in the business press? A retrenchment like that would be a bad trend.

There are various "trend gurus" who track psychological trends in the American public. Is there a "cocooning" trend, where people are staying home more? What does that mean for your proposed new restaurant? How about for a family-oriented cable station? You can find books by these gurus in your library. You need to know if one of their trends is in tune with your start-up—or working against it; your potential investors will know.

If your business fits in with the trend, you will find it easier (although seldom easy!) to get capital. If your business goes against a trend, you'll need to recognize that and deal with it through more research and/or an explanation of why it isn't pertinent in your case.

Check out books by Gerald Celente (*Trends 2000*) or by Faith Popcorn (yes, that's her real name) and, if your library has it, look at a few issues of the *Trendletter* newsletter.

Market Penetration

Once you have a pretty good idea of how many of your market targets exist and/or are likely to come to your specific location, you can calculate how many of them you could reasonably expect to get as customers.

The lower the percentage of a target market you need, the better. If you need to get 90% of all your potential customers to have a successful business—bail out now.

Niche-oriented (special interest) consumer magazines—like *Audio* or *Popular Photography*—generally look for 2%–4% market penetration. A $3,000/year electronic newsletter giving hourly price changes in crude oil may get 35%–40% penetration of those people whose job requires they have this information frequently.

If you were the only dry cleaner in a city of 15,000, and the nearest city with a dry cleaner was 60 miles away, you might get

Free Stats

You can find demographic information in your library or at the answer desk on the home page of *www.sba.gov*.

95% of the dry-cleaning business. But the dry-cleaning business will probably not be as robust as in other cities. Your "indirect competitors" in this case will be washing machines and clothes that look good without dry cleaning.

If you're opening a bagel shop, you'll need to know:

- How many people within a five- and 10-mile radius *buy* something to eat for breakfast.
- How many of them eat bagels.
- How many places serve breakfasts within that same radius.
- All the same info regarding lunch sandwiches, which could be replaced by your bagel sandwiches.

The Competition

This is another critical section of the business plan. And it's one that has been ignored.

If you're seeking investors, the easiest way to get them to throw away your business plan is to claim you have no competitors. There are always competitors. Horse-drawn carriages were competitors to the automobile. Calculators were competitors to the first computers.

Another mistake that will make potential investors doubt you is to mention your competitors, but show by your analysis that you think all you need to do to compete is to provide a quality product/service. In fact, if you have a wonderful product and you work hard—you can still fail miserably.

You need to know exactly who your competitors are. Their strengths and weaknesses. Their plans for the future. Their financial situation. Their goals. Their key personnel.

Sound difficult? It's not, really. You'll be amazed at all the ways you can gather critical information about them—as shown in Chapter 4 of this book.

The Product/Service

This section should open with your mission statement. Then you describe exactly what you will be offering—and how it will be

created. Will it be high quality and expensive? Low quality (but reliable) and cheap?

- **Service businesses:** Describe the service, describe how it will be performed, and how it will be priced. If you already have one or more customers lined up, they go in here.
- **Product businesses:** Describe the product, where you will acquire the components of it (and how stable those suppliers are), how you will manufacture it (and at what cost), equipment needed (and its cost), etc.

Your Marketing Plan

No business succeeds without bringing in customers, so here's where you describe exactly how you plan to do this.

- **Advertising:** Identify how leading competitor companies are advertising for customers and relate your advertising plans to theirs. If advertising is not a part of how competitors attract clients (e.g., if you're a software or crafts designer), say so and state your alternatives.
- **Public relations:** If your potential customers read the local paper or specific trade magazines or special interest magazines, you may wish to create a program to get yourself mentioned in these publications. Publicity can work well if you're a local company and a simple call to Information will yield your phone number. It may not be worth your while if you're a national company, because national publications often don't identify locations for companies they mention. An 800 number may do the trick, as a call to 800 Information would bring in your company.
- **Electronic promotion:** If there's any chance some of your customers might look for you (or your type of products) on the Web, you should have a Web site.

If you only need a basic one and if you're willing to create it yourself, it will cost you about $200 up front and maybe $30 a month to maintain it on a server. It will take roughly a full weekend

Business Is Like Sports

Too many people think business is like golf: you just play your game as well as possible and don't worry about how to outfox your competitors.

Business is more like being on a special version of the tennis tour. There's four or five players you have to play every tournament (your direct competitors). And five to 10 more you play every third tournament (your indirect competitors).

Each of your competitors has different abilities. Some are stronger. Others more crafty. Some have great forehands but weaker backhands. Others the reverse. Some you need to lob. Others you need to try to overpower. But you won't know how to compete against each of your competitors unless you've studied them very carefully.

of work to create a Web site. The Web authoring software FrontPage 2000 is about $100, and has ready-made templates to help you create the site.

AOL promotes a deal that enables you to get a business site up and running for a small up-front fee and $30 a month. Most ISPs (Internet Service Providers) give you Web site space for free. But make sure it's one where you can get your own domain name. You want to be able to take it with you if you change your ISP. You don't want to have a bunch of strange location codes before your name. My site is NewsletterGroup.com. Yours should be something equally straightforward. Registering the name costs $70, and the AOL service will handle it for you as part of the package.

You can use your Web site as a fishing site (seeing what kind of "fish" it attracts) and as a place to send people in e-mail promotions. With no promotion whatsoever, I pulled in two subscription orders to a new newsletter in five months—which brought in enough to cover my Web site expenses for a year. Now, as I'm gearing up for promotions, the site should do much more business.

- **Pricing:** Part of any marketing plan is your pricing strategy. Don't try to invent it from thin air; wait until you've done the competitive analysis so you can see what your competitors are charging for similar products. You'll learn more about pricing strategy in the chapters on marketing.

The Management Team

This is a critical section in your business plan if you are trying to raise money. Venture capitalists (and other investors) look to see if your management team has all the required skills to pull off all the production, marketing, and financial activities outlined in your plan.

If you are the sole employee in this business, take a careful look at your résumé. Are you missing any key skills that will be needed in the business?

- Do you have any financial background? If so, list the facts. If not, have you done anything that would show financial skills? For instance, I had an editorial and marketing back-

ground in publishing and decided I wanted a financial job to round out my knowledge. How did I get such a job? By telling my potential boss that I had done my own corporate tax returns for a previous company of mine. He figured if I could do that, I'd be a safe hire. If you've kept any books for anyone, served as an executor for a relative's estate, taken night courses in accounting—anything to show potential investors you understand the concept of money and accounting—list it.

- Do you have a sales or marketing background? If so, list it. If not, you'll need help in this function. Selling Girl Scout cookies just won't cut it—unless you won an award for selling more than anyone else in your state!

- Do you have a background in delivering whatever your product is—be it information (as a consultant, a writer), design, or manufacturing? If not, you'll need help in this function.

If your background is remiss in one of the above functions, you can still shore up your management section—without hiring staff. You need to find a mentor, advisor, or consultant with the needed expertise.

Does anyone in your extended family have this expertise? A former boss? A former teacher? These are the people who might be willing to advise you for free—or almost free. You could establish an "Advisory Council" and put them on it; but you need their permission to list them, and their expertise, in your business plan. Advisory Council can mean whatever you want it to mean. Usually it gives you the right to call the people and ask specific questions. If you expect them to spend a couple of hours in a meeting—maybe you need a "think tank" to deal with a broad problem—you should pay them some sort of fee— maybe $100 to $300, assuming they're all local.

Occasionally people who have sought help from SCORE (see page 39) strike up a rapport with the person who helps them and that person turns into a mentor. Under that scenario, you might also come up with someone willing to be on your Advisory Council.

Advisors and consultants will cost you money, but they can usually save you money costs by shoring up the areas in your business where your expertise is weak.

PR Requires a "Hook"

Remember, you need a "hook" for a public relations mailing to succeed. If you don't offer information of value, your chances of it getting published are slim to none. Ask yourself about each effort:

- Is it real news?
- Is it results from any kind of study/survey/research?
- Is it an opinion from an industry leader?
- Is it some tidbit that will help the publication's readers?
- Is it some tidbit that will shock/surprise/infuriate/titillate the publication's readers?

If it is none of these, don't waste the time and postage sending it.

Financial Statements

Here's where you find out what all of the above will mean on the bottom line. Don't expect the first set of financials you create to become your bible; you'll probably have to rework them at least once. That's because you'll likely discover something wrong about all your assumptions—something that means the business will fail if it isn't changed.

Aren't you glad you'll be changing the business when it's just a computer document or ink on paper instead of after you've wasted money you couldn't afford to waste on something that would never have worked?

Assumptions

Financial numbers for a new business are all guesses. They're completely meaningless unless you include the *assumptions* they are based upon.

For instance, you could show a positive cash flow of $100,000 in the first year. Or a million. It all depends upon the assumptions you're using. Business plans are evaluated looking at the assumptions.

- Can you *really* pull in 500 new accounting clients in a year?
- Can you *really* price car tune-ups at double the price your competitors are getting?
- Is it *reasonable* to expect the direct mail you send out will pull orders from 50% of the people who receive it?

(You'll find all you need to know on financial assumptions in Chapter 11 of this book.)

Cash Flows

Cash flows are just what they sound like. You count cash received in the month you receive it and cash expenses in the month you pay them. Credit card charges can be counted in the month you pay for them or when the charge is entered. The IRS allows you to count a year's expenses in credit card charges, entered right up to December 31.

Accounting Definitions

Double-entry bookkeeping: This is the standard accounting method used to track company receipts and disbursements. Every financial transaction requires two different entries: one a "credit" and one a "debit." For example, a cash expense would debit cash (lower it) and credit the expense account, say for "telephone." A cash receipt would credit cash (raise it) and debit the revenue account, say for "consulting sales."

What makes the double-entry bookkeeping system so confusing is that debits can be both "good" and "bad," as can credits.

"Good" (meaning more money to the company) is a debit to cash and a credit to sales.

"Bad" (meaning less money to the company) is a credit to cash and a debit to sales.

If you find this confusing, don't feel bad. There's an old accounting joke about the CFO of a company who had a special drawer with a key. Each morning when he sat down at his desk, he would unlock the drawer, look inside, then close and relock it. One day the staff received word the man had a stroke and wouldn't be returning. The employees quickly gathered at the desk and forced open the drawer. Inside was a note saying, "Debits are on the window side."

With great software available today like Quicken and QuickBooks, you almost don't have to know debits and credits—the program handles them for you. You just make entries like writing in your checkbook and it posts them as debits and credits.

Accruals: Expenses entered into your books for bills you haven't yet paid. They are entered into an Accrued Expenses account. When you actually pay the bill, you credit (lower) cash and debit Accrued Expenses (removing the amount from that account).

Deferrals: Expenses already paid but not expensed on your books. They are entered as a credit to cash (reducing it) and a debit to Prepaid Expenses (increasing it). When the month comes when you want to "book" the expenses, you remove the amount from Prepaid Expenses (via a credit) and enter a debit to the actual expense account.

Cash flows will tell you if you'll have enough money coming in to pay for your expenses. They'll tell you how much cash needs to be put in before the company starts breaking even. Cash flows are how you judge the success of your work—your new company.

P&Ls (Profit & Loss Statements)

P&Ls are cash flows that also include deferred and accrued items (see page 37). If you're not trying to raise money, you can ignore P&Ls and just base your business decisions on cash flows—UNLESS you have one of the following financial situations, which require—and maybe mandate—using deferrals and accruals:

- Any subscription business requires (says the IRS) deferring the revenues over the life of the subscription. That is, a one-year subscription received in September should book $1/12$ of the revenue in September, another $1/12$ in October, etc. So, in this case, $4/12$ of the *cash* received is *revenue* in the first year and the remainder is *revenue* in the second year.
- Large, infrequent expenses may be spread over a period of time to "even out" financial statements. Here are some examples:
  - Consumer magazines do huge subscription mailings in January and July. The thousands (or millions) of dollars spent in January are spread equally over the six months of January through June. The additional thousands/millions spent in July are spread over July through December. Otherwise the financial statements would look like a disaster in January and July when in reality those months might be very profitable compared to other months—except for the timing of the promotional mailings.
  - Book companies spread author advances over the "life" of the book—however long they expect it to continue bringing in revenues.
  - If you have specific expenses incurred in generating a specific product, you might want to tie both the revenue and the expenses together. Thus, if you sell bathing suits to stores in April, you would want to *defer* all the expenses related to it (materials, designers, etc.) that were incurred before April.

That way, the revenues and the expenses both show on your books at the same time.

- If you have inventory (e.g., for a retail store) you will need to put those expenses into an inventory account and only show as an expense (on your P&L statements) the costs of items *when you sell them.*

Appendices

You use appendices (or appendixes) at the end of your plan to add detail to back up what is in the business plan. If you quoted an article from *BusinessWeek,* for instance, on how demand is growing for your type of product or service, you might include the full article here if it makes your point even more forcefully (if you obtain permission first).

If you want to launch a magazine or consumer newsletter, you would add tables of contents for three sample issues here.

If you already have a product design of some sort, a rough of it could go here. However, *do not* put product designs you wish to keep secret in your plan. Even though potential investors sign non-disclosure agreements, the information in business plans almost always gets out.

If you're entering a market with over twenty competitors, you might put all the details here of who they are and summarize the competition in the body of the business plan.

SBA Offerings

The Small Business Administration (SBA) has a number of offerings for entrepreneurs, including SCORE. You can research what they have to offer at *www.sba.gov.* The site is pretty impressive and I highly recommend you visit it. If you don't have access to the Internet, go to your local library and they'll show you how.

Here are features you can find at the SBA Web site:

- **SCORE**. More than twelve thousand volunteers donate their time to help people like us start a business. Click on "Local SBA Resources" on the SBA home page.

SCORE

Service Core of Retired Executives (SCORE) is funded by your tax dollars through the Small Business Administration and is staffed by volunteers—all retired former executives.

There's probably someone (or several someones) currently aligned with SCORE who can answer those seemingly impossible questions of yours. If they don't have a SCORE office in a city near you, call a more distant office and get advice via the telephone. It's well worth the price of long distance! Call (800) 827-5722 to find the SCORE office nearest you.

Getting Help

When I launched
Sportswoman magazine,
I had no clue about how to
process subscriptions. How
do you keep track of who
gets each issue, and when
they expire, and who has or
hasn't paid? Now I wouldn't
dream of doing it without a
computer program, but
back then they didn't exist
except as large, very expensive programs.

I was to learn that there
are a large number of outside
sources of free help available—whether you are
looking for a specific answer
or for a broader overview.
How specific can it be?
Incredibly.

- **Answer Desk.** This button is available on the SBA home page. Clicking on it will get you answers to the SBA's "10 Most Asked Questions" and directions for e-mailing other questions (*answerdesk@sba.gov*) or for calling in: 800-UASK-SBA. Representatives are available to answer your questions between 9 A.M. and 5 P.M. eastern standard time.

- **Small Business Development Centers (SBDCs)**. There is at least one SBDC in every state of America. Click on "Local SBA Resources" on the SBA home page. Some of their services are free, provided by volunteers. The centers also provide corporate and education consulting on a fee basis. The program is a joint project between the SBA, state, and local governments and state colleges and universities.

- **Women's Business Centers (WBCs)**. A network of more than sixty WBCs provide a wide range of services to women entrepreneurs. If a WBC is not near you, check out "Women Online." Click on "Local SBA Resources" on the SBA home page.

- **Business Information Centers (BICs)**. Another local offering for current and future business owners. Click on "Local SBA Resources" on the SBA home page.

- **U.S. Export Assistance Centers (USEACs)**. These centers offer a full range of federal export programs and services from a number of federal agencies. Many locations have a new-to-export program called E-TAP. Click on "Local SBA Resources" on the SBA home page.

- **PRO-Net.** This free service will list your company so that those looking for specific suppliers can find you and contact you. It lists over 171,000 small and/or women-owned businesses. The button for this service is on the SBA home page.

- **Loans and loan-guarantee programs.** The SBA offers loans and loan guarantees. Learn more by clicking the "Financing" button on their home page. (Note: Due to freedom of the press restrictions, you cannot get an SBA loan for funding a publication.)

CHAPTER THREE

Learning the Industry

Identify Your Industry

If you're putting up all the money for your business, spend at least a day or two researching your industry. If you're raising outside capital, you'll need to spend several days or more.

Researching your industry can help you avoid launching a scooter company just as the accident rate is hurting sales. Even if you think everything is rosy, it doesn't hurt to hear or read about warning signs on the horizon. After all, those warning signs might point your industry in a particular direction for the future. You might even be able to capitalize on that by incorporating them into your business strategy—your scooter comes with a helmet.

What exactly is an "industry"? It's the category of usage for your product or service. Here are some examples:

Business	Industry
Pet stores, veterinarian offices, and doggie treat manufacturers	Pets
Cooking schools, cookbooks, wok manufacturers, and spice bottlers	Cooking
Apparel manufacturers and clothing stores	Apparel
Diamond cutters, jewelry designers, and jewelry stores	Fine jewelry
Auto parts stores, auto dealers, tire manufacturers, service stations	Automotive
Nurseries, garden stores, outdoor furniture, and plant fungus killers	Garden

Why does it help to look at your business in such a broad stroke? This macro look—which means looking at the big picture, compared to "micro," which looks at a small detail of the macro picture—takes in a lot of businesses that may seem dissimilar to yours.

For example, if you're planning to create a gourmet dog treat product, why would you care about what's happening at vet offices (Pets)? If you're going to sell tires, why would you care about auto dealers (Automotive)?

The answer is that each of the businesses grouped under Pets has one common feature: pets. If people stop having pets, they're out of business. And though that isn't likely to happen, there could be a trend to fewer people having pets. Or people switching to different kinds of pets—over the past 20 years, cats have superseded dogs as the favorite pet. A change such as this could mean your company will be fighting against established companies for a smaller and smaller amount of business.

How to Find Trends

If you can find a knowledgeable librarian, your task of learning about industry trends is infinitely easier. Usually there is too much information in a library for you to find your way to what's usable. But you can try. But you also have the Internet, trade associations—and even the Yellow Pages!

On the Internet

Since searching for "cooking" or "pets" will produce millions of listings, you'll have to use a lot of qualifiers with most search engines in order to find anything usable. Try adding one or more of the following words in the search box to narrow your search:

Trend
Association (may help you find an industry or trade association)
Statistics
Sales
Industry

Usually you do this by adding the word AND, as in "pets AND sales."

Also, look at the Web sites of the leading Business-to-Business publications in your industry (*Advertising Age* and *Ad Week* for the advertising business; *Jewelers' Circular Keystone* for the jewelry industry, etc.). You can find which publications are in your industry by looking at *SRDS Business Publications Rates & Data*—available in your library.

You might also try large-city newspaper Web sites. As this book went to press, you could still search by topic and pay by the article on the *New York Times* site, though not on the *Wall Street Journal (WSJ)*.

Change Can Affect an Industry

- What happens to your auto parts store if people stop having second cars and use bikes for in-town errands? Conversely, what happens if more people get a car of their own, so you have more families with two or three cars? What happens if more people buy recreational vehicles in addition to their cars?
- What happens to sales of your garlic peeler if more women are working full-time and cooking less?
- What happens to sales of your garden sundial if more people are spending more time in their gardens and decorating them more?

In all of these examples, you can see that changes and trends can point to more or fewer opportunities for your business.

However, you can get a free two-week trial for the WSJ, during which you can see what you can find. Try to search both newspapers at your library.

Also try the *Forbes*, *Fortune*, *BusinessWeek*, and/or the *Economist* sites. If you find good articles about your industry's trends in any of these sources, print them out as possible appendices for your business plan, citing appropriately.

At the Library

I recommend throwing yourself on the mercies of business section librarians. Tell them what you want and they will probably have some good ideas on where to find it. If you run into an indifferent librarian (which I never have!), try the library's indexes for the *Wall Street Journal*, *Forbes*, *Fortune*, *BusinessWeek*, the *Economist*, or the business-to-business publications in your industry.

To find the leading publications in your industry, look at the *SRDS Business Publications Rates & Data* (a huge directory, updated monthly) to find the Business-to-Business publications in your industry. They're arranged by industry, in alphabetical order, and include apparel, architecture, automotive, general business, computers, electronic engineering, financial, maritime and marine, sales management, safety, telecommunications, etc.

Industry publications print any sales or trend information they can get their hands on, so you should read at least a few recent back issues and look at the annual index. Sometimes one particular issue each year carries all the sales and trend information for a particular industry. If you can't find what you're looking for, call the editor and ask if the numbers you're looking for are available anywhere.

From an Association

Trade associations usually have good industry trend information—or at least as good as is publicly available. Don't forget, however, that trade associations are formed to promote their industries. You may not hear about bad news or bad trends from them. One way of assessing the state of the industry is to look at their current membership directory and compare it to one three to four years old. Do they have more or fewer members? Does the directory have more or less companies advertising? Each of these is an indication of an industry on the rise—or on the decline.

Help from Gale

While you're in the library, look at *Gale Directory of Associations*, which lists all the associations in the USA. Associations frequently have good trend information on the industry.

In the Yellow Pages

If your type of business is listed in the Yellow Pages, look at this year's book and compare it to one two to three years old. You can probably get an old book from your library; if not, the publisher will probably sell you one. How many companies in your line of business are listed in the current book compared to an older one? How many of them have display ads compared to before? Look at the display ads in the old book, then see if those same companies: 1) still exist in the new book; 2) have larger (or smaller) ads in the new book; and 3) have added (or subtracted) color in the new book.

A Business Plan's Industry Profile

Here is a sample industry profile from a business plan to launch a business aviation magazine. It will give you an idea of the type of information wanted by investors. If you are funding your own launch, there is no need to be so thorough; however, every new business plan should include some thought on industry trends.

THE BUSINESS AVIATION FIELD

Far from being the playthings of the chairpeople and CEOs of major corporations, business aircraft are operated in as professional and as sophisticated a manner as the major airlines. Basic to their use are some obvious facts:

- Most commercial airlines now use hub and spoke systems to carry passengers—there are just 55 of these commercial hubs nationwide. "Hubs" serve three-quarters of all airline passengers and some 669 "spoke" airports. As efficient a method of operation as it is for the airlines, the hub and spoke system is terribly inefficient for the traveler. It offers a limited number of destination airports, proving to be both time-consuming and inefficient while breeding traffic and congestion. By contrast, business aircraft may choose as their destination any of more than 5,500 airports in the United States. The ability to use these smaller, less congested airports located closer to the final destination is a vital part of the utility and flexibility of business aviation.

Advertising Definitions

Line ads: In telephone directories, line ads list the company name, the address (usually), and the phone number. The listing may be in boldface type (which costs more) or not. In other publications, such as magazines and newspapers, line ads are any ads that are just words (text) in the one typeface and style the publication uses for all line ads.

Display ads: These ads may have one or all of the following: pictures, art, text in different typefaces, larger words, words arranged on the page in a different order, background tints, colors, etc.

- Over 90% of the *Fortune* 500 "honor roll" companies operate private aircraft—not coincidentally, these corporations consistently earn the most profits for shareholders.

There are some 11,000 turbine-powered (jet or turboprop) aircraft in the United States and Canada in the corporate fleet, with some 6,000 more based internationally.

These planes are mostly owned by the major corporations. They employ their own flight crews, service technicians, and other support personnel. The cost of each plane ranges from $500,000 to upwards of $50 million with direct hourly operating expenses of $500 to $5,000. Not only are they used by their corporate owners, but they are often leased on a per-flight basis to other corporate users during their off periods.

Aircraft operations normally report to the CEO, EVP, CFO, or other top officers. Use is carefully controlled. Only a handful of individuals are allowed to fly in them. The number of key people in any company who can fly together is strictly regulated.

The average number of passengers on a flight is very small, no matter the size of the company or size of the plane. Seats are normally left empty rather than have them used by nonqualified people. The use of the planes is carefully coordinated with the use of scheduled airlines in many companies.

The reasons for this careful monitoring of the use of the planes is obvious—the operating expenses are considerable and it only pays to use these facilities for the most highly paid employees whose time is most valuable, or when time is of the essence in being at certain places at certain times.

Time spent in transit can be categorized as "outbound" or "inbound." Outbound time may often be used for discussing and working on company business. The privacy of the corporate aircraft cabin is often necessary for top executives in these discussions. Inbound time is normally spent in relaxation, and passengers may take advantage of the aircraft's entertainment facilities, which often include a full bar and galley, and a TV/VCR/Stereo system.

Pilot training procedures and methods, as required by the Federal Aviation Administration (FAA), are virtually identical with those of the commercial airlines. Most aircraft are maintained to the rigorous standards imposed by Federal Aviation Regulations (FAR), which, except for certain rules relating to the much larger passenger capacity of commercial passenger aircraft, are essentially the same as for airlines.

Efficiency reports are required in most companies and there are internal chargebacks to the departments using the planes.

Industry-Profile Basics

A good industry analysis demonstrates:

- How solid your industry is.
- The industry's trends.
- The size and importance of the industry.
  - Your competence—which shows in how you analyze your industry.

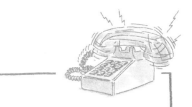

Finding Your Customers

In order to estimate how much money you can make from your business, you will have to come up with a total number of potential customers—people who are good prospects to buy from you.

Who is most likely to buy your product? Men or women? Young or old? Rich or poor? Homeowners or renters? People first to jump on a new fad, or people who like to stick with tried-and-true products? Homebodies or partygoers?

Some say why worry about it—why not just put the product out there and see who buys? That's the wrong approach. Understanding your potential customers can dramatically increase your chances of success. It does so in two ways:

1. By focusing on who is most likely to buy your product, you will likely uncover ways you can make the product more appealing to them—which should increase your sales.
2. You will save a lot of time and money in promoting your product if you don't waste time and/or money on prospects who are less likely to buy.

Your Customers and Your Business Plan

At the end of this chapter are sections from three different business plans. In the first plan, the emphasis is entirely on demographics (vital statistics). The second relies mostly on demographics, with only a paragraph at the end on psychographics (how people behave psychologically). In the third plan, the demographics section is quite small, followed by a much more important psychographics section.

What you do in your own plan should depend on what the most important defining qualities are of your potential customers. If your product is homeowners insurance, the most defining characteristic of your potential customers will be home ownership. If your product is a wrinkle-removing cream, you have both important demographics (e.g., women 35–60) as well as psychographics (desire to look younger).

What about for business services? If you're selling financial consulting services to corporations, does any of this demographic and psychographic stuff matter? Yes, it does. Who are your potential customers? Are they CEOs or accounts payable managers? Are they CEOs who are in

Characteristics of My Potential Customers

	My customers
Demographics	
Age Range	
Sex	
Married?	
Kids at home?	
Geographic location	
Own home or rent?	
Household income range	
Psychographics	
Homebody or party animal?	
Follows fads?	
Splurger vs. tightwad?	
List other important traits for your marketplace:	

their sixties or CEOs in their twenties? In each case, how you sell to each group will be very different. You won't want to e-mail 60-year-old CEOs, for example, whereas that is probably the only way to reach CEOs in their twenties. Also, your business plan for reaching CEOs would require more expense than a plan to reach accounts payable managers, because CEOs have people in place to screen calls and unwanted mail from salespeople, while accounts payable managers don't.

The Demographics

Demographics—the "demos"—are the vital statistics of a population, such as age, gender, income, and so forth. The narrower your target group—teenage girls only, for instance, instead of every human on the face of the earth—the easier and cheaper it is to market to them . . . if you can find them.

Suppose you want to introduce a new razor blade, with some new dazzling feature that makes it less likely to nick while shaving with it. Because it can be used by almost anyone, you'll need millions of dollars to market it nationwide. You could start selling it in one city and hope to later expand, but as soon as Gillette and your other competitors hear about it, they're going to try to match it and your advantage will be quickly gone. So the ideal marketing plan for such a product is millions of dollars, spent to create a big splash across the country, in every city at the same time.

However, if you want to launch a product that is only for left-handed women experiencing hot flashes, you would need far less in marketing—if you could find lists of your targets, which you can't with such narrow demographics. But there are lists of other narrow demographic groups, such as students about to enroll in Harvard. If you had a product that would help orient them better—perhaps a book titled *What You REALLY Need to Know About How Harvard Works*—you could probably market it to everyone interested with just a couple hundred dollars.

And the advantages of "narrow-niching" don't only apply to direct marketing. If you've developed a great-looking model train station, there are probably no more than 500 stores nationwide who are likely to carry it, plus a couple of big catalogs. You could send

all the dealers flyers about your product and call all of them to follow up for a thousand dollars or less. Quite a bit less, if you're doing it all yourself.

Demo: Gender

Are the users of your product or service likely to be male or female—or both? If both, is your product likely to be equally attractive to each? Maybe your business plan should say, "The likely buyer is female, although we anticipate up to 30 percent of the purchasers will be male."

The advantage of knowing the gender of your potential buyers extends to where you would market the product, to knowing how many potential buyers there are in your city, and to whether that group is likely to expand or contract.

Demo: Age

Age is a key demographic that should be carefully considered. One of the biggest mistakes new business owners make is taking on too large a group as their potential market. Entrepreneurs hate to write off a potential group of buyers, but usually they would see more profit if they did. If you believe all ages will buy your product, try this exercise to see if you can't narrow your focus.

Narrowing Your Customer Base

Product: A shaving cream product, which could be used by men and women over the age of 12. Ask yourself about women buyers over 60: While maybe they could use your product, the question is *will* they? What about male buyers over 80? Are they currently using a similar product? Go somewhere—say, a busy train station or an airport—where you can talk to a lot of people in one age group and ask them if they currently use your type of product. If over 50% don't, maybe you've just narrowed your focus. What about buyers under 18? Can you write them off as unlikely?

Product: Pink hair dye, which conceivably could be used by everyone over the age of 2. But will it? Can you write off anyone under the age of 12? Can you write off males? What about anyone over the age of 30? Over 25? Maybe you can write off males and

females who are employed, no matter their age? Perhaps an 18–22 group, generally unemployed but maybe attending college, are likely candidates, while those in the same age bracket who are employed are not likely targets?

Once you know the age and gender of your prospects, you can track how many of them there are right now and how many there will be in 10 years.

Demo: Homeownership

There are many products that only homeowners are likely to buy, such as new fixtures, carpeting, tile, wood flooring, trees, ground covers, and on and on. The U.S. Census tracks the number of homeowners nationally, by state, and for the top 75 metropolitan areas. This is valuable information in figuring out just how many good prospects you have for your product.

Demo: Household Income

The U.S. Census tracks household income by race and by state.

You won't be selling $10 jars of baby food to low-income homes, so you can eliminate that large group from your potential targets. However, don't assume that *all* products sell better to those in the highest income brackets. And they might be less inclined to buy a product whose marketing strategy is that it's cheaper than other products in the category—even though that marketing strategy could be very successful to another economic group.

Also remember to look at *disposable* income, not just income. Disposable income is what's left after shelter and food are covered. How large that number is doesn't depend just on the income coming in, but also on the local costs of shelter and food. For example, take-home pay (after taxes) is lower on average in Oklahoma than in Connecticut, but so is the cost of shelter and food. Someone in Oklahoma could earn thousands less than someone in Connecticut and still have more disposable income.

Further, if you're selling to teenagers, their cash coming in could be very small—but it may *all* be disposable income.

Survey the Market for Your Product

It is very important for you to verify your assumptions about who is likely to buy your product. As the entrepreneur, you are likely to overestimate potential buyers.

When students in a direct marketing program were asked to determine the market for a book designed to improve health, they overestimated its appeal. Specifically, they felt students of their own age would buy it. Yet, research says that 20-year-olds almost never buy health publications. They may buy magazines that emphasize beauty (females) or muscles (male) but not magazines that tell them how to protect their immune systems.

If students studying marketing overestimate what people *like themselves* will buy, imagine how inaccurate they could be about people *un*like themselves!

Why don't they know that 20-year-olds are unlikely to buy health publications? They say things like, "Young people today care about their health, and want to live a healthy lifestyle . . ."

But what they should ask themselves and their friends is: "How many health books did I buy this past year?" That would bring out the fact that, though they are interested in the topic, they're not interested enough to spend much, if any, money on it.

Likewise, for any product you are considering launching, talk to people in your target age and sex group. Ask them how many similar products they've bought in the last three months or 12 months. If you ask them if they're *likely* to buy a product you're describing, they'll give you more "yes" answers than are correct. Maybe they don't want to disappoint you on your idea. Maybe their definition of "likely" is whether there's any chance *at all* that they might buy such a product.

The only important answer for you (unless your product is so new and so unique there is nothing remotely like it) is whether they're already buying a similar product on a regular basis.

Demo: Geographic Location

Where are your potential customers located?

If your business is a local one, the geographic location is within a certain mile radius of your store—say, everyone within 14 miles, or within eight miles. Or perhaps you plan to draw customers from farther in one direction than the other, because you have a competitor in one direction. Talk to potential customers. Where do they currently shop? How far will they drive for your type of product? How far will you drive for certain products?

You'll find that people are not willing to drive as far for products they buy often as for the products they buy only occasionally. Superstores have changed these patterns somewhat, in that people will buy in large bulk at CostCo and similar discount stores and shop for perishable items at the nearby grocery store.

If your product will be sold nationally, you may still wish to consider geographic distributions. Perhaps your product is for use in the snow, in which case your market will exclude states where it seldom snows. Perhaps it's a "New Age" product, and you'll want heavier distribution in California and the Southwest. Perhaps your product will sell better in large cities? Perhaps it will sell better in rural areas?

How Reachable Are Your Targets?

Access to a particular market is not normally a part of demographics investigations, but it should be. For example, if your product will sell through stores or distributors, how open are they to new products? Launch a new breakfast cereal without the distribution muscle of a big line, and you'll find yourself paying huge premiums—stocking fees—to get your products on the shelf. Premiums like this could ruin your chance to generate a profit.

If you're selling a service to pharmaceutical marketing executives that requires a face-to-face meeting, will you be able to get to them? Marketers at pharmaceutical companies are renowned as the hardest people on the face of the earth to get a sales appointment with.

If you will be marketing by direct mail, e-mail, or telephone, are there lists available of your targets? If not, you're in trouble.

- **Consumer Lists:** There may be no way at all to cost-effectively find names of some groups of consumers. For example, if you're trying to market to single parents, nobody—to my knowledge—has yet figured out a way to get substantial lists of these people. Without lists, your business is in trouble.
- **Business Lists:** In this market you at least have a chance of generating a list yourself, if one doesn't already exist. But you'll have to pay a hefty fee up front to get the names. For example, a newsletter company named IOMA wanted to market to company office managers, but no lists were available. So it set up a telemarketing operation that telephoned companies (there are of course lists of companies, but not of office managers at those companies) and asked them for the name of their office manager. They entered the name in a database, then talked to the person and tried to sell them the newsletter. Thus they got two benefits from the same call: a sales attempt and a name in their database that they could mail further offers to. For your budgeting, know that telephone sales calls run about $30 an hour. However, you don't spend any of that for dialing numbers that don't answer; the big telemarketing companies have automated dialing equipment that places the calls and sales reps only pick up if someone answers.

The Psychographics

Psychographics is a term used by marketers to describe the psychological aspects of a specific group of people—your customers—as compared to demographics, which deals with statistical aspects. Psychographics categorizes types of people by analyzing what is important to them.

When I was publisher of *Home Mechanix* magazine, we did psychographic research on our subscribers to better understand them. We were able to categorize subscribers in three psychographic groups:

1. **Neighborhood gurus:** It was important for this group that their neighbors looked up to them as individuals who

Help from the Census

The U.S. Census tracks Americans by age and projects the numbers into the future. You can access this information online at *www.census.gov*.

If your target market were all Americans, here are the projected numbers that would help you calculate future profits:

Year	Americans
2000	275 million
2005	288 million
2010	300 million

It's simple to analyze numbers when looking at all Americans; the number just keeps rising. But if you are looking only at Americans aged 12–20, that number may rise or fall over the next 10–20 years. Looking at the census numbers will tell you that.

Also, the U.S. Census breaks out the numbers for individual states. If your business is local, you will need those numbers to work with.

Unexamined Assumptions Can Be Dangerous

We often assume other people are like us. This is a *very* dangerous assumption when you want to market a product. Yes, there are other people like us—our friends! Seriously, however, the differences can be astounding.

Watch out for your assumptions. For example, if you want to create crafts, I highly recommend you work in a crafts store for at least a couple of months. It will give you an opportunity to see the broad range of people buying crafts products. It will also let you see what kinds of products are selling better than others. If something somewhat similar to your product is in the store but isn't being bought—consider it a strong warning sign.

(continued on next page)

could answer questions about home repairs or remodeling, furniture building, or car repairs. Neighborhood prestige was their motivator.

2. **Money savers:** This group was motivated primarily by saving money. They wanted to know how to repair their house and car so they could do it instead of paying more for someone else to do it.

3. **Dreamers:** This group seldom did any of the building or repair projects in the magazine. This group was a complete surprise to us. Why would someone read plans to build a project—if they never built anything? We found that the magazine was a "wish book" for them. It's why some people read *Architectural Digest* even though they know they'll never have a home that looks like any of those in the magazine. Or why others read about sexy celebrities they will never know.

So, what good is all this information? When you want to sell to people, it matters. If your home product was primarily of interest to money savers, you'll stress how much money they'll save by doing it themselves. If instead your market is primarily motivated by neighborhood prestige, you'll want to talk about how this product will help the customer avoid mistakes the average person makes, how using it is the smarter and more effective way to get something done.

Where can you get good psychographic information? You can't get it on your exact potential target without spending a lot of money in custom market research—money which, in most cases, would be better spent elsewhere.

However, you can look at national trends in psychographics. For example, the national trend toward "cocooning," where people stay home more and cook more, seems to have crested. People are now starting to eat out more.

If you're planning to launch a restaurant, you should mention this trend in your business plan. If, on the other hand, you're planning on launching a kitchen cooking utensil, this trend is not going to help your product.

Where can you get national trends in psychographics? At your friendly library. Read the latest book by Faith Popcorn. She has identified many psychographic trends and she's a fun read. You can also check out *Trends 2000* by Gerald Celente. He reports psychographic trends, and points toward products he believes will succeed in the future.

One-on-One Research

Spend as much time as possible before launching a business talking to potential customers. Ask them why they buy particular products. Ask them what's most important to them in buying products like yours.

How can you get cooperation from strangers? Well, you won't get it from someone running to catch a bus. But, if you don't take too much of their time, and you're considerate about when you ask (not interrupting a fancy dinner, for example), most people are willing to answer a couple of polite questions. Especially if you preface it by saying, "I'm planning to start a business doing (*fill in the blank*) and would really appreciate if it you would answer three quick questions for me. Is this a good time?"

A man ahead of me in a grocery checkout counter said he worked for Yoplait and wanted to know how I used the extra large tub of yogurt I was buying. I told him.

A friend, planning a restaurant launch, went out for three weeks to similar restaurants in her neighborhood and struck up conversations at the bar with people waiting for their dinner partners. Those people gave her valuable feedback on what they liked best about the restaurant and which restaurants they didn't like. She learned how her potential customers defined "quality" in a dining experience. She then used those same definitions to hold up as performance standards for herself and her employees in the restaurant she opened.

Before launching *Media Marketing* newsletter, I called 30 publishers and ad directors and asked for five minutes of their time; 20 of them gave it to me. It had been awhile since I sold advertising (the topic of my newsletter), so I needed to know what was most important these days to people selling ads. I asked them the following questions, some of which may help you in your research:

- What do you like most about your job?
- What do you hate most about your job?

Unexamined Assumptions Can Be Dangerous

(continued from previous page)

You probably won't make a financial success selling only to enlightened souls (such as yourself!). See if the masses agree with you. If not, you'll at least learn your product has a smaller potential customer base and needs to be targeted specifically to a subgroup of customers. Then you can figure out how best to reach those customers and how not to waste money reaching the masses who aren't interested.

- What do you wake up in the middle of the night in a cold sweat about?
- If you could have a top consultant working for you for free for six months, what would you have that consultant do?

I also gave them 10 potential topics that might be covered in the newsletter and asked them to rank those topics from 1 to 5, where 1 means they have no interest in it and 5 means they are extremely interested in it.

Get creative in how you get feedback from potential customers. For example, you can go to work for a month or two in a place offering your kind of service or product and ask the customers you deal with what is important to them.

Using Your Data in a Business Plan

Following are the demographic and psychographic sections from three different business plans. The first section focuses on demographics. The second has a small paragraph at the end on psychographics. The third is primarily psychographics.

THE LING GARDEN RESTAURANT

National spending patterns are important when evaluating the local demographics of the surrounding towns that frequent the Ling Garden. Table 1 displays incomes and ages of households from the neighboring towns. Assuming that national trends are applicable to this area, then it is apparent that households in the surrounding towns will mature into age groups that spend higher than average amounts on food away from home. In addition, household incomes in the surrounding neighborhood are also above average in amounts spent on food away from home.

With a planned marketing campaign, increased tourist trade, neighboring residential areas representing groups (age, income) that spend higher percentages of income on food away from home, the prognosis for steadily increasing revenues is very promising.

HEART & SOUL MAGAZINE FOR BLACK CONSUMERS
THE MARKET

The 34 million black consumer market has increased its purchasing power 54% in this decade, from $304 billion in 1990 to an estimated $470 billion in 1997—faster than the total purchasing power of the nation, up 43% during the same period, and greater than the GNP of all but the top 15 countries in the world. Strong population growth and continued economic gains will contribute to 6% annual growth in the purchasing power of black consumers, reaching $593 billion during the year 2001.

There are 18.1 million black females, representing 53.4% of the total black consumer market, and the lion's share of its purchasing power. Nearly 40% of the black population is under 20 years of age so that the median age of 28.4 years is significantly lower than the 33.9 years for the general population. Another 42%, however, is 25–54—the target age group for the *Heart & Soul* market. The black population is growing twice as fast as the general population and is expected to reach 35.9 million during 2001.

The fastest-growing segment of the black consumer market is affluent households earning more than $50,000 a year, up 46% from 1970–1990. The number of college graduates doubled in the 1980s. *Heart & Soul* readers are representative of this segment.

This market consumes more print media than the overall U.S. population. A Simmons Market Research Bureau survey found that 46% of the black consumer market rely on magazines and newspapers for their information needs. With a preference for black-oriented media, 29% named magazines as their preferred medium of choice versus 20% of the total U.S. population. *Heart & Soul* is the fourth-largest magazine in this market.

Sources: 1997 Packaged Facts; Selig Center for Economic Growth, University of Georgia.

TEMPO MAGAZINE FOR WOMEN

Tempo's target is women, 25–54, in households with income exceeding $50,000 a year. Only 55,000 of these women need purchase *Tempo* to achieve 5-year profit goals.

There are 92 million women in the United States, 51 million of whom are in the 25–54 age bracket. There are almost 15 million women in

households earning over $50,000. The goal is, therefore, to reach less than 0.4% of that 15 million.

The anticipated demographics include:

Median Age	*36*
Median Income (married)	*$56M*
Median Income (single)	*$35M*
College Educated	*65%*
Employed	*80%*
Professional/Managerial	*35%*
Metro Area Residence	*90%*

This journal is not for everyone. Our target audience is an intelligent woman strongly moved by romance, who wants a journal that reflects her values, tastes, and interests. Her attitude is more important than her demographic profile.

Her values, like most women today, are a curious mix of old and new. She has more choices now. Whether she assumes traditional roles, forges new ones, or shows a combination of both, it is her ability to choose that sets her apart. She's conscious of the delicate balance she maintains as part of a generation redefining notions of femininity and sexuality.

Nowhere is this more apparent than in her relationships. For example, she can be assertive sexually yet feel vulnerable. She might be making $100,000 a year and secretly longing for Prince Charming.

As a consumer she knows what she likes. She is stylish and up on the latest trends. She is interested in the arts, goes to museums, attends the theater, ballet, and movies. She is discriminating, self-indulgent, and spends a fortune on luxury goods that she views as necessities of life—clothes, travel, health clubs, manicures, massage, entertaining, favorite restaurants.

When she picks up a magazine it is *Elle, Vanity Fair, L.A. Style, Vogue, Money, Interview,* or *Architectural Digest*.

Self-confident, successful, complex, she will respond to these key words: *grace, womanliness, whimsy, caprice, lushness, dessert, fun, intimacy, lust, strength, heart*. And she will love a journal that will allow her to embrace and express her sexuality with sensitivity and dignity.

Evaluating Your Market

The two most important things to come out of a market evaluation are:

1. Whether the market is growing or shrinking.
2. How much penetration of the total market is needed for success.

By "penetration" we mean what percentage of the total market you need to get as your customers. For an example of how market penetration is used in a business plan, look at the excerpt in the previous section for the women's magazine, *Tempo*. The second paragraph presents a compelling argument that this magazine requires only 0.4% market penetration to be a success. Here's how you can calculate a number like this—or better—for your business:

Size of Your Market

The first part of your market penetration number is arrived at by calculating the total number of potential buyers for your product. Let's look at ways of estimating that figure:

- **For a local product or service:** How far will people drive to buy from you? Or how far will you drive to sell to them? Then, how many people are in that area? Let's say you establish a 15-mile circle and there are 200,000 people living (or working) within that circle. Are all of them potential customers? Should you cut back, say, 17,000 for children? Maybe another 3,000 for people in nursing homes? This would leave you with a potential market size of 180,000 people. Will men *and* women buy your product? If not, cut back accordingly. What about household income?

- **For a national product or service:** First, narrow your potential demographic groups to match your potential customer. For example, you might decide your target demographics are: men, 18–35, single, not homeowners. Or, they could be: women, 45–60, married, with household incomes of $45,000 or more. Check the U.S. Census numbers and calculate how many people are in your market. For a rough calculation,

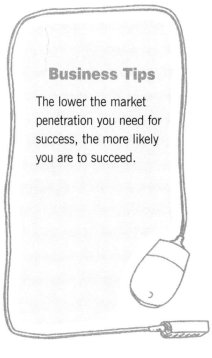

Business Tips

The lower the market penetration you need for success, the more likely you are to succeed.

there are 100 million households in the United States, with an average of 2.7 people per household. So, if your target is all adult women, you'd start with 100 million. Of course, some of those households have only adult men living in them, but some also have two or more adult women, so it will even out in your rough figure.

Using "Norms"

If you're selling a consumer product, normal market penetration—the "norm"—is in the 2%–6% range. If you have a true monopoly, you may get 7%–8%. Thus, if you've calculated that you have 900,000 potential customers, you'd take 2% of that number and get 18,000, and take 6% of that market and get 54,000. That leaves you with a "reality check" for your business plan figures. Can you succeed if you can get 18,000–54,000 customers? You'll find out in Part 2 on marketing.

If you're selling a business-to-business (B2B) product, market penetration can range from 10% up to 40% or more.

These numbers (2%–6% for consumer products and 10%–40% for business products) are not infallible. Your business could easily get lower market penetration or in some cases get higher. However, these are numbers that investors find reasonable on business plans—higher percentages set off their warning alarms, as they should yours.

When you calculate your potential profits later, the figures will be based upon how many customers you can get. If you find you need 25,000 customers to make a profit, and 25,000 customers are 75% of your total number of prospects—a 75% penetration rate!—your business will probably fail. But if those 25,000 customers are just 1.5% of your total prospects—your business has a much better chance of success.

CHAPTER FOUR

Learning from the Competition

Direct and Indirect Competitors

A common mistake many entrepreneurs make is believing their product is so unique that they have no competitors. Never forget: you *always* have competitors, even if they're only indirect competitors.

All products have some commonality. Even those on the cutting edge of innovation, such as:

- The computer, which at first indirectly competed with adding machines and typewriters.
- Virtual reality headgear and software, which at first indirectly competed with video games. Now, instead of saving the galaxy from evil invaders by blasting them out of the sky using a joystick, you're "participating" in blasting them out of the sky!

Your potential customers are already satisfying some of the needs your product or service will address through indirect competitors. Studying these competitors can give you great advantages. You'll see what customers like about a current product, and you can thus apply features, where appropriate, so your product seems more familiar and thus more comfortable to them. This is particularly important if your product is substantially different from anything else on the market.

You'll also see what customers don't like about the current product they're using—which will help you to clarify or emphasize how your product eliminates or eases that problem.

Let's look at some examples of competition.

Crafts Kit Business

Say your product is a crafts kit to make elegant Christmas tree decorations.

Your direct competitors are the makers of other Christmas tree decoration craft kits. You'll want to study them to make sure:

- Your product is different
- Your product is similarly priced—or if higher priced, it's for a reason that makes obvious sense to the consumer

Your indirect competitors are:

- Child-oriented Christmas tree decoration kits
- Hallmark Christmas tree ornaments and other ready-made, top-end products

Your study of your indirect competitors will help you:

- Make sure your product sharply distinguishes itself from child-oriented kits in product, packaging, colors, price
- See what is selling in elegant, ready-made ornaments, information you can use to:
  - Brainstorm ideas for future kits to develop
  - Pick up ideas for ad copy to sell your own product
  - Inspire packaging design and art ideas
  - Use your packaging/sales message to emphasize your strengths—handmade = family heirlooms, love, etc.—over ready-made.
  - Do a reality check on your prices

Restaurant Business

Let's say your business plan is for a diner. Your direct competitors will be any other diner within a few miles of your location. If there aren't any diners, you will doubtless have some strong indirect competitors: fast-food restaurants and low-end regular restaurants.

What can you learn from these indirect competitors? You can learn exactly what dining experiences your potential customers are already having. Such things as:

- How long does it take to get served breakfast at 7–7:30 A.M.? At 7:30–8 A.M.? At 8–8:30 A.M.? Each group will present a different experience, based on how crowded the restaurant is, and each group is unique—someone who has breakfast 7:30–8 will probably do so each workday because he or she has a work start time to meet.
- How's the food?
- How's the experience? (waitstaff, ambiance, cleanliness, odors, etc.)

Don't Go Overboard

Too much novelty doesn't always attract. If you can make it feel comfortable—even though it's new—you'll be ahead of the game: "Just like with the old Widget, you'll learn how to use the Acme Widget—only QUICKER!"

Types of Competitors

Your closest competitors are direct competitors. Those not so close are indirect competitors.

- Example: You want to start a consulting business specializing in utility bill analysis. You look at a company's utility bills and find ways they can save money or recoup money incorrectly billed. Your direct competitors are anyone doing the same service. Your indirect competitors may include anyone offering general financial analysis consulting for companies, or programs offered by utilities to help their customers save money.

(continued on next page)

If you can chat with diners near you, you can get even more information. Say, "Would you mind if I asked you three questions? I'm thinking about opening a restaurant and I'd like to get your opinion."

1. What do you like best about this place?
2. What do you like least?
3. If you could change anything, what would it be?

Most people are happy to give their opinions, as long as they know you won't tie up too much of their time (hence the "three questions" line). If they feel like it, of course, you'll be happy to get all of their opinions!

Spotting Competitors

Your competitors are anyone or any company providing a product or service that serves a similar purpose to yours. Try to look at it from the *customer's* point of view—not yours.

By looking at competitors with this broader stroke, you can save yourself the disaster that befalls many companies that have too narrow a view of what they're selling. For example, Amtrak's competitors include automobiles and airplanes, because the customer thinks only of how they're going to get from one location to another. To stay in business, Amtrak had to do a lot of advertising and deliver better service.

If you're selling chocolate chip cookies, your competitors may include candy, cakes, Hostess Twinkies, and more—anything your customer may think of when they want a sweet treat.

If you're selling consulting services, your competitors may include people who have your expertise who are willing to become employees. Look at it from the buyer's viewpoint. Say Famous Amos is thinking about adding ice cream to their product line and they need someone to analyze if this makes sense. What are the advantages of having an outside person do it? What are the disadvantages? Or say they want to train their salespeople to improve their skills. Do they have enough salespeople to make this an internal position? Or can they get better, cheaper service by using outside trainers?

Seeing Your Competitive Environment Graphically

Sometimes displaying a subject graphically can pull everything together. This exercise will open your eyes to who your competitors are as well as opportunities.

On a piece of paper, list all your direct competitors. If there are fewer than 10, add your most important indirect competitors. List the price each charges for a product or service comparable to yours.

If you don't know the price, call and find out. Give some thought to the quality of the company's product or service. Then draw a quick square and vertically list the range of prices at the left margin (as in the example on page 66) and write the quality measures horizontally along the bottom. Draw a center vertical and horizontal line in the box, dividing the box into quarters—this is your matrix. Then locate each competitor in the matrix where their price and quality would put them. Use abbreviations to identify each competitor.

What does this graphic tell you? That a number of competitors (Co. E to Co. H) are high priced and high quality, a few are low priced and low quality (Co. B to Co. D), and some are confused. Here are some questions to ask yourself:

1. Does this matrix environment show an opening for a high-quality but medium-priced product?
2. Where would your company show up in this chart?

Types of Competitors

(continued from previous page)

- Example: You want to open a pet store. Any pet store within 20–30 miles is probably a direct competitor. Indirect competitors would include pet stores outside that range, the local pound, individuals using newspaper classifieds to sell or give away pets, and—for purebreds—classified ads in newspapers, magazines, or Web sites.

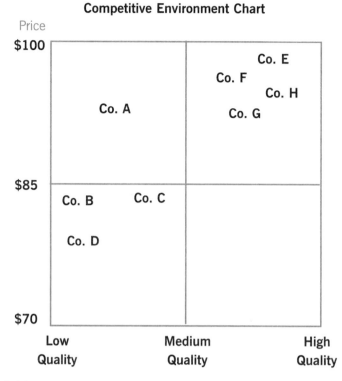

Competitive Environment Chart

Note: "Co" is company: Thus Co. A is company A, etc.

3. Is your company's quarter of the matrix a crowded area? If so, you're competing head on with a lot of competitors.

4. If there are no competitors in the quarter of the matrix where your company is, why is that? Perhaps there are no low-cost, low-quality competitors because this product is too critical for buyers to risk the lower quality? Think about other reasons why.

You can make marketing decisions based on your matrix positioning. Here is how to interpret your position:

- Upper right quarter: You'll be marketing to people whose first concern is quality—more than price.
- Lower left quarter: You'll be marketing to people whose first concern is price—more than quality.

- Lower right quarter: You'll be marketing to people who care a lot about quality, but for whom price is slightly more important.
- Upper left quarter: You'll be marketing to idiots willing to pay top prices for low quality. Hint: there aren't too many of these people. Company A may not be long for this world!

Customizing the Price/Quality Chart

The chart you just made ranks competitors in two areas that are almost always part of the competitive environment: price and quality. If you have specific, quantifiable measures for quality, however, it is much better to adapt the chart to those measures. For example, specific quality measures are:

- How quickly can a customer get what they ordered?
- How good is your guarantee? Your returns policy?
- If a food product, what ingredients are used?
- If a manufactured product, what specs are used?

Customize the chart by using these different measurements instead of price and/or quality. For example, if your product is software, count the customer-desired features and rank how many of those features each competing software package has. That could be one side of the matrix, with price as the other side.

Proving Your Quality Claims

"Our product/service will be better quality than the competition's . . ."

Frankly, a phrase like this in a business plan sends shivers down my spine. I suspect it also lights up the b.s. detectors of investment bankers and others considering lending a new business money. Never, ever use it without concrete, specific examples of that superiority.

The problem isn't the goal—to produce a better quality product/service—which is an admirable one. The problem is that *everyone* thinks their product/service is better than the other's product/service. Most consumers don't see much difference between those very same "superior" products and their competition.

Following are concrete examples of quality measurements from a business plan for a gardening service business. This business intends to distinguish itself on quality, and the plan gives exact details of what that quality is based upon.

PLAN FOR A GARDENING SERVICE BUSINESS
TRAINING

Building a sense of teamwork among all personnel is an essential component for the success of Lawn Masters of Newton. By allocating significant time and resources to staff training, we expect to increase every employee's ability to provide valuable services for our customers, and to feel that he or she is an important, contributing part of the organization. Responsibility for training will come under Operations (Ed Davis), but all three members of the management team have taken part in developing or reviewing training materials or in actually delivering training sessions as appropriate.

Due to the short seasonal nature of the business, all employees need feedback on their performance with a much greater frequency than the normal annual review process. Lawn Masters of Newton uses a standard form, completed on a weekly basis by the crew leader. This form contains specific feedback on job performance, and also makes summary recommendations as to areas for improvement.

SERVICE DELIVERY

Here are standards we have adopted to ensure that we provide high-quality service:

1. *We will answer our phones within three rings.*
2. *We will provide a free, written estimate within 48 hours.*
3. *We will begin work within three days of receiving a signed agreement.*
4. *We will not interrupt work for any reason until we finish a job.*
5. *We will use the highest quality equipment and supplies available.*
6. *We will leave the property clean and neat at the end of each day.*

7. *We will follow up after every job to be sure the customer is completely satisfied.*
8. *We will guarantee satisfaction for all of our work.*

Our strategy is built around offering highly personalized service to our customers. Integral to this approach is the careful selection of field staff, in-depth training so that they may respond quickly to customer requests, and in-depth backup support for more difficult requests.

QUALITY-CONTROL CHANGES

Overall responsibility for control is handled by Ed Davis. After a major review of our current procedures, which included soliciting input from customers, we have redesigned certain aspects of the process. In particular, we will institute new incentive programs and emphasize training and rewards to help motivate employees to ensure that our high-quality standards are being met.

CUSTOMER SERVICE/SUPPORT

We intend to prioritize customer service and make it a key component of our marketing programs. We believe that providing our customers with what they want in the area of lawn maintenance, when and how they want it, is the key to repeat business and to word-of-mouth advertising. Not only will we train our employees to deliver excellent service, we will give them the flexibility to respond creatively to client requests. In addition, we will continually monitor our clients' level of satisfaction with our service through surveys and convenient feedback opportunities.

We plan on using the World Wide Web for a significant portion of our service/support effort. On the Web we can offer support 24 hours a day, 365 days a year, and customers won't have to wait for the next available service representative. Once the service area of our Web site is up, the cost to maintain it will be minimal. On our Web site we will offer a choice of text options explaining basic service issues, a list of frequently asked questions and answers about lawn maintenance, and e-mail capabilities for help with highly specific questions and any requested changes in the scheduled maintenance plan.

Getting Info on Your Competition

"Your mission, should you accept it, is . . ." Yes, consider yourself under the employment of a top spy master (yourself!). Your assignment is to get all the information you can on your competition. However, you have one small additional consideration not faced by the Mission Impossible team: You have to do it legally. You'll be astounded at how much you can learn about your competitors without breaking and entering or wearing a pull-off rubber face.

Don't put this off until you're starting up your business. You'll never be able to get as good information on your competitors as you can when they don't know you exist. Once you launch, and especially as you start to grow, you'll find a number of your information sources disappear. So take advantage of your anonymity now—while you still have it as an advantage. Don't procrastinate!

Work for Your Competitor

There's nothing you could do that will help your business succeed more than working for a company that does the same thing your business will do. It doesn't have to be a company that will become a competitor. It could even be in a different city from where you plan to set up your business.

What you can learn by working for a competitor:

- Manufacturing processes that work or don't work. Or, if you won't be manufacturing your product, you can learn which manufacturers in your industry do good work and which don't.
- Which vendors are reliable, and which to avoid.
- The feedback from customers on how the products or services did or did not please them.
- Marketing results: What methods of selling the product work best?
- Pricing results: What prices worked well and/or made the greatest profit?

Competitor Files

There are a number of ways you can get competitive information—legally. What do you do with this information? Start a folder—now—for each of your direct competitors. In that folder will go everything you read about them, what you hear about them, and the results of your investigations. These folders will come in mighty handy when you start your marketing campaign, and may be handy for much, much more.

- Personnel management techniques: What are the particular problems that crop up in your industry, and how is the company trying to manage them?

Also—an added bonus—if you impress clients and/or the competitive company with how good you are, they may become clients of your new company.

Avoid Legal Trouble

If you go to work for a company that will become a competitor, there are two things you have to avoid doing so you don't get sued: stealing trade secrets and stealing clients. If you're planning something that could even possibly violate either of these two areas, consult an attorney who specializes in this kind of law before proceeding. Your state's bar association should be able to point you to someone appropriate.

Here is more on the two categories that could pose legal trouble for you.

Trade Secrets

Trade secrets are any business practices or information a company keeps secret. If you learn a trade secret, you can't then take that information and use it in your business. For example, if you worked at McDonald's headquarters and learned the ingredients of their "secret sauce," you could not use it in your new, competing restaurant or McDonald's will sue you—and win.

Here are guidelines to what is *not* secret:

- Any information that is published or available to the public cannot be a trade secret.
- Any information announced in a press release can't be secret.
- Anything that can be seen by the public can't be secret. For example, I can pick up an issue of *Sludge Weekly* magazine and see who their advertisers are and roughly how much money those clients are spending

Work for Competing Consultants

If you're selling consulting services, it will be hard if not impossible to get your hands on a report prepared by a competing consultant. Yet the knowledge you could gain from seeing one is astronomical.

So, if you can't get a full-time job learning from a future competitor in your line of consulting service, you can offer yourself to consulting service companies for part-time work or for project work. That way you can see how the competitor does the following:

- Prepares proposals
- Establishes fees (if you're lucky enough to have access to this)

(continued on next page)

(by looking at the size and color of the ad and their rate card, which is available in advertising directories).

- What a company does in marketing is mostly visible and not a trade secret. Ads and direct mail campaigns are not something that can be considered a trade secret.

If there are any doubts about something being secret, consult a lawyer who specializes in this kind of law before proceeding.

Clients

There are two ways you could steal clients from a company that are illegal: taking customer lists and contacting company clients as your potential clients *before* you leave the job.

- Client lists that are kept secret cannot be taken. How do you know if they are secret? Has the company announced names of clients? Or have they appeared in print, written up in articles regarding the business and its clients? If so, those clients' names are not secret.

  As a rule of thumb, legal representation is seldom a secret, because the attorneys' names are filed on court documents. If you're planning to open a new security company—not one with highly visible (thus not secret) guards—the names of those clients may be carefully protected by your competitor, and thus a secret.

  A list of a magazine's advertising clients is not confidential because they're in the magazine, which is printed and distributed. But a list of subscribers *is* confidential—unless they print it for public dissemination.

  Note, however, that you can always promote your company to any outside lists of suitable targets, which will undoubtedly include many names of your former company's clients.

- Contacting clients before leaving and trying to get them to go with your company is also illegal. Once you leave, you can promote your company to any potential clients, including clients of your former company—as long as you didn't find their names on a kept-secret list. And clients of the former company will be free to contact you and decide if they want to go with you.

Read Trade News

Read the trade publications for your industry. Whether it's *Metal Finishing* magazine or *Children's Apparel*, these publications cover your market (giving you trend information) and your competitors. Clip out any articles on your competitors and save them. You can find which publications serve your industry by going to the library and looking at *SRDS Business Publication Rates & Data*. This directory lists all the magazines serving businesspeople—by industry. Yours will doubtless be included.

An astonishing amount of "confidential" information is published by outside research firms and/or magazines and newsletters. You'll often find it published in industry publications, or at least referred to in them.

For example, in the publishing industry, you can guestimate pretty closely what profits any magazine makes by gathering information on the following:

- **Ad pages:** The bigger magazines report their number of ad pages to Publishers Information Bureau (PIP) or Media Industry News (MIN), two reporting services. But even if they don't, you can buy or check out in the library a year's worth of issues and count the ad pages.
- **Ad rates:** You can get the competition's ad rates in SRDS (a directory in your library) or from the publication's Web site.
- **Subscriptions:** These are audited by audit bureaus and, again, listed in SRDS. Some publications are not audited. They list a "sworn" circulation in SRDS.
- **Newsstand sales:** This information is again in SRDS. What it does *not* tell you is how many copies magazines send out to dealers in order to be able to sell what they do (lots of copies to dealers never sell and are trashed). However, that information is listed in the November or December issues of any magazine that is mailed at Periodicals rate. It's in the tiny-type "Annual Statement of Ownership" required by the Post Office.
- **Manufacturing costs:** You can get a print bid for a magazine similar in coloration, number of pages, and number of copies from either a competing magazine's actual printer or another using similar equipment.

Work for Competing Consultants

(continued from previous page)

- Establishes guidelines or parameters for:
  - Proposals for new business
  - Price quotes and payment schedules
  - Work scheduling

- Presents the findings, including style, format, and quantity of material in final report

Similarly, if you want to sell accounting services, you could probably get yourself hired on a temp basis at a similar firm— during tax season.

- **G&A (General and Administrative) costs:** This is the only thing you can't get elsewhere, but you can see the number of names on their masthead, which gives a small clue. You really don't need this information; just figure out how many people you'd need to do the same job.

Not everyone is going into the publishing business, of course, but several of these categories will apply to your new business, no matter what it is. Add information categories of your own to correspond to your industry.

Search the Web

The World Wide Web is a virtual gold mine of information on other businesses. If you don't own a computer, go to the library and use theirs.

There are three excellent ways to acquire competitor information on the Web.

1. Visit the Web sites of your competitors. If you can't find one at the logical place (e.g., *www.ibm.com*), use the Web search device or call each company and ask for their Web site address. What can you learn from a competitor's Web site?
   - Who they're targeting as customers. Note what audience the site is designed to attract.
   - Their line of products, and what they are emphasizing as special features.
   - Special deals or offers they are making.
   - How many salespeople they have (usually all are listed by name and by geographic region).
   - Their prices.
   - Sales trends. Look at what is featured for sale on the site. Is it the same thing that was featured last month? Last week? While small companies generally keep the same products displayed, sharp Web "e-tailers" see what is selling and give it more prominence, pushing

Hard Facts from Trade Associations

Many industries have some regulatory body—either governmental or voluntary—that receives input from companies and reports on it.

Many trade associations do a confidential financial study of members. In this study, participants can see what the average company in the association pays for various expenses—such as marketing, manufacturing, and G&A (General & Administrative expenses, which usually include salaries, telephone, rent, etc.) as a percent of revenue.

Frequently the numbers are broken down by size of company. So if you see that the average small company in your industry spends 33% of its revenues on marketing costs, that will tell you that the 55% you're planning to spend (or the 15%) is not realistic. From the many business plans I've looked at, I usually find entrepreneurs underestimating what they'll need to spend on marketing. Often, they overspend on G&A, usually with too much staff.

Often trade association financial surveys will detail:

- Profits or revenues per employee
- Profits or revenues per profit center
- Return on sales (the amount of each dollar you receive as revenue that you end up keeping as profit)

Find out if the main association in your field does such a study and how you can get a copy of it. Frequently you will be required to participate in the study in order to get it, though often the association will make an exception for someone who has just joined the group—allowing you to get the current study. This can be worth the cost of joining the association all by itself.

lower-selling products to the background, or even off the site. Profit from their knowledge.

2. Use a search engine. My favorite one is AltaVista (*www.altavista.com*), but there are a variety of good ones. Go to a search engine and type in the business name of your competitor. See what the search engine finds for the company.

    This is great the first time you do it. But when you do it again a month later to see what's new, you may have to read through all the old stuff again. See if you can find a search engine that lets you search for information posted after a specified date. The help screens for the search engine or a savvy librarian should be able to tell you how.

3. Get regular news on your companies. If your competitors are public companies (listed on a stock exchange) you can get an e-mail from the *Wall Street Journal* every time any article runs about that company. Just visit *www.wsj.com* and sign up.

Examine the Product

You can't beat firsthand examination of a competitor's product. You want to see it. Hold it in your hand. Personally evaluate its quality.

There are three ways you can do this:

1. Visit a store and view the item. If your competitors make clothing, go into stores and look at the product. Handle it. Look at the seams. How well is it constructed? What colors are they using? What designs?

    If the product you want to examine is complicated, buy one and take it apart to see how it is made and the quality of the components. You'll see where your competitor cut costs and where they spent for quality. This is important because you'll need to do the same. An entrepreneur in the bed linens marketplace told me her biggest surprise was that quality doesn't always sell. Buyers—even rich ones—have a perceived idea of what something is worth, and even if you use extra quality components people won't pay the higher price needed to cover those costs.

2. Buy the product via direct marketing. If your competitor doesn't sell in stores, you'll have to go after their product where they sell it. Don't skip this chance because money is tight. If money is really that tight (and if so, are you sure you should be launching a business?), you can always return the product for a refund (you pay shipping). You can't take the risk that there's something about a product you should know but don't.

3. Examine the products in the office. If your products or services are used in offices, go in and see them in use. If need be, pester your friends to let you hang out at their offices. Call in markers. Pressure acquaintances. For example, when a friend of mine first joined a large business, she found herself kept out of the loop. So she got a list of alumni from her graduate school who worked there and contacted them all, asking for their help. It worked. Find contacts through your church or synagogue. The Rotary Club. A friend of a friend of a friend.

Get a Personal Assistant

There are "personal assistant" sorting engines you can pay for that will search the Web daily and bring you everything it finds on selected companies or keywords. Yahoo! allows you to set up a page (My Yahoo!) that will bring you daily news on companies you select (if they're publicly traded).

Spying!

I'm always astonished at how few people adopt the spying tactic. They're either intimated or they give up and claim the information isn't available, when clearly it is—if you're willing to work for it.

Not every industry's sales are visible, but many are. You can easily—and legally—spy on competitors:

- If they are retail stores
- If their products are sold in stores
- If their services are sold in storefronts
- If their services are performed in homes

Let's break that down into some examples.

On Retail Stores

Unless you have a relative in the business—and maybe not even then—nobody is going to tell you how much money they're making. But you can get a good idea if you're willing to do the grunt work.

Retail stores can't sell to customers who don't walk in the door. Thus, if you count the number of people entering the store over a week or two, you'll have very valuable information. Yes, it will be incredibly boring to sit in your car or on a bench in the mall and count their customers for 10 hours a day. But if you find they're only getting 430 people a day, and your business plan assumes you'll be able to get 700 people, you might have just saved yourself from a bankruptcy. By the way, if you try to delegate this spy job to one of your children, make sure it is a very responsible child—and give them frequent breaks. The only thing worse than *no* numbers is *wrong* numbers.

While you're counting customers, you might want to add some additional information. Unless it's a jewelry store, where most purchases go into a handbag or pocket, you might want to look at the size of the bags customers come out with. You could have a note pad with you where you make a mark for every customer going in. On another page you'd indicate the shopping bags they come out with: 0 = none, S = small bag, M = medium or two small bags, L = huge bag or many bags. If it's an ice cream shop, it will be easier. Count the scoops and toppings! A tailor shop? How big a clothes bundle is carried in?

With an apparel store you could examine their merchandise beforehand and estimate their average price was $30, or $200, etc. Then multiply that figure times the number of purchases that would fit in each size of bag coming out. Then you'd have a rough idea of how much sales they were making.

On Products Sold Retail

Many products sold in retail stores can be tracked for profitability as well. Ask the retailer questions. If you're a regular customer, the retailer may be kindly disposed to help you. Retailers might also help you even if they don't know you—if there's nobody in the store needing their attention at the time. What should you ask?

Sales Per Square Foot

Many retail industries track sales per square foot of store space. Talk to your trade association and to the magazine editors in your industry to see what averages they have. With the size of the store you're spying on an easily known quantity, you can then estimate what sort of a profit the store is making.

Hear It Through the Grapevine

The Former Employee

A great way of getting confidential information is interviewing—and perhaps hiring—former employees of your direct competitors. Part of any interview process is asking potential employees what successes they've accomplished and what failures they've experienced. Some of the answers may contain confidential information or your competitor's business practices. You could pick up some valuable do's and don'ts.

If you hire people away from a competitor, you learn more about the competition—and help yourself—and you'll hurt your competitor at the same time. Of course, expect that the competitor might try the same tactic on you!

The Loose-Lipped Rival

Hang out in places where your competitors hang out and listen to the scuttlebutt.

One of my bosses often ate lunch in an out-of-the-way restaurant where our biggest competitors frequently ate. One day, in the booth right behind him, two employees were discussing budget numbers for one of our biggest competitors—a magazine on mechanics. My boss motioned to his lunch partner to be quiet, pulled out a pen and paper, and wrote down everything he could hear. Some of it was eye-opening information for us.

Some people frequent bars where midlevel employees of competitors hang out. They strike up bar friendships with these people and gossip about the imaginary company they work for—hoping to get reciprocal gossip in return. (How many movies have used exactly this scenario to move the plot along?) You might dig up something interesting this way. Or you might get nothing but a big bar tab and trouble focusing on work the next morning.

For a product sold only in a few stores in your town, tell the retailer you're planning to create a line of products—say, a new kind of floor wax. You're working on the business plan and you have no idea what to estimate for sales. Tell him you're trying to track all the sales of floor waxes in your town. By telling the retailer all of this, you can impress him or her with your seriousness, and you'll be more likely to receive an answer for these two crucial questions:

1. How many of these products do they usually sell in a month?
2. Is that number steady, increasing, or decreasing?

Now you can add up the sales figures from all the local retailers selling floor wax (estimating a number for any who won't give you an answer). Divide that number by the population of your town. If you're in an area far from another city, take part of the outside rural population—out to half way to the nearest other cities. That gives you local monthly sales per person—it will be a small fraction, not to worry.

Multiply that number by the U.S. population to get a figure for estimated national sales. NOTE: If your product is only sold in certain regions—such as if it's snow-related, or a marine product—adjust the population numbers accordingly.

Finally, reduce that number by 25%—just to be conservative and stay on the safe side. You'll end up with a very rough national sales figure for an established product (in this example, floor wax). Don't create a business plan that depends upon your competing product having a similar sales number, however. Regard the numbers you come up with as sales estimates and see how they compare to your planned sales (see Chapter 11).

What if you can't get sales numbers from local retailers? You can still gather information on:

- Whether the store increased or decreased the shelf space devoted to a product
- How fast the merchandise is moving

For perishable products, you can see how many organic donuts, for instance, they put out first thing in the morning and how many are on hand when they close. Ask if they put out all the donuts in the morning, or hold some back and replenish during the day.

For nonperishables, ask a store employee when they might be getting in new stock. Then watch how fast (or slow) the current stock moves.

I can't recommend the following, but I do know an entrepreneur who did it. She made a tiny little mark in the corner of bath oil products on the shelf and checked back each day. That way she could count how many bottles of bath oil were sold over time, without being fooled by a new batch coming in and being put out on the shelves.

On Storefront Services

What if you want to open a copy shop? A picture framing business? A tax accounting service?

How can you tell how many customers similar businesses are getting? As in retail spying, you can count people going in or out, and look at what they carry out. For a printing business, you could go into the store four times a day for a couple of weeks to make a copy (of anything). While there, take your time and see how much business they are doing. For example:

- How many of their copy machines are busy?
- How many of their printing presses are running?
- How many employees are on duty?
- How many customers do they have in the shop?

Use your imagination. Think of how you can track customers for a potential competitor.

If you can't think of a way, drive to a competitor in a nearby city and offer your services free for a month. (Or at minimum wages, if you can get it.) Tell them you're planning a similar business in your hometown and you want to learn the ropes. A friend who wanted to open a pizza business in Hawaii—where they don't have too much pizza!—worked free at a New York City pizzeria and learned the business from top to bottom in a month.

Getting the Skinny on Distributors

If you tell a store manager you're planning to introduce a new line of XYZ products, and ask about distributors, he'll probably tell you one, two, or more distributors his store uses for competitive products. Many of the stores will tell you which distributors are better than others, and maybe throw in the skinny on any distributor that's in trouble.

Now, call and ask those distributors what kinds of products they would most like to add to their lines. The answers will reflect the type of products that are selling best, or those products that stores want but they can't seem to supply. Factor this information into your business plan. You might want to reconsider a few things—or you might want to jump with joy.

Discovering the Competition's Marketing Plan

To know a competitor's marketing plan—and ad budget—is extremely valuable information—and it's usually quite easy to acquire. If your business and your competitors are local, buy all the local papers for two months. Go through the papers daily and clip out any ads for your competitors, mark the dates of the ads and where they ran, and stash them in the folders you've made for each competitor. (In fact, this is a good procedure to continue doing as long as your business is operating. You'll want to know if your competitors have increased or decreased their ad budgets.)

Summarize the ads in an organized fashion. Make a sheet for each competitor and list dates of ad appearance, size of ad, and where it ran. (See sample spreadsheet for determining advertising schedules on page 83.)

Here's what you'll learn from this process:

- **How much money each competitor is spending on print advertising.** (You will of course be missing the figures for radio or TV). You estimate their ad budget by counting up the ads and looking at a rate card for each publication (easy to get—just call the newspaper and say you're interested in advertising and want to see their rates). You'll find each publication charges different rates for different sizes and frequencies of ads (e.g., an ad run in every issue costs less per ad than an ad running only once a quarter). Find the appropriate ad rate, multiply it by 0.85% (to eliminate the ad agency discount), and multiply it by the number of ads that company is running *per year*, assuming the rest of the year is similar to the two months you studied. As you continue to track this information over future months, your estimate will get closer and closer to the actual ad budget figure of your competitor. Be aware that publications sometimes discount their rates, so your competitor(s) may be paying a little less. Tip: When you're ready to advertise, try to get extra discounts yourself. Ask if they're available.

Home Services

Planning a home cleaning service? An appliance installation or repair service? A decorating service? First, call all your potential competitors and get their prices. Ask some (or all) of them to come to your home and give you a bid on providing their services to you. Ask how the work will be done. Ask about their employees. Ask about their insurance in case of problems. Ask how long it will take to complete the job. You'll get great competitive information, right in your own house.

Competitors' Marketing Plans: Advertising Schedule

A spreadsheet similar to this will help you track competitors who advertise more than one day a week. If your competitors advertise only in weekly or monthly publications, you can simplify this report considerably. The reason for getting weekday totals is to see what days your competitors have determined are best for advertising.

You can add columns to this spreadsheet to track competitors' ad budgets and places they advertise. You can also use a spreadsheet to design your own advertising plans.

| Date | Day | Competitors | | | | Total Ads Mon. | Total Ads Tues. | Total Ads Wed. | Total Ads Thurs. | Total Ads Fri. | Total Ads Sat. | Total Ads Sun. |
		1	2	3	4							
6/1	Monday					0						
6/2	Tuesday	¼ pg.		⅛ pg.			2					
6/3	Wednesday	¼ pg.	¼ pg.	¼ pg.				3				
6/4	Thursday	½ pg.	½ pg.	½ pg.	¼ pg.				4			
6/5	Friday	½ pg.	½ pg.	½ pg.	¼ pg.					4		
6/6	Saturday										0	
6/7	Sunday	Full pg.			Full pg.							2

- **Which publications your competitors have determined are the best to advertise in.** By the way, your competitors could be wrong on their choices. A local newspaper may be a good place to start when you launch your business, but eventually you'll want to test other options to see if they work better for you.
- **The seasonality your competitors recognize.** Do they advertise more in the spring and fall and less in the summer or winter? Do they skip ads in February and March? Do they run twice as many ads in September or December? Not only will these patterns give you guidelines for your own advertising, but they will also give you major clues as to what months produce more sales and what months produce less.
- **The days of the week that pull best.** If none of your competitors advertise on Tuesdays, but they all advertise on Saturday and Sunday, you'll probably want to plan such a program for yourself at first.
- **The size ad to run.** If nobody runs less than $1/4$ page ads for your product or service, you'll know you either need to budget for a similar size or come up with something unique in a smaller ad that would get noticed.
- **What color ad to run.** Are they basic black and white? Do they add one more color, like red? Are they in full color? Color is something to consider for your own ad budget.
- **What copy and design to use.** Do your competitors sell a specific product with a lot of copy—or do they just try to build traffic in general with a big flashy design, the name of the company, and the address and phone number?

How Information Helps You Get Investors

Imagine you're an investor and two entrepreneurs come to you with two ideas that look roughly equal in potential. Each entrepreneur has a business plan, but the sections on competitors are vastly different. One would-be entrepreneur listed his main competitors and the fact that there were no publicly available sales information for any of them.

The other would-be entrepreneur had experienced the same scenario and said so. But this entrepreneur had gone out and done some footwork. She:

- Counted customer traffic in the shopping area.
- Tracked the amount of shelf space devoted to different types of products at similar shops in neighboring towns.
- Talked to two key distributors in the field and got their advice as to which types of products were moving the fastest, and which types of sales promotions seemed to work best.
- Tracked advertising by shops in neighboring towns for three months, and detailed how her marketing plan would agree with what was being done by others—and what she would be trying that was different.

Which one of these entrepreneurs would get your money?

Investors know that by using the right financial twists, anyone can produce a business plan that will make money on paper. And they know that lots of businesses fail that could have been successful. The key ingredient is the entrepreneur. The investor will assess an entrepreneur on more subjective qualities:

- How determined is he/she?
- How resourceful?
- How willing is he/she to work hard?
- How creative is he/she at finding new solutions to problems—such as finding competitive information when none is "available"?

Your business plan will be evaluated more for what it says about you and the answers to these questions than what it says about the business.

Digging up the kind of information about competitors we've discussed in this chapter says you're smart, creative, willing to do the hard (grunt) work, and relentless. You couldn't ask for a better calling card.

Trash Collector

All right, searching your competitors' trash for information about how they run their business might be a *little* extreme. I've never done it, but I know of people who have. So you *could*, if you are so inclined. Remember, however, if companies in your area recycle office paper, you'll have to look in an office paper recycling bin or bag instead of the general trash. That's where you'll find discarded correspondence, bills, names of vendors, distributors—even marketing plans.

Warning: Do not go onto someone else's property to get a bag of trash, say, out of their basement area. It's illegal. But anything left at the curb, or left in the spot where the garbage (or recycling) trucks pick up can be presumed to be thrown away and thus no longer protected. However, if I was planning such a raid, I'd call a local lawyer first, just to make sure there aren't any local ordinances I'd be breaking.

The Gold in Key Statistics

A spreadsheet of key statistics about your competitors in your business plan is essential if you're trying to raise capital—and smart to have even if you're not. We're talking about a single page of paper, listing all the key statistics about your competitors.

What are key statistics? Whatever elements that are important for your marketplace.

If your business will be manufacturing, such as clothing, you'll want to include:

- Your competitors' prices for similar products
- Their distribution channels (retail? wholesalers? direct marketing?)
- Who sells their line (chain stores? specific wholesalers?)

At a glance, such a spreadsheet would tell you which wholesalers carry your kind of merchandise. But it would also give you an idea of *how* to sell chains on your merchandise. For instance, if a chain carries your competitors, you would market your line to that chain as a "natural fit with the kinds of clothes that are already selling to your customers."

If they don't carry your competitors, but do carry clothes for the same sex, age, style as those your clothes are targeted to, you would sell them on your line by saying your clothes are "covering a niche your current customers are buying—but which you aren't offering."

If you're planning a retail or storefront operation, your key competitive statistics might include:

- Square feet of the competitors' stores. Measure the outside or inside of their building by stepping it off. (If you practice, you can learn to step at one-foot intervals.) Multiply the width times the length for the total square feet. If you measure the outside, deduct 10%–15% for unusable space.
- Product lines carried.
- Amount of advertising running in the local papers and where.
- Store hours. If none of your competitors are open after 6 P.M., for example, it might reflect a lack of buyers at that time—or it could be an opportunity to pick up buyers your competitors are ignoring.

Competitor Analysis: Health Newsletter

For some new businesses, there are too many key statistics—and too many competitors—to fit on one page. In the example that follows, part of a business plan for a new health newsletter, notice how the publications are grouped by price range.

General Health Newsletters (Indirect Competitors)

Newsletter	Price per yr.	Issues per yr.	Year Established	Corporate Owner
Heart Sense	$100	12	1995	Phillips Publishing
Nutrition Research Newsletter	$96	10	1982	LYDA Associates
Earl Mindell's Joy of Health	$69	12	N/A	Phillips Publishing
Health Wisdom for Women	$69	12	N/A	Phillips Publishing
Longevity Letter	$47	12	1983	Am. Longevity Assn.
Personal Fitness	$47	12	1983	Cromwell-Sloan Publishing
Women's Health Letter	$39	12	N/A	Soundview Publications
Health & Longevity	$39	12	N/A	Agora Inc.
Health Alert Newsletter	$39	12	1984	Bruce West
Men's Health Confidential	$36	12	1985	Rodale Press
Nutrition Forum	$35	24	N/A	Nutrition Forum
Health Confidential	$30	12	1987	Boardroom Reports
Harvard Health Letter	$24	12	1990	Harvard Medical School
Harvard Women's Health Watch	$24	12	1993	Harvard Medical School
Mayo Clinic Healthletter	$24	12	1983	Mayo Clinic
Nutrition Action Healthletter	$24	10	1977	Ctr. for Science in Pub. Int.
Living Health Bulletin	$24	24	N/A	GOTACH Center for Health
Univ. Berkeley Wellness Letter	$24	12	1984	Health Letter Assoc.
U. Texas Lifetime Health Letter	$24	12	1989	Univ. of Texas

Consumer Reports on Health	$24	12	1989	Consumers Union of U.S.
Good Health Bulletin	$20	12	N/A	Harvey W. Waft & Co.
Hope Health Letter	$20	12	1979	Int'l Health Awareness Center
Public Citizen Health Letter	$18	12	N/A	Public Citizen Health Group
Healthlines	$15	12	1982	Fitness Research Ctr. U. Mich.
Average Price:	$37.94			

Alternative Health Newsletters (Direct Competitors)

Newsletter	Basic Price	Intro Price	Issues per yr.	Year Established	Corporate Owner
Health & Healing	$69	$39.95	12	1991	Phillips Publishing
Dr. Atkins Health	$69	N/A	12	N/A	Wellness Communications
Naturally Well	$69	N/A	12	1994	Phillips Publishing
Second Opinion	$49	$39	12	1991	Soundview Publications
Holistic Medicine	$30	N/A	6	N/A	Am. Holistic Med. Assn.
Health Facts	$21	N/A	12	1976	Ctr. for Medical Consumers

Source: Hudson's Subscription Newsletter Directory, 1994

Ads in the Top 10 Alternative Health Magazines

Magazine	Total Circ (000)	Est. Ad Pgs./Issue	Rate	CPM*	Est. 1995 Ad Revenues (000)
Prevention	3,428	75	$46,800	$13.65	$42,120
Vegetarian Times	343	57	$8,390	$24.46	$4,600
Let's Live	1,239	40	$10,680	$8.62	$5,126
Energy Times	575	35	$7,849	$13.65	$1,648
Natural Health	243	83	$13,020	$53.58	$3,486
New Age Journal	200	73	$5,075	$25.38	$2,964

Body Mind Spirit	150	55	$3,600	$24.00	$1,188
Health World	120	35	$2,860	$23.83	$601
Total Health	91	30	$2,200	$24.18	$396
Yoga Journal	83	53	$2,125	$25.60	$676
TOTALS	6,472	54 Avg.			$62,805

*CPM – Cost per thousand readers. This calculation allows advertisers to compare ad prices for publications with varying numbers of readers.

Circulation in the Top 10 Alternative Health Magazines

Magazine	Total Paid Circ. (000)	Basic sub. Price	Total subs.	Est. sub revenue (000)	News-stand price	Total single copies	Est. N/S revenue (000)
Prevention	3,428	$21.97	2,812	$41,392	$2.25	616	$9,148
Vegetarian Times	343	$35.40	300	$7,115	$2.95	42	$743
Let's Live	1,239	$19.95	N/A	N/A	$2.50	48	$720
Energy Times	575	$15	430	$4,322	$2.50	145	$743
Natural Health	197	$12	185	$1,487	N/A	N/A	$0
New Age Journal	185	$24	150	$2,412	$3.95	35	$553
Mind Body Spirit	150	$21	50	$704	$3.95	100	$1,185
Total Health	91	$16	32	$343	$3	49	$441
Health World	87	$10.50	43	$302	$2	34	$204
Yoga Journal	83	$19.97	43	$709	$3.95	31	$367
TOTALS	6,378	$19.58, av.	4,055	$58,786	$3.01, av.	1,100	$14,449

Analysis: Chinese Restaurant

COMPETITORS FOR THE LING GARDEN

There are several direct competitors. Geographically, the closest Chinese restaurant is the Asian Kitchen, located approximately one mile away on Route 16. This restaurant appears small since most of the parking area is in front of the building and it is placed back from the roadway. Inside the restaurant are two dining areas divided into smoking and nonsmoking sections. The smoking section has five tables, which seat 25 people, the nonsmoking section seats 20 people at four tables. The exterior of the building is plain. The interior decor is red and black with lanterns, fans, framed tapestries, and Chinese wall hangings. The two dining rooms are narrow and not as bright. Also open seven days a week, the hours are shorter than the proposed Ling Garden hours.

An analysis of the menu prices for similar items at both restaurants reveals that neither restaurant is consistently higher or lower. The prices vary up to $1.25 depending on the menu item.

A second direct competitor of a Chinese restaurant with table service is Polynesian Paradise, located five miles southeast from the Ling Garden. The one-story building is surrounded on three sides by its parking lot. The restaurant is sectioned into three areas: the bar and lounge, and two dining areas. The dining areas have 16 booths and six tables, which seat approximately 100 patrons. A metal serving table on which Sunday brunches are displayed is in the center of the first dining area. The table sits empty in the dining room when not in use. The decor is black, red, and green with mirrors and other Chinese ornaments. There are no windows except those in the front door.

A comparison of the menu shows that the prices are less than at the Ling Garden. An additional difference between the two restaurants is the Sunday brunch: $7.99 for adults, $4.50 for children.

Indirect competitors include G. Willikers, the Golden Cup Restaurant, Rosie's Diner, India Mahal, Linda's Spa, and the fast-food chains on Rte. 16.

PART II:

Success in Marketing

CHAPTER FIVE

Your Marketing Strategy

(continued on next page)

Seven Rules of Selling

Nothing happens for a business until someone buys something. If your background is in sales, you already understand this. If your background does not include sales, this chapter may be the most important one for you in this book.

The following principles must be taken to heart:

1. "Quality" doesn't sell itself.
2. Just because I like something doesn't mean anyone else will.
3. People may like a product without being willing to pay for it.
4. People may just say they'd buy my product because they don't want to discourage me.
5. People may think they'd buy a product, but when given the chance they might not.
6. Asking people if they would buy a product is a poor predictor of whether or not they actually will buy it.
7. People may say my price is too high, even if that's not the reason they won't buy it.

Test First, Launch Later

Nothing predicts success like people actually buying your product. If there's any way to make that happen before you launch a business, you can save yourself a lot of money by doing it. If your product will be sold via direct mail, telephone, on the Internet, or person-to-person, you can easily do a market test of your product before committing to a launch.

Some entrepreneurs appear to be afraid of test-marketing their idea—they fear a negative response might inhibit their drive to start a business. But consider the upside of a negative response:

- Not proceeding with a "loser" idea will save you a fortune—which you can use to fund your next new business idea, which will probably have a much better chance of success knowing what you know now.
- You can still proceed with an idea that tests poorly, but at least you'll know where the danger lies, and you can take steps to compensate.

- The response to a new business idea isn't always yes or no. Sometimes you learn things that should be changed, which can greatly increase your chances of success.

Do-It-Yourself Telemarketing

IOMA, a large newsletter company, tests about fourteen new newsletter ideas every year via the telephone. They have their own in-house telemarketing staff, but you could do a similar test by yourself.

IOMA puts six telemarketers on the phone for two hours, trying to sell the new newsletter. After two hours, they meet and discuss the reaction they've received. Here are some of the types of things that they—or you—discuss:

- Is the demographic group we're calling correct for this product? Do they instantly relate to the idea or do they seem confused as to why we are calling them for this?
- Does the title of the newsletter grab them—or does it require more explanation?
- Do they gasp at the price, or pay little attention to it?
- What other problems cropped up in the phone calls? Perhaps this week/month is an extraordinarily busy month for the people in this business sector and we shouldn't contact them now (e.g., calling corporate accountants near or right after year end, or even month end, or calling tax accountants in March or April).

Based upon the results of the discussion of the test calls, they may or may not make changes to:

- The product they're offering
- The title of the product
- The way they describe the product
- The price
- The type of business or individual they sell to
- The offer—guarantee, terms, etc.

Definitions

(continued from previous page)

- **Measurable response and/or transaction:** Sometimes direct marketing is not trying to gain an immediate sale. If you are selling printing presses for $500,000, you will never close a sale from a direct mail piece or an ad in *Printers* magazine. Instead, you use the advertising to get someone to request more information—a "lead." Then you follow up on those leads and try to close a sale.
- **Database:** Direct marketing tracks individual leads or sales in a computer database. That database allows the direct marketer to look at which mailing lists (or other media) pulled best, and what their profit per dollar spent is. It also informs direct marketers about media that isn't profitable.

If the telemarketing group decides to make changes, they then retest with the changes and meet again to review. If nothing they do is improving potential sales of the described product, they kill the idea. If the changes have caused enough people to be interested enough to buy it, they launch the product.

Never Say Never to Test Marketing

If you think your product cannot be test marketed, try to think of a way it can. Use that creativity that inspired you to think of launching your own business. Remember the determination you have to make your business succeed. Use that energy here to come up with a way to test your product.

If your product is to be a service, try to sell it even though you're currently employed. Here are two ways you can do that—you may think of several more:

1. Sell services that can be performed by others you hire, while still in your current job.
2. Sell services only you can perform—for delivery starting in three months. If you line up enough customers, you can quit your job and have your new business already launched.

If your product will be sold nationwide in retail stores, make up a smaller batch of the product and try to sell it in local stores. If you encounter strong resistance from retailers—which could be a warning sign—you could offer it to them free—in return for sharing the sales figures with you. How quickly did it sell? The figures will tell you.

Armed with actual store sales figures (assuming they are good), you should be in good position to interest national retail chains and wholesalers in your product once you actually launch.

Test-Marketing on the Internet

As almost everyone on the planet knows by now, selling opportunities on the Internet's World Wide Web abound. But you can test-market on the Web as well.

What will a World Wide Web site cost you to set up, assuming it's only for test purposes at first? You can get your own domain name for under $100, and find a company that will host (maintain) your Web site for under $100 in setup fees and $30 or so a month. You can do it even cheaper if you use the free Web sites offered by most Internet Service Providers (ISPs, such as AOL or EarthLink), but those sites don't let you have your own domain name. Instead of *www.yourname.com* your address would be something like *www.earthlink.net/xyz/yourname.html*. Avoid this if at all possible, not only because it is so awkward and difficult to type, but also because you can't take it with you if you move to a different ISP.

You can find a decent Web hosting company through America Online. Ask for their Web hosting service for businesses, and they will introduce you to the Web hosting company Verio, which did my Web site for the costs mentioned above.

Once you have the domain name and the hosting company, you can create your own Web site for $100 and a weekend or two of work—using Microsoft's FrontPage 2000 or Adobe Page Mill, which are the easiest Web design programs to use. Netscape Composer and Front Page Express are two smaller programs you may have on your computer already, if it's a Windows system.

What you'll have is a Web site that people can use to look at your products and click to e-mail you that they want to buy. It won't include a "shopping cart" or "secure link" for taking credit card payments. Those are add-ons that will cost extra, but Verio, or whoever your Web host is, can put you in touch with "package" programs that will add those functions.

Even without credit card service, you can test a "bill-me" product. Naturally, not all products lend themselves to selling by credit over the Internet; products sold to businesses in the moderate price range will have the best results.

Test-Marketing in the Movies

The 1987 movie with Diane Keaton called *Baby Boom* offers an opportunity to see test-marketing in action. Watch Keaton test-market her baby food product, testing not only the desire for it, but also getting feedback on how much parents were willing to pay for it. If you can't test a product on your friends, make a friend out of a couple of store managers; you may be able to test prices at their stores.

Alternate Days, Alternate Products

The ideal way to test two different products or sets of prices would be to alternate offers to Web visitors: the first visitor gets offered product X, the second visitor gets offered product Y, the third visitor gets offered product X, etc. However, such an ideal state is technically a challenge on the Web.

The easiest way to test on a Web site—with some degree of comfort in the reliability of your numbers—is to alternate offers on different days. For example, depending on whether you were testing interest in different products or testing different prices for the same product, you could set up a schedule like this:

Monday:	Offer product X (or price 1)
Tuesday:	Offer product Y (or price 2)
Wednesday:	Offer product X (or price 1)
Thursday:	Offer product Y (or price 2)
NEXT Monday:	Offer product Y (or price 2)
NEXT Tuesday:	Offer product X (or price 1)
NEXT Wednesday:	Offer product Y (or price 2)
NEXT Thursday:	Offer product X (or price 1)

Why nothing on Friday or the weekend? Because the response on those days is likely to be different than the responses on Monday through Thursday. Note, also, that the second week, started with product Y instead of product X to see if Mondays had a different response pattern than other days.

By using the schedule above, and adding up the results, each product or price will have been tested on each day of the week.

What we're trying to do here is to compare apples to apples and make sure any differences we see are due to the customers' responses to the products or prices—and not due to external factors. If you only tested on only two days—Monday for product X and Tuesday for product Y—you wouldn't be comfortable that differences in how much customers liked the two products were real differences. That's because any of these external factors might have caused you to get more or less orders on any given day:

- A snowstorm across much of the country.
- Heavy rain in the Northeast. This could cause more people to stay home and shop on their computers.
- Heavy computer traffic. If too many people are on America Online at the same time, for example, more people will be signed on at lower speeds and experience slowdowns, factors that could make a person give up and quit your site without ordering.
- A computer glitch anywhere in the system.

Direct Mail Testing

The easiest way to understand how direct mail testing works is to take you through a case study.

Let's say, for the purposes of this demonstration, that you want to market new, high-tech swim goggles that truly don't fog up, unlike others that simply *claim* not to. The product is more expensive than products currently in the store.

Let's also assume you've found lists of people who belong to swim clubs, as well as lists of triathletes, because you're smart enough to know only the most dedicated swimmers are likely to pay the higher price for your product. Let's also assume the total number of swimmers on those lists is 200,000.

Let's say the direct mail piece you want to send to all of these people would cost you roughly $125,000, including printing, postage, list rental, and creative design.

Being smart, you want to test a small group of these people before investing $125,000. But you want to be sure that the results you get from the small group will be the same results you'd get on all the names. That way, you can project the results from your test onto the rest of the names and know what kind of profit (or loss) you would get from mailing the rest of them.

Random and "nth" Name Selection

If you want to test 20,000 names from a 200,000 list—and make sure the results you get from those 20,000 names are the same results you'd get when you mailed the entire 200,000 list—you must make sure that the names you test are identical in kind to the remaining names.

If you just grabbed 20,000 names at random from the larger list, you could encounter problems:

• Geographic differences. If the 200,000 list was in zip code order, and you picked the first 20,000 names, you'd get only New England area residents. People in New England might respond differently than people in other areas, so your test wouldn't be valid for the remaining names.
• If the list is in alphabetical order, your 20,000 test might include an extra-large amount of people of a certain nationality. That might also affect your results.

You have two choices: if the names are in a computer, the computer can be programmed to assign each person a number on a random basis. In that case, you could pick records 1 to 20,000, which should reflect the remaining database.

Or, you could put the list in zip code order and take every *nth* name (*n* stands for a "number to be identified"). For example, if you're testing 20,000 names from 200,000, that means you would pick every tenth name. So *n* becomes 10. If you were testing just 10,000 names from the 200,000 database, you would pick every 20th name, so *n* becomes 20.

Small Price-Test Mailings

Now, suppose you also want to test three prices for your swim goggles to see which works best. And you want to mail the smallest number possible of direct mail pieces (to save yourself money) and still get reliable results.

You can make a grid to estimate the minimum quantity of mail you'll send out. Here's one designed for the swim goggles:

	$52	$59.95	$69.95	Grand Totals
Swim club list	2,000	2,000	2,000	6,000
Triathletes list	2,000	2,000	2,000	6,000
Other list	2,000	2,000	2,000	6,000
TOTALS	6,000	6,000	6,000	18,000

To read this grid, the prices you want to test are across the top. The lists you want to test go down the side.

Under the $52 price, you've chosen to test 2,000 names at that price from the Swim Club List, 2,000 names from the Triathletes List, and 2,000 names from a third list, for a total of 6,000 names. You've done the same for the other two prices.

The grid tells you that you can mail 18,000 names and have a pretty accurate picture of what results you'd get if you mailed the entire 200,000 names. From this mailing you'll know if it's going to be profitable to contact the rest of the list.

Does it have to be 2,000 in each test cell? After all, you'd save good money if it were only 500 names. A direct mail marketing rule-of-thumb for small tests is that you need to have enough names so that you get at least 50 orders for each test mailing. If you were to get a 1% paid response on 6,000 names, you would get 60 orders. When you're testing prices, it is better to mail more than needed.

Reading Your Direct Mail Responses

Remember how we said that test marketing doesn't only say "yes" or "no" but that it can also point the way to changes that could make you more successful?

Suppose you decided that in order to make a profit—and therefore launch your swim goggle business—1.6% of all people receiving your direct mail test offer need to buy it.

Then, suppose you mailed the test and got these results:

	$52	$59.95	$69.95	Total Averages
Swim club list	1%	0.7%	0.3%	0.67%
Triathletes list	3.5%	3.6%	3.4%	3.5%
Other list	0.2%	0.2%	0.1%	0.2%
Averages	1.6%	1.5%	1.2%	1.43%

Direct Mail Response Rates

(continued from previous page)

- For business-to-business mailings: Normal *paid* responses for B2B products are in the 0.25% to 2% range, although they can be further outside this range than consumer products—again depending on how targeted the list is and how expensive the product. A B2B newsletter costing $300 per year can pull just 0.25% paid response, while B2B offers for a "free" sample issue (where you have to write "cancel" on the invoice if you don't want to continue the subscription) can pull 10%–15%, though the number of people who pay can be substantially less.

The percentages represent those people who bought your swim goggles in the test mailing. What do the results tell you? You could read them in a number of ways:

- The overall response rate for the mailing was 1.43%, which is not the 1.6% you had hoped for—so the test could be called a failure.
- You got 1.6% for the $52 price test, so you could decide to go ahead and launch at the $52 price.
- Or—the smart choice—you could look at the Triathletes List, which averaged 3.5%. Obviously those people love your product, and just as obviously, the other two groups of people aren't particularly enthusiastic.

Making Changes Based on Test Results

Do you therefore have a potential business selling goggles to triathletes only? Here are some additional things you could learn from your test results:

- How many triathletes do you have in the full list? If you have only 2,000 triathlete names in total, you don't have a big enough market to make a profit. But if you have 100,000 names of triathletes on your list, then you do have a business.
- The triathletes don't seem to care much about the price. The response rates were so close for the three prices that the difference is negligible. That means you might be able to sell them goggles for an even higher amount.
- Because the triathletes don't seem to be price sensitive, you may be able to develop even better goggles (which would cost more) and they might well pay more for those extra features.
- If you eliminate swim clubs and your other targets, you can cater more to triathletes. For example, triathletes compete first in swimming, then move to biking. Maybe there's a clip or something that could allow the goggles to be stashed somewhere on the bike after use.
- Because you are focusing on triathletes, you might also sell them products for biking and running.

More Benefits from Test Results

To start, you were thinking about a business selling goggles to swimmers. If you hadn't tested the idea, and instead just launched the business, you would have found sales to all swimmers to be marginal and your business might have failed, or limped along at breakeven.

However, after reading the test results, you were able to:

- Raise your price—increasing your revenues.
- Mail to fewer prospects—saving costs to prospects who weren't likely to buy.
- Launch with a different name—Tri-Goggles—that positioned you to triathletes.
- Create packaging materials that appeal more to triathletes.
- Have a clear company focus on what kinds of new products you want to acquire or design for the growth of your new company.

In short, your new business is far better positioned to make a profit than the business idea you were first considering.

As a further benefit, with direct mail testing, you have results that can interest investors. You now know that when you mail to your entire list of triathletes (100,000 names) what percent response you will get. Using the above results, you got a 3.4% at the $69.95 price. That means when you mail 100,000 names and get 3.4% paid, you'd get 3,400 orders at $69.95—for total revenues of $237,830. You've already calculated the costs of mailing, which would be $70,000 for 100,000 pieces. If your cost for the product, packaging, and shipping was, say, $35 each, that would be $119,000. That would leave you with a profit of $48,830.

$237,830	Revenues: 3,400 orders @ 3.4% paid response on 100,000 mailed
- 70,000	Direct mail costs: paper, printing, assembly, postage
- 119,000	Product, packaging, and shipping costs
$ 48,830	Profit

Definition: Factors

Suppose you don't have the $70,000 for the direct mail costs or the $119,000 for the goggle manufacturing costs? If you have test results that were reliably done—you used an *nth* name selection and a sufficient sample size—you can find people who will lend you the money for this follow-up mailing. These investors are called "factors" and you can find them through the DMA (Direct Marketing Association). Factors advance money for direct marketing—and take their repayment plus 7%–8% interest from the money received from the mailing.

Pricing Strategy

Pricing is one of the hardest, most critical decisions you can make for your product or service. If you overprice, you'll lose customers. If you underprice, you'll lose profits—and may even lose customers as well.

Making the decision even harder is that pricing is not a simple matter of costs plus a reasonable profit margin. People who think they can add up the costs of their product, add in a "fair" profit margin—10% or 15%—and come up with the price to charge are doomed to failure.

Pricing must be related to the customers' *perception* of what a fair price is. Their perception may be completely wrong—but it's a very real factor you have to deal with. Here are two completely different examples:

- **Customers won't pay for highest quality:** A friend with a line of top-quality bed linens found that she couldn't use the highest-quality products because it would push the price over the limit of what customers perceived as a fair price for top-of-the-line linens. Yes, even rich customers have limits as to what they're willing to spend for products—even though the actual dollars are pocket change to them.

- **Customers wary of a lower price:** I launched *Ancillary Profits* newsletter at $97 a year for 10 issues. Coming from the magazine business, I thought $97 was a very high price (I was used to consumer magazine subscription prices of $10–$30). Then I listened to other newsletter publishers who told me a newsletter rule-of-thumb: You always *over*estimate how many subscribers you will get and *under*estimate how much your subscribers are willing to pay. So I tested a $127 price and found I got many *more* subscribers at that price. That's because my customers' perception of a fair price for my newsletter was in the hundreds of dollars (eventually, I found the best price was $197). Seeing a newsletter for less than that price didn't excite them about the great bargain they'd found; it made them think my newsletter probably wasn't very good.

Pricing Based on Competitor Pricing

How do you find out what your customers think is a fair price? The best way is to look at what they're already paying for a similar product. Take your competitor analysis (developed in the exercise in Chapter 4) and look at it. Arrange the prices of your competitors in descending order. Note which competitors are successful, and which you've scarcely heard of.

Use a successful competitor's price as a starting point for your price. If your product will be high quality, use the price of the successful competitor who also sells high quality.

If you are selling high-quality products, there is usually no benefit whatsoever in pricing your product slightly lower than your closest high-quality competitor. Match their price. At first you may have to give higher discounts than your competitor to get wholesalers to take your product—those discounts could make a difference in getting wholesalers to take on your line. A small end-user (see sidebar) price difference for quality products usually only cuts your profits without increasing sales.

Instead of cutting your price, think of something you could add to your product that would make it look more valuable than your competitors' product. Is there a small additional feature you could add? Better packaging? More user-friendly design? Maybe a small extra that complements your product could be packaged with the product?

Factors Affecting Price

If your product is fungible you'll have few options in pricing. "Fungible" means there's no perceived difference between your product or any of the others you compete against. In hardware, nails are fungible. In office supplies, staples are fungible, and (to many people) so are cheap pens, cheap paper, etc. In the supermarket, flour is fungible. The more distinctive your product can be from other products, the more likely you can charge a premium price for it. Here's an example: Before Frank Perdue, chicken in the grocery store was fungible. You never asked where it came from or if you could buy chickens from a different company. Chicken was chicken. Perdue spent a fortune making consumers believe there *were* differences in chickens—which allowed him to charge a premium price for his.

Definitions

- **Wholesalers**: They buy products from manufacturers and sell those same products to retailers.
- **Retailers**: They buy products from wholesalers, and (often) manufacturers, and sell those same products to consumers.
- **End users**: Buyers who will actually use the product bought—instead of selling it to someone else. End users can be consumers or businesses, but in each case the buyer bought the product for use, not for reselling. The buyer is the "end" of the line as far as selling the product.

If your potential clients can easily find out what prices are offered by others. If your products and your competitors are in catalogs—or on a Web site—where a purchasing director can easily price compare, you will have to price closer to your competitors than if, for example, your product is car detailing, where each job is somewhat custom and there's no easy way to compare your prices versus a competitor.

If you're selling a service, you'll have a little more pricing flexibility if your qualifications and product are not directly comparable to your competitors'. If you offer bookkeeping services, you can be compared directly to others offering the same services. But if you consult on stock acquisitions, the qualifications and background you bring to the table will be different from those offered by your competitors—sometimes very different and sometimes just marginally. Those differences mean one company might value your background more than your competitors', or vise versa.

General Pricing Guidelines

Even if you aren't competing in the high-quality arena with your product, your competitors' prices are the best starting point for your own prices. You can raise the price you want from that point—recognizing your product's extra features, higher quality, and more personalized service. But you can only do this if those extra features can be easily perceived by your customers as adding value to your product over the competition's.

Before you even think about competing by setting a *lower* price than the competition's, ask yourself the following:

- **Do most buyers of these products even notice the price?** For example, do people notice the price on razor blades they buy? Or on muffins? If you were selling cut flowers along the side of a road, would $3 get you more customers than $4? Or are customers willing to pay either of those prices? Probably the critical question to ask in that situation pertains to how many customers you could expect to get—whether or not the people driving by are the kind who would be willing to stop and spend money on cut flowers.

- **Do most buyers of your products choose among your competitors based upon price?** For example, if you are selling baby clothes, customers might consider all of them to be overpriced. But would they really pick yours over another because yours were $2 cheaper? In the lower-end products—definitely. But in the higher-end products? Or, within a certain price range, do customers buying baby clothes select more on style?

- **If you enter with a lower price and start being successful, what would you do if your competitors matched your price?** Would you lose that business? Remember, established businesses have deeper pockets than most start-ups. They can afford to lower their prices—in some cases to cost or below—easier than you can. Competing on price is usually a losing proposition for a small company, because it is easy for a larger competitor to take away that advantage.

Sustainable Competitive Advantage

A *sustainable competitive advantage* is what you most want for your new business. That's an advantage over your competitors that you can maintain—sustain—over time, one that will be very hard for your competitors to match.

A sustainable competitive advantage: I built up a business consulting on newsletters for magazine companies. There are a lot of newsletter consultants, but I'm the only one with a strong magazine background. That's a sustainable competitive advantage because other newsletter consultants would have to spend 15 years publishing magazines to match my background. Or magazine consultants could match me if they would first spend eight years publishing newsletters.

Is there something in your background—education, experience, awards, etc.—that makes your services of more value to your customers? Something other service providers in your area can't easily match? If you can find a needed niche, even if it is small, where your credentials beat those of anyone else—you've got a sustainable competitive advantage. Which means you can price accordingly—higher.

Another example: Product designs you create give you a competitive advantage, especially if you can patent them. Even if you can't patent them, your ability to create new designs that appeal to those who bought the first, gives you a sustainable competitive advantage.

Protect Your Prices

A sustainable competitive advantage is seldom a lower price. An exception is Wal-Mart, which developed a sustainable competitive advantage on pricing—but it was based on their inventory and delivery systems that allowed them to cut their costs of operations below that of almost any other company. Those lower costs let them offer customers lower prices, while still protecting Wal-Mart's profit margins. So it was sustainable. And it worked for quite a while. But now, with CostCo and other discount stores having their own lower-cost warehouse and inventory systems, Wal-Mart has a lot of new competitors over which it no longer has that big advantage.

(Lots of people create nostalgic children designs on clothes, mugs and greeting cards, but if you like Mary Engelbreit you'll want only hers.)

The Discount Factor

People love to get "deals." Even when we know it's so much hype, a deal still attracts buyers. That's why magazines offer subscriptions at 50% off the basic price. How can they do this and still be profitable? Because new magazines figure out what kind of revenue they need to get and set a "basic" price that is twice that number. (Of course, they also have to price close to what their competitors' prices are.)

If you're selling a luxury status item, you probably won't want to discount it—although stores selling it can do so and increase sales.

If you're selling a cheaper item—say, a soft drink, a $4 knick-knack—a discount of a few cents won't mean a thing. That's why fast-food chains offer free toys with purchase—it's still a discount, but it's more appealing than 15 cents off.

Also, how you word a discount can mean a big difference. Which of these offers would you be more attracted to?

- 50% off—for a subscription to *Tempo* magazine!
- Get one year FREE of *Tempo* magazine!

The second offer would be much more compelling, although they're really almost the same offer. The one-year-free offer is with a two-year subscription, so what you're really getting is 50% off.

Which of these two offers sounds more appealing?

- 50% markdown
- $1.50 off

Yes, the first sounds more impressive. If the product price is $2.50, $1.50 off is a better deal. But small dollar numbers don't sound impressive.

Which of these two offers is more appealing?

- 25% markdown
- $75 off

You may vote for the second offer here. If the dollar amount was $300, you'd almost definitely vote for the dollar amount. Yet, that 25% markdown could be more than $75 if the product price originally was $350 or higher.

The point is that large numbers sound better than small ones when you're offering discounts. So use whichever number sounds the most impressive to you. It may be a dollar amount, or it may be a percentage discount. Again, this goes to the buyer's *perception* of the offer—which is as important, or even *more* important, than the actual offer.

No Einsteins Needed—Just Test

You don't have to be a genius in order to figure out the best price for your product. In fact, it wouldn't help you at all—geniuses don't have a clue what the best price for your product is.

Beyond having a price that is comparable to your competitors', based upon quality and additional features, you'd be surprised at how different a price could be.

Be wary of research that asks people what price they would pay for a product such as yours. People lie. Friends, or people you're sitting with in a focus group, may lie on the high side to make you feel better. Most people will lie on the low side. People have figured out that if they say a higher price, you may price it that high; so if they give you a lower price they'll be able to get it cheaper.

The only real research on pricing is what people actually pay for an item. If there's any way you can figure out to offer your product at different prices and see what happens, do it.

Here's an example that might surprise you. Magazines are in direct marketing, so price is something they test regularly. When some of the big consumer magazines got frustrated many years ago because they couldn't go over $9.99 or $19.99 for a year's subscription, they started testing what you or I would consider silly prices. The magazines that couldn't sell for over $9.99 started testing $9.99 versus:

- $9.98
- $9.97
- $9.96
- $9.95

Most of us would never have tried such insignificant differences. But—surprise—the magazines found real differences. Prices ending in a 7 tested significantly better than any other number. That's why to this day you'll see a large number of magazine and newsletter prices ending in a 7.

This might work on other, nonsubscription products. Of course, you may have much bigger questions for price testing, such as $325 vs. $275, where the results would be much more significant than whether the number ended in a 7.

Round Off the Price

If your product is over $100, don't add on cents into the price. Don't, for instance, charge $152.99. Just charge $152 or $153. Adding cents affects a buyer's attitude toward you. Although most people wouldn't consciously think this, their subconscious is saying: "This company is already getting $152 of my money for this product. I can't believe they're trying to grab another 99 cents on top of it. I better protect my gold fillings, or they'll try to come after those as well!"

Even if your product is $20, consider hard whether to charge cents in your price. Consumer newsletters in that price range have found $22 or $24 works better than $21.99 or $23.99. Think about your prices. Consider the pennies.

The worst culprit is the marketing department that raises the prices on established products a fixed percentage a year—and keeps the pennies. For example, if you had a product priced at $60 and you wanted to raise the price 7%, your calculator will tell you the new price is $64.20. Don't allow that to go through as your new price. Make it $64 or $65, but never $64.20.

You may not believe it, but I've seen large companies with products priced at $342.76 or $488.91. When your price is this high, you need to change more than the cents. $342 or $488 are not good prices, either. You need to round up and get $345 or $490, which just look like a more "professional" price from a professional company.

You'll also see that some foolish companies price using cents—when they're not charging any. Look at these two prices:

$325
$325.00

Did the second price look bigger to you? It does to most people. Yes, we know they're the same amount. But those extra zeros make the number longer—physically bigger. They also beg the question of why those extra zeros are there. Did the manufacturer *plan* to add some cents to his price but forget to do it? Don't get into this kind of mistake; eliminate cents altogether—unless your price is under $100. Even then, think about it unless your price is under $20.

Reality Check: Your Costs

After all the suggestions in this chapter about how you can't price based on your costs, the truth is that you nevertheless do need to figure out your costs per product. That's to ascertain if you can make a profit at the price the market is willing to pay.

Don't assume because others are making a profit at that price that you can too. If raw materials make up a big part of the price of your product—as compared to products where time is the key expense—large companies may well have a big cost advantage over you because they can buy in bulk. For example, General Motors can probably get a much better price on steel than you can.

However, it doesn't always happen that way. When I headed up acquisitions and new product development for CBS Publishing, management always assumed cost savings in printing when we looked at smaller companies to buy. Those cost savings were to come from our muscle power, the "buying in bulk" we did of printing for some of the biggest magazines in the world—*Woman's Day, Field & Stream, Road & Track*, etc. Surely we were getting a better price from printers.

In fact, we weren't. I never saw an outside magazine that was paying more for printing than we were. Maybe that was due to our print buyer; more likely it was due to our need to have reliable printers even more than the cheapest deal. Small companies are much more maneuverable and can sometimes find supplier prices that the big guys can't risk going with.

So, after you decide what price the market is willing to pay for your product, how do you calculate whether or not that will let you make a profit?

Reason Aside

Remember that pricing is not always logical or rational. Pricing is based upon what the buyer thinks is a reasonable price, and that "reasonableness" could be a lot more irrational than you would think. Test your price wherever possible.

When Your Product Is a Service

If you're selling a service, you may have seriously undercalculated your actual "cost." The sample worksheet that follows will help you figure out your cost if that service is consulting. You can adjust this worksheet to fit your own service, but it will help you avoid underestimating your time costs.

CALCULATING COST FOR A SERVICE BUSINESS

These costs are designed for a consulting business: you can adapt them for your different service business.

Item	Calculation	Description
A:	40	Working hours per week
B:	x 52	Weeks per year
C: (A x B)	2,080	Potential hours/year for work
D:	10	Holidays
E:	10	Vacation days
F:	5	Sick days
G: (D+E+F)	25	Total DAYS off for holidays/vacation/sickness
H: (G x 8)	200	Total HOURS of holidays/vacation/sick time off
I: (C-H)	1,880	Total working hours/year
J:	_____	Hours per day spent prospecting for clients (networking, writing materials, updating your Web site, sending out direct mail, telephoning, speaking at conferences, etc. Note, if this number isn't at least 2 hours a day, use how many hours you should be doing these things!)
K: (J x 5)	_____	Hours PER WEEK spent prospecting
L: (K x 47)	_____	Hours PER YEAR spent prospecting (excludes holidays, vacations, sick days)
M:	_____	Total working hours NOT spent prospecting
N:	_____	MONTHLY number of specific bids or proposals created for potential clients
O:	_____	Time (in HOURS) required for preparing EACH bid/proposal, including telephone follow-up
P: (O x N)	_____	Hours spent per MONTH bidding on jobs
Q: (P x 12)	_____	Hours spent PER YEAR bidding on jobs

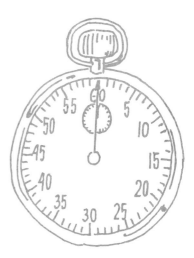

R: (M - Q)	_____	**TOTAL WORKING HOURS NOT SPENT PROSPECTING OR BIDDING ON JOBS**
S:	_____	How much money you want to make PER YEAR
T: (S ÷ R)	_____	Amount you must earn PER HOUR to make the annual salary you want
U: (T x 2 or 3)	_____	**Hourly amount you must earn—if you're not fully busy**

Shocked at the results? Many consultants are. But remember, these are your costs—NOT what you should be charging. If you charge this amount and it is less than what other consultants charge, potential clients may think you're not worth it.

When Your Product Is Bought or Manufactured

When you manufacture (or buy) a product for sale, there are several different types of costs. Each of those must be calculated differently—so you know what your product really costs and thus can easily figure what it would cost if you were to make (or buy) a larger quantity at a time.

Indirect costs: Those costs that are not directly spent on the product you're selling. They include sales costs, office expenses, telephone, salaries (of anyone not directly creating the product), etc.

Direct costs: All the expenses you incur in creating or buying the product itself. They include:

- Raw materials—cloth and thread for clothing; paper, ink, writing, and photos for books; flour and eggs for food products, etc.
- The product itself—if you sell animals, for instance, the cost of the animals and the food you fed them are all direct costs

Direct costs break down in most cases into:

- Fixed costs: Setup charges that stay the same if you make (or buy) one product or 100,000 products. (If you're publishing a book, for example, your printer will charge

you a fixed amount to set up the book so it's ready to be printed.

- Variable costs: Costs that are per unit of what you make or buy. In the example of the book printer, she might quote you $800 in setup charges and $10.49 per book. These costs are variable because they vary depending on how many units you make/buy. If you printed one book, you'd pay $800 plus $10.49. If you printed 100 books, you'd pay $800 plus $1,049.

CALCULATING COST FOR A MANUFACTURED PRODUCT

If you are buying the products you sell, you may be charged a flat amount per product. In that case, ignore the first box on this chart.

Item	Calculation	Description
A:	$____	Fixed manufacturing costs PER MONTH (or other period) Add all setup fees and other costs you incur regardless of how many products you buy or create. (Example: editorial costs are fixed for a magazine: no matter how many copies you print, the cost of the stories, photos, and artwork still remain the same.)
B:	$____	Variable manufacturing costs PER PRODUCT Add all costs for manufacturing that increase or decrease depending on how many products you buy/create.
C:	$____	Number of products produced LAST MONTH (or other period)
D: (A ÷ C)	$____	Fixed manufacturing costs PER PRODUCT
E:	$____	Nonmanufacturing costs PER MONTH (or other period used in A and C) (Example: rent, telephone, salaries of nonmanufacturing people, advertising, etc.)
F: (E ÷ C)	$____	Nonmanufacturing costs PER PRODUCT
G: (B+D+F)	$____	Total costs PER PRODUCT (for period used)

Note: Remember, these are your costs—not what your price should be. For a real eye-opener, double the number of products you create per period (item C) and see how it lowers your total costs per product item (item G).

CHAPTER SIX

The Art and Science of Sales

Selling Your Product

Products almost never sell themselves. That means you'll need some manner of salesperson or marketer to sell it for you.

If you're a consultant, the person selling will be you, at least at first. If you're launching a new product on a shoestring, the seller might also be you.

This chapter will look at the science and art of sales. Even if you plan to hire other people to sell for you, you'll need the basics of how to sell, so you can monitor the performance of your salespeople.

Some of you may have a negative idea about sales, based upon dealing with car salespeople, or others using high-pressure tactics. *Sales need not be high pressure.* Here's some reassurance for you: the best salesperson I ever saw was a 55-year-old grandmother selling magazine advertising space who probably never used a high-pressure pitch in her life. Her whole mission in life was to help her customers. She'd call them to:

- Alert them to deadlines.
- Alert them to special deals.
- Alert them to special issues in which she thought the client would want to be represented.

She'd also send them:

- Copies of their ads when they ran
- Copies of anything unusual or any research she found that might help them:

  1. Sell more products
  2. Design ads that would sell more products for them

She became part of their business lives. Clients believed she really cared about their success. How did she convince them of that? Because she really did care.

The result? She got the lion's share of their business. The clients always took her calls—unlike those of other salespeople, who they would dodge. They knew she always called with something specific for them and would get off the phone quickly once she'd communicated the message, not tying them up in the chat that some salespeople use to pretend they like you.

Prospecting: How to Find Potential Clients

If you're a local business, you will advertise in the Yellow Pages, the local papers, maybe local radio, and maybe local TV (see Chapter 8 on advertising). You might also set up a Web site. Flyers distributed around the city might also work—especially for the grand opening and for special sales or events.

If you're a consultant or offering a service (like tax preparation or accounting services), you can "cold call" (contact people you don't know with no introduction) and you can network. You can also set up a Web site, but you'll need to cold call and network to get people to visit your Web site in the first place.

If you're going to sell prospects via direct marketing (including direct mail, telemarketing, Web site marketing, etc.), you will find potential customers by renting lists of names. Even if your primary sales tool will be your Web site, you will probably still want to mail (e-mail and postal mail) lists of people who might be interested in your product(s), so you can tell them about your Web site.

If you're a national business in a specialty field, but don't sell via direct mail marketing because people won't buy a $40,000 piece of equipment through the mail, you can sell via:

- **Lists of people.** Only, in this case, you direct market the lists asking the prospect if they want to receive free information about your products. Once people receive your information packets, you assign salespeople who call, and then, if the potential client is really interested, make an appointment to try to make an in-person sale.
- **Sales reps.** These salespeople, who may be your employees or not, have territories where they contact all your potential customers and try to make the sale.

Contacting Prospects

If your business requires contacting people you don't know (cold-calling) to let them know about your company, here are essential guidelines:

Reach the right person.

When telephoning businesses, make sure you are speaking to the right person. Sometimes the job title doesn't tell you if the person is really the one you need to talk to.

It can be as simple as asking, "Am I speaking to the person who buys photocopier products for the company?"

In letters, use names when you have them; letters addressed to a previous occupant of the job get thrown away more frequently than letters addressed to the current job holder. However, if you don't have names—or if the names you have might be old—you can try addressing it to the job title alone: for example, Marketing Director, XYZ Company, Street. . . .

The letter can open with "Dear Marketing Director" or you can just skip the salutation and start right in with the message.

You can do a great job "selling" somebody, but if he or she is not the somebody who can make the purchase decision, you've wasted your time.

Respect prospects' time.

Whether you're writing a letter or telephoning, come to the point immediately. Wasting a potential client's time makes them more likely either to toss your letter unread or turn antagonistic on the phone.

Tell the prospect why you're calling. *Immediately.* If the prospect has no interest in your message, you might as well find that out right away rather than after an artificial "make-nice" chat about the weather that wastes both of your time.

In a letter, you respect the prospect's time by keeping the message short and to the point, or by coming to the point quickly—in the first paragraph—in a longer letter. Sometimes a short two-to-three-paragraph letter can be supplemented with two or three additional pages that give more details. Longer letters that don't hit the point immediately are almost always tossed.

Respect prospects' interests.

Probably the biggest mistake people make in sales is assuming potential clients have the slightest interest in anything about you, your company, or your product. Believe me, they do not. They are interested in:

- Themselves
- Their company and their sales (if businesses)
- Their lives and their interests (if consumers)
- Protecting their pocketbooks or budgets from salespeople

Given this, how receptive do you think they will be to a letter or telephone call that starts out by talking about your company? Not much!

A short training course in direct mail marketing would show you in black and white by response rates what works and what doesn't in trying to sell a prospect. If you get letters from people selling you subscriptions, take a look at those letters. In instances where you've already gotten the same letter before, it tells you that they tried the letter and it *sold*, which is why they're using it again.

Look how that letter talks to you. It probably doesn't even mention their product anywhere on the first page. Instead, it talks about *you*. *Your* problems. *Your* interests. *Your* opinions. *Your* worries.

Steal some of that technique for cold-call telephoning and letter writing.

For example, which of these telephone call opening lines do you think is more likely to interest businesspeople who send out fax marketing to their clients?

A. "I'm calling from ABC Direct, the largest fax broadcast service provider in the United States."
B. "Are you paying over 10 cents per minute to send broadcast faxes?"

The winner, of course, is B. If I *am* paying over 10 cents a minute, I want this call because I could possibly save money. Then, naturally, the caller would have to convince me of the quality and reputation of her company. But the interest is there. If the call

---

Artificial Niceties

There's nothing I hate more than a telemarketer asking, "How are you this morning?" I know they don't care about the answer. They are already telling me they don't value my time. Expecting me to chat with someone I don't know assumes I don't have more important things to be doing with my time. It's insulting.

recipient was currently paying 8 cents a minute, and your service costs 9 cents, you would immediately disqualify him as a potential customer.

Which of these telephone calls would more likely interest a consumer?

    A.   "DEF Cable company is launching a new direct line service to the Internet. It will give you high-speed access and . . ."

    B.   "Would you like to try three months of high-speed access to the Internet—for no risk? DEF Cable company is . . ."

CAUTION: I've said these exact words many times to students in direct marketing classes. I've seen students nod in understanding, then submit copy that ignores what was said and talks about their product instead of the customer's wants and needs.

Talking customer benefits instead of product features doesn't seem that difficult to understand, but I guess it goes against the grain of human nature. We are fascinated by our product and just can't believe—on some gut level—that others won't be equally fascinated by it. Or we can't escape our wants enough to look at someone else's wants.

Because so few salespeople do this correctly, if you do it—you'll be ahead of the others who don't. Try it.

The Meeting
Getting a Meeting

If selling your product(s) requires a face-to-face meeting, then all your prospecting should have only one goal: to get the meeting.

With some products, it isn't difficult; you're selling to purchasing agents, for example, whose job is to meet with people like you. But if you're selling an idea or another intangible, getting the meeting can be both difficult and essential.

There are tactics that can get you in the door of key decision makers who are not purchasing agents:

1. You tell them enough in the letter or phone call to let them know one or both of the following:

   - They stand to gain from meeting with you
   - They stand to lose if their competitors meet with you and they don't

2. You do *not* tell them enough about your idea/product that they can make a decision before meeting you. For example, if you're selling clothing to potential chain buyers, you can tell them you want to show them a line that was tested in four stores and sold X number of items in X number of days with no advertising or promotion whatsoever behind it. You do not enclose pictures or drawings of your clothes, thus giving the prospect the opportunity to reject the meeting.

Presenting at a Meeting

Know the key ways of making your presentation appear better than others':

- **Do your homework.** You need to have researched the company and found out what you can about how they operate, how profitable they are, what their corporate goals are, etc. The Internet can help in providing this information, as can talking to people/companies who do business with the company. If you can talk to some customers of the company you're meeting with, you will have the rapt attention of its executives on what you have to say.
- **Start your presentation by addressing the needs of the company.** When I was selling advertising for magazines, I often found myself competing against Ziff-Davis ad salespeople. Ziff-Davis trained its salespeople to start with the customer and the customer's needs, and only at the end to explain how their magazine(s) could solve those needs. If their presentation took 12 boards (or PowerPoint slides), only the last three or four were about Ziff-Davis magazines.

Presenting to Investors

Presenting to potential investors requires a different strategy. You get those meetings once they've seen your numbers, so you've already passed one hurdle before meeting. At those meetings, they primarily want to evaluate you; they want to see how well you know the business and how well you can anticipate future problems and opportunities.

- **Get feedback.** The more you can get the decision makers involved in your presentation, the better. The goal is not to complete your "show" but to get a sale. If their interaction takes you off in another direction that could still lead to the sale—go there with it! As you define their needs, they may interrupt and say their needs right now are different. Ask them to tell you more about their needs. How are they planning to solve them? What are they considering? The more they talk about their problems, the easier it is to see a way where your product or service could be tailored to solve at least some of their needs. You may pull an information tidbit from later in your presentation to make a new point, or you may throw out the prepared presentation entirely and draft a proposed new plan right there on a pad of paper.
- **Get the company to customize your proposal for their needs.** The more influence the customer has in what is offered, the more likely the customer will accept the plan. Get them to customize it with you.

Customize for the Customer

Say you're trying to sell a bookkeeping service to a company.

Prospect: That's an interesting proposal, but I need someone who can handle my payroll for me.

You, getting out a pad and pen and writing: OK, you want payroll handled. Are there key numbers, beyond the P&Ls, that would be helpful to you? Do you want to track inventory?

Prospect: Yes, I want to look at inventory every 15 days.

You, writing: Inventory, every 15 days. What about aging of your accounts receivable?

Notice that this prospect has never said he wants your service. All he's talking about is what he wants in any service. But, as you get more and more of his wishes and needs, the prospect starts feeling as if he's getting a customized product—containing *exactly*

want they want, and *nothing* they do not want. Once the prospect has finished this exercise with you, assuming your price is not a problem, he will have a strong inclination to go with the program that *he* designed.

Another example. You're trying to sell knit vests to a chain store:

You: Your Web site has a trendy design that appeals to girls 14–19. for whom these vests were designed. Are girls a big market for you?

Prospect: Yes, they're a big market . . .

You: Am I hearing a "but . . ."?

Prospect: Yes. It's just that we're having a harder time finding good products for women 25 to 40, who are an even bigger market for us.

You: That group of women would probably want more conservative colors than those in these vests, don't you think?

Prospect: Yes, they would.

You: What colors are most popular with them?

Prospect: Peach is hot right now. And so is ecru.

You: What about the styling of these vests? A tighter knit might make them more appealing to that group?

Prospect: Yes. And they'd want it machine washable.

Again, you have your potential customer helping you design exactly the product she wants to buy. See if you can customize this technique to suit sales calls for your product.

The Close

A *close* is where you ask for the order. A *trial close* is when you ask for the order, expecting that your prospect might not be ready yet to give it. By trying to get the order, you can pull out any remaining objections they have to buying from you.

Selling Big-Ticket Items

If you are selling expensive or "intangible" items, you might want to toss out most of the techniques in this chapter and check out a book called *S.P.I.N. Selling* by Neil Rackham. The acronym S.P.I.N. stands for Situation, Problem, Implication, and Need-payoff. It's a way of making the sale without even trying to close. Instead, you advance the process by questioning the situations, problems, implications, and need-payoffs.

This technique of selling has become the technique of choice among *Fortune* 500 companies. This method would also be good if you are trying to sell to *Fortune* 500 companies that use it themselves.

**Definitions:
Tangibles vs.
Intangibles**

Tangibles: Things you can hold in your hand and examine. Something that has actual form and substance.

Intangibles: Things that cannot be touched. Something that cannot be easily defined, formulated, or grasped. A corporation is an intangible. It only exists on paper; it's not something you can actually touch. Another example is goodwill. When you buy a company, you pay a premium for "goodwill," which is the positive impressions that company has built up with consumers over time. It's nothing you can actually put your hands on.

(continued on next page)

You might say, "So, would you like to order 100 units at $1,000, or get 200 units at a 10% discount?"

They might say, "I don't know. Your price is better than Martha Stewart's, but she's always been very reliable. I don't have to worry about whether or not the product will show up."

Then you know you still have to sell them on your reliability.

You want to pull out any remaining objections, so you can deal with them to the prospect's satisfaction. Only then can you make the sale.

Asking for the Order

There are a number of ways to ask for the order. More important than which close you use, is that you do ask for the order.

Salespeople are human, and like all humans they don't like to be rejected. If you don't ask for the order, you won't get told no. That's why a shocking number of salespeople don't do it.

When I became associate publisher of *Audio* magazine, whose ad sales were going down the toilet, I made a sales call with the publisher. We took two key executives from an audio components company to lunch. After the lunch, as we were walking them back to the office, one of the executives turned to the other and said, "You owe me a bottle of champagne." When we asked why, the executive said, "I bet him that you wouldn't ask for the order." My boss had not asked, and you could tell that the other executive couldn't understand why that had not happened. He *expected* to be asked for an order. That's what salespeople should do.

Once I became publisher, I and the other salespeople always asked for the order. The sales jumped over 60% in a single year.

Different Ways to Close

1. When you're using the customization approach described earlier, the close becomes part of the customization process. You're already writing down exactly what the customer wants. Now add to it. Say something like, "How many units would you like to start with?" Or, "When do you want your first shipment delivered?"

2. After you've covered the basics and your potential customer is raising objections, use a closing tactic that lets you discover whether or not the objections raised are the real objections. Sometimes customers raise price objections just to get rid of a salesperson, when price isn't the real problem.

Example #1:

Prospect: Our customers won't buy rayon.

You: If it came in silk, would you buy?

If the answer is "yes" you have an order. If "no," you then know that the fabric is not the real reason why your prospect is not buying.

Example #2:

Prospect: Your price is too high.

You: What price would be reasonable?

Prospect: $100 per thousand.

You: If the price were $100 per thousand, would you order?

Even if you can't deliver it at $100/thousand, this question can flush out a no that will allow you to find out the real reason—which often has nothing to do with your price.

Definitions: Tangibles vs. Intangibles

(continued from previous page)

Consulting services are usually intangibles. A created software program is tangible; you can hold it in your hands. But consulting on how to better integrate software programs is intangible.

Most people consider advertising sales to be intangibles. I can sell you six pages in *Time* magazine, and the six pages are tangible—you can hold them. But what I'm really selling you is access to *Time* subscribers. And access to people is an intangible.

Learn from Top Car Salespeople

If you've ever read a book by leading car salespeople, you'll see that their kind of sales pitch requires a technique all its own. Here is some advice from several of the top car salespeople:

- **Visibility at the time of purchase.** You can't know when people will decide to buy a new car. Sometimes it's a snap decision, such as somebody driving past a car dealership, seeing the new models, and starting to think about his dissatisfaction with his old car. Sometimes his engine goes, and the cost of repair makes the driver consider a new one. Heck, some people probably decide they need a new car after a social rejection. As a result, you need your company name to be where it will easily be seen by someone newly looking for a new car. That means Yellow Pages, ads in the automobile section of the local paper, maybe billboards, and a good, highly visible location.

- **Personal relationship.** People are generally uncomfortable making a big-ticket decision, and thus prefer to deal with someone they already know. Or at least someone they've met who has made a positive impression. Someone they think would make the process easier and more enjoyable. That's why car salespeople hand out business cards to everyone they meet. Most of those people aren't looking for a car now, but they will be eventually.

One top car salesman, after receiving good service from a waiter, writes, "Thank you for your good service" on the back of his business card and gives it to them. Given the choice of buying a car from an unknown salesperson or someone who wrote you a note about how good you are at your job, which would you pick?

The Sales Force

Before you think about hiring salespeople or sales reps, you need to decide what TYPE of salespeople you need. Basically, there are "gunslingers" and "maintainers":

Maintainers do best at servicing accounts that already exist. They cultivate their clients, remember their interests, develop a long-term relationship that leads to repeat sales. They are not as good at getting new clients.

Gunslingers are best at landing new business, and usually not so great at keeping business you already have. Gunslingers bag their targets in a variety of ways:

- Usually they create instant rapport with people they've never met. Telephone gunslingers create instant rapport with people they will *never* meet.
- They're fearless; they'll call the president of the biggest company in your industry and assume that person will be happy to talk to them once she finds out what your company can do for her.
- They present well. Whether it's a fancy presentation or just sitting and talking, they know how to condense pitches for products and services that either don't exist yet or are brand-new into a simple, compelling opportunity for the prospect.
- They're relentless, though in a pleasing way. Prospects don't usually try to dodge calls from gunslingers.

As a new entrepreneur, you will probably be looking for gunslingers, which may be a problem because good ones are very hard to find. I've directly managed about 50 salespeople in my life (excluding telemarketers), and just four of them were gunslingers.

How can you find gunslingers to bag new business for your company?

- **Check their resume.** Look for people who have worked on start-ups—new companies, new divisions, or just new products.
- **Check their results.** Gunslingers rack up good numbers pretty quickly. They don't increase business by just 5% in a year. Don't be too concerned if they've jumped from

Sales Reps vs. Employees

In general, reps (representatives) usually sell less for you than employees. However, there are some instances where that is not the case. And there are a number of instances where reps are a better solution for you than employees. See the table on page 131.

company to company every two or three years. Gunslingers do best where there's lots of new prospects to land; they wilt in mature selling environments where you're trying to eke out another small increase from your clients.

- **Check their references.** While nobody will tell you (in these litigious days) that the person is a dog, watch out for faint praise. If they say the employee was good but you don't hear enthusiasm in their voices or get any elaboration about how good they are—worry! Also, ask the references if the employee was better at breaking new accounts or servicing existing accounts.
- **See how they "sell" you.** If they're seeking a job, they're trying to sell themselves to you. How well do they do it? Do they follow up? Have they established a rapport where you'd like to hear from them again? Do they sound awkward in their phone calls to you—or do they sound confident? Do they try to pin you down as to when you might be making this decision?
- **See how they want to be compensated.** Gunslingers usually like a bigger piece of their payment in commissions because they will do better if they sell more.

Paying Your Salespeople

The most important thing you can do in order to have satisfied salespeople is to talk to others in the industry and see what they are doing about compensation. If they're competitive with you, they certainly won't give you confidential information, but if you phrase your questions to sound more general you may get valuable information.

Ask, "How are salespeople in this industry compensated? Salary and commission? What are the norms?" Ask as many people likely to know as possible. That protects you against a sneaky competitor who might try to mislead you.

When you interview salespeople, ask for the details of their previous compensation:

- How much salary?
- How much commission?

- Was commission a percentage of sales?
- If so, what percent?
- Were other bonuses given upon meeting certain criteria? If so, what were they?

Then, when you check their references, call their former employers and verify those details. It's a matter of record what a person was paid. You can say, "Jane Doe says she was paid $30,000 in salary and $45,000 in commissions in 2000. Do your records verify that?"

The Importance of a Base Salary

While the best salespeople want to earn the biggest part of their pay in commissions instead of a salary—so they have the potential to make more money—most salespeople have earned a healthy wariness about companies paying only commission (unless it is the norm in your industry).

They've been burned themselves (or heard of someone who was) by a company with no money who got a lot of work out of salespeople and left them with little reward to show for it.

Plus, some beginners who have great sales potential can't afford even a month without money for rent. If you don't offer a base salary, you'll never get either of these desirable sales types.

To get the best salespeople, and good-potential beginners, you'll probably need to have a base salary level that's at least high enough to cover rent and food.

Commissions vs. Bonuses

Salespeople have also learned a healthy skepticism about bonuses. That's because bonuses are often:

- All or nothing. If you reach a goal, you get it; otherwise you get nothing. Salespeople can't tell initially how reasonable (or unreasonable) your goals are, so they'll probably believe your goals to be unreasonable.
- Outside their control. This includes bonuses based upon the company having achieved a specific level of profits. The

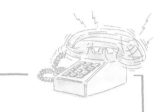

salesperson figures if the company were to reach that level, it could buy an executive car or a new ad campaign to use up the profits and they wouldn't make their bonus.

- Fixed—with no upside. A "flat rate," say $10,000, that they get if their sales go over budget.

    Further, salespeople find it hard to stay motivated for a full year on a single payout number.

Commissions are a percentage of sales. That percentage may vary, and it may or may not be on all sales, but commissions have these advantages:

- Usually salespeople can earn something every month—more or less depending on their results. That keeps them more highly motivated. Picture greyhound dogs: If you trained them to expect a rabbit at the end of every lap of the racetrack, they'd probably go for it. But not with anything like the motivation that comes from sticking a rabbit in front of their noses and then leading them around the track with it.
- If a salesperson on a percent-of-sales plan increases a company's sales by 20%, they're going to make a windfall of commissions. The company should be happy about it, because they'll be making a fortune off the salesperson's sales.
- A commission is generally perceived as fair by salespeople.

Kinds of Commission Plans

This first kind of commission plan—for a fixed percentage of sales—works best in advertising sales; you may have a better one for your industry, or you could adapt parts of this one.

For a start-up—commissions are a fixed percentage of all sales. Say the norm for sales compensation in your industry is a $70,000 package (package means base salary plus expected commissions). You decide to make it a $40,000 salary and a $30,000 commission. You expect your sales in the first year to be $200,000 (see Chapter 11 on cash assumptions, where you will estimate your sales). Divide the $30,000 commission by the $200,000 sales estimate and you get

Should You Hire Employees or Reps?

Situation	Employee	Rep
I have zero money to pay an employee.		Only choice
My current sales are $50,000 or less.		If they take you, they'll want a monthly fee. Reps seek firms with ongoing business where their 10%–20% commission will give them a base salary.
I have direct marketing sales in the same state where I need in-person sales staff.	If you hire an employee in another state, you will be establishing a "nexis," which means you will have to collect and pay sales taxes on products sold in that state via direct marketing.	Hiring a rep firm may not establish a nexis. Consult a tax accountant.
The people I have to sell are swamped with sellers like company. There are rep firms that specialize in the exact people I want to reach.		Sometimes a rep firm that already knows the key players in your industry can give my your company's sales a jump start.
I have a few sales from Arizona, and could probably have more— but never enough for a full-time employee.		This is the perfect reason for hiring a rep firm in that geographic area.
My company's goods are premium-priced, because it includes a lot of personalized service with it.	Employees' servicing of your customers can be monitored much more closely than reps can.	
My product is complicated and requires a lot of training to understand how to best communicate its advantages over other products.	99.99% of the time you'll be better off with an employee. The other 0.01% of the time is only if you get a rep who spends *all* of his/her time on your products.	
I'm in a fast-changing industry where customer feedback is critical to my ability to develop good new products.	Use an employee. The feedback you get from reps is seldom equal to what you get from employees.	

15%. That means you would offer your salespeople 15% commission on all sales for the first year.

If they sell $100,000 instead of $200,000, they would earn only $15,000 in commissions. If they sell $300,000, they'd earn $45,000 in commissions. The important thing to tell a salesperson is that *they* control how much they make. A big selling point to potential salespeople is that you have no "cap" on their earnings.

A cap means there's a limit on how much a salesperson can make. In this example, a company might decide that they'll pay 15% of all sales, with a cap at a $45,000 commission. That would mean that if the salesperson sells $400,000 in revenues for the company, they'll only get a commission on the first $300,000 ($45,000 commission at 15%). This is not a good idea. How likely do you think it is that salespeople, having made their $45,000 commission for the year, would continue working hard to make more sales for the company when they don't earn anything for it? Not very likely! Wouldn't it be smarter to trade an extra $15,000 to the salesforce for an extra $100,000 sales?

For businesses that already have sales—pay sliding-scale commissions. Say your business already has $200,000 in sales, which your new salesperson would be responsible for maintaining, in addition to selling new business. You expect your salesperson to sell another $200,000 this coming year, for a $400,000 total. You want to pay $40,000 in base salary and $30,000 in commissions. You set up a plan like this:

- No commissions paid if total sales are less than 85% of last year ($170,000 for the year)
- Once sales for the month/quarter/year are *over* 85% of last year's, you pay 13% commission on all sales *over*. (The expected sales over is $230,000: $30,000, which is 15% over last year's sales, plus $200,000 for this year's.)
- For sales *over* the expected $400,000, you pay a higher commission. In this example, you might boost the 13% commission on expected sales to 15% on sales over expectations.

Commission Payout Schedule

Last year's sales: $200,000. Expected sales this year: $400,000

If sales are:	Potential Commission	Explanation
$160,000	$0	Not 85% of last year's sales
$200,000	$3,900	13% of sales over $170,000
$400,000	$29,000	13% of sales over $170,000
$450,000	$37,400	13% of sales over $170,000 plus
		15% of sales over $400,000

Avoiding timing differences with a sliding-scale plan. You know salespeople need at least monthly reinforcement, so you want to pay monthly on all sales over 85% of last year's (while saving the higher percentages for sales 5%–20% over expectations until the end of the year, when you know if the year actually was that much over).

However, there could be a problem with doing this. What if a salesperson talked people who were going to buy that year anyway into buying earlier rather than later. So you were 120% ahead of your business plan in the first three months, then only 80% of plan afterward. (Yes, I've seen salespeople do exactly this!) Theoretically it wouldn't matter. Each month you'd look at sales year-to-date and what their commission should be. Then you'd deduct what they'd already received that year and figure out what—if anything—you owed them for the new month. However, in the scenario just described, they might owe *you* money.

Commission Payout Schedule

Month	Sales This Yr.	Sales Last Yr.	This yr. Better/(Worse)	Commission Due	Commission Explanation	Paid	Commission Held for Year End Accounting
January	$15,000	$10,000	$5,000	$845	13% of $6,500	$634	$211
February	$20,000	$20,000	$0	$390	13% of $3,000	$292	$98
March	$5,000	$10,000	$(5,000)	$0		$0	$0
1st Quarter	$40,000	$40,000	$0	$780	13% of $6,000	$926	$309

Note: At the end of the first quarter, the commission actually due is $780. Because of the timing (good first month, bad third) the salesperson has actually been paid $926, with $309 held back for an overpayment of $146. But the overpayment would have been $455 without the 25% held back.

It's hard to get money back from salespeople. Psychologically, nobody wants to write a check to their employer; they figure money should be traveling in the other direction. The solution is to hold back 20%–25% of the amount due the salesperson each month until the end of the year. Then you look at the full year's sales and see whether or not it was earned. If so, the salesperson gets the lump sum. See the table that follows for an example that tracks the first quarter of this year and last year:

Adding Bonuses on Top of Commissions

Your company may have additional goals for its salespeople. Sometimes those goals warrant a bonus payment on top of the commission structure. Here are some examples of bonuses paid on top of the normal sales commissions:

- **New account bonuses.** When *all* your accounts are new, this sort of bonus makes no sense. But if you have a number of established accounts and feel your salespeople are primarily selling them, and aren't doing enough missionary work to land new accounts, you might wish to establish a flat-fee bonus for every new account of a fixed amount or more that a salesperson signs.
- **Share of market bonuses.** Again, this bonus is for more mature companies with established competitors. If your industry is one where it is easy to get information on how much sales your competitors are getting, you might want to establish bonuses for every share of market point increase in a salesperson's territory (see page 136).
- **Particular product bonuses.** Suppose you have six products your salespeople are selling and one of those six isn't doing very well. If the product is a dog, kill it. However, the problem might be that the product requires a more complicated sale, and your salespeople are focusing on the easy-to-sell other five. If so, you might want to pay a bonus on top of commission for selling a certain number of the more difficult-to-sell product.

Paying Reps and Distributors
Negotiating Fees/Commissions/Discounts

After negotiations with a sales representative, you'll have an agreement to pay the rep a fixed percent of his or her sales. The number varies by industry. Advertising sales reps get 10% to 20%—depending on how much sales they have in their territories. You'll need to talk to reps in your markets and see how much they are asking. Then ask others in your industry what the norms are.

Negotiations with distributors will center on how many clients they have and what kind of purchase volume they can generate for you, along with what their discounted price will be.

You can negotiate better deals with both reps and distributors if you ask them to list all the services they'll be providing for commission or discount. Check the list for the following:

- Does their fee/commission/discount cover everything you want them to do, or will you get unpleasant surprise charges for what is not covered?
- Does their fee/commission/discount cover things you do *not* need them to do? If so, negotiate with the company. They may be willing to reduce their fees in return for not having to perform certain services.

Bonuses and Incentive Programs

Just because they're not employees doesn't mean you should neglect your sales reps and distributors when designing sales incentive programs. In fact, you may need to consider them even more than employees—so you don't lose a handle on what is happening with the clients they cover for you.

Bonus programs for reps are often the same as those for employees (new account bonuses, SOM increase bonuses, etc.). Programs to motivate distributors are usually designed as incentives for the distributor's salespeople. For example, you might offer a sales contest that provides a trip to Disneyland or a $1,000 gift certificate for the distributor's salesperson selling the most of your product.

Definition: Reps vs. Distributors

- **Representatives** "represent" your company both to clients they have developed and to new clients they find for you. They earn a percentage of their sales and—if your sales are small—a "base" amount they negotiate with you to cover their initial expenses.
- **Distributors** actually buy your product from you—for resale to their customers. They get a reduced price from you and profit when they resell your product at a higher price. Their customers might be retail stores—who will mark up your product a second time before they sell it—or their customers might be company purchasing agents whose company will use the product without reselling it.

Tracking Share of Market

Share of market (SOM) tracks how many sales your company has relative to its competitors. For example, let's say you launched a new magazine last year called *Loving Gerbils*. You have two established competitors. Let's further say that *Loving Gerbils* got a 19% share of the 2,930 ad pages sold in the market:

	Ad Pages	Share of Market
Gerbil Life	1,500	51%
Gerbils Today	870	30%
Loving Gerbils	560	19%
Total	2,930	100%

Why is it important to track SOM? Why not just measure a salesperson on whether or not they've sold more ad pages for *Loving Gerbils* than last year? Because that might not be a complete picture of how good a job the salesperson did.

What if your salesperson didn't increase sales at all this year. He might have done an excellent sales job, but the economy went bad or the demand for gerbils dropped due to a *60 Minutes* TV report on a gerbil biting a baby. The other two competitors might have lost 20% of the ad pages they had the previous year. If your sales-person "stayed flat" in that situation, he did a great job. Tracking SOM changes will alert you to this. Here's another example:

	Last year Ad Pages	Last year SOM	This year Ad pages	This year SOM	SOM Changes
Gerbil Life	1,500	51%	1,675	48%	-3 points
Gerbils Today	870	30%	1,200	35%	+5 points
Loving Gerbils	560	19%	600	17%	-2 points
Total	2,930	100%	3,475	100%	0

In this example, your salesperson (on *Loving Gerbils*) sold 40 ad pages more than last year. You might think he has done a great job—but it isn't true. Both you and *Gerbil Life* have been outsold by *Gerbils Today*, which went up 5 SOM points.

What can you do? Look at what *Gerbils Today* is doing. Do they have a new sales program that's working? Can you steal part of it and make it work for you as well? Or do they have a new salesperson who's landing clients right and left? Maybe you should try to steal away that salesperson?

CHAPTER SEVEN

The Different Channels of Marketing

Marketing via PR

An alternative to paid advertising is getting free publicity for your company by articles or mentions placed in newspapers and other media. This is known as public relations, or, more commonly, PR. You can use PR and you should, but there are catches.

1. It's not that easy to get free publicity.
2. Companies that advertise in a publication usually get a little more free publicity than those that don't.
3. If you aren't a local company serving a local area, publicity is not as effective.

The Press Release

The method of getting free publicity in newspapers, magazines, radio, and TV is through press releases. These sing the praises of a new company or product and are written either by you or a firm you hire to write them and sent to various editors and producers on media lists.

The grim reality is that most press releases are tossed in the trash. After a time, if you continue sending press releases that editors don't want, they'll recognize your envelopes and toss them without even opening them.

How to Get the Media's Attention

How can you avoid that fate? By trying to put yourself in the editors' shoes. Remember they couldn't care less about your company; they care only about their readers. What would interest their readers? What would surprise them? What would they like to read? What do they need to read?

Study your targeted publications and other media carefully. See what kinds of articles or stories they run. Could there be anything similar from your company?

For example, the business section of your local paper likes to announce new projects, new appointments, anything new. You could send them releases on:

- New research you've conducted (*Tip: You might be able to do a series of inexpensive research studies whose primary purpose is to get you press in the local paper.*)
- New partnerships you've formed
- New (local) vendors you've hired
- New employees you've added
- New (local) clients you've signed with
- New office space you're expanding into, which you got from (local) company

Say your company is a gym. Your local paper does frequent features on improving health, so you send out periodic press releases on:

- National statistics on Americans' growing waistlines
- Local statistics from local hospitals on the increasing number of heart attacks in the city
- Report from a national association on how stress is a contributing factor to heart attacks, along with an exercise for relieving stress

You might want to hire an artist and illustrate a series of exercises to relieve stress, protect your heart, lose weight, etc. You could offer one a month to your local newspaper. Even though they would be things that can be done outside a gym, the exercises would be identified as coming from your gym—which would keep your gym in the minds of exactly those people who are thinking about exercising.

Format for Print Media

Editors expect press releases to follow a particular style; if yours doesn't, you won't look professional. There are a number of books on the topic available in the library and you should check one of them. Here are some basics:

1. Double-space everything. Editors want room to make edit changes on what runs in the newspaper (that's why they're called editors!). If your press release is single-spaced, it will increase its chances of ending up in the trash.

2. Remember the old rule about the five Ws for newspaper reporting: Who, What, Where, When, and Why? That rule works. Your release should answer each W.

3. Stack everything critical into the first paragraph. Each succeeding paragraph should add to the story but add less the further it goes. That way the editor can easily cut it to fit whatever "hole" in the paper she or he needs to fill.

4. Two pages are an absolute maximum. Most press releases need only be one page. If the editor wants to learn more, they're quite capable of picking up a phone and calling you.

5. At the top right of your press release put:

- Contact name and phone number. Who to call if they have a question.
- Company name.
- Company address.

6. Just under that, and justified to the left margin or centered, put your headline.

7. At the end of the press release, centered at the bottom, put "End." That assures editors that they're not missing a page.

Format for Local Radio and TV

You can send the same style of press release to your local TV and radio stations—after assuring yourself that it fits in with the type of information reported by each. You're much more likely to get airtime with an audio or video tape, however.

Local stations need clips to fill time. Watch to see which reporters cover the kinds of stories that would fit in with the kinds of information your company could provide.

You may be able to adapt what national PR firms are doing. They're providing audio and video "interviews" to stations across the U.S. that are ready for the local reporter to insert themselves as the questioner.

It works this way. You are taped "answering" five or six questions. Your taped answers are sent to local stations along with the "questions," which their local reporter can ask. Put together, it looks as if the local reporter is interviewing you.

Contacting Media People

Don't just pick up the telephone and call media people. It's only likely to get you remembered as someone to avoid. There's an entire science of who to contact and how to contact. A newsletter titled *Bulldog Reporter* does nothing but interview newspaper and magazine editors and report how they want to be approached by PR firms. Professionals buy it to increase their chances of getting press for their clients.

If PR will be a strong component in your marketing plan, you will probably need to hire a PR firm. If you have little money, or if your PR chances are small, you'll probably want to do it yourself.

Do-It-Yourself PR

You can increase your chances of positive attention from media by following these tips to make it happen:

- Send a press release, doing your best to make it focus on key interest to the publication's readers or the local audience and putting it in the right format. If they run it, great. You're doing it right.
- If they don't, try another release. If it also doesn't get printed, send a copy of it back to the reporter/editor with a self-addressed, stamped postcard. At the top of the postcard, put something like:

Please help me send you only the kind of releases you'd like to print. You didn't run the enclosed release. How could I have made it better for you?

Then put some check boxes to get their feedback, such as:
❏ Format wrong
❏ Not of interest to my readers
❏ Not news
❏ Other_____

Hire a PR Firm

If you think you have lots to say that would be of high interest to local listeners, find a PR firm that has experience doing this. It's too expensive to create tapes that nobody will run; by adding the expense of a PR firm, you increase your chances of getting the clip to produce airtime for you.

Because the idea is to get the media person to respond, don't expect to get their names. If you're sending several of these cards to local media, make sure you put a code for the contact (name of publication, TV station, etc.) somewhere on the front of the postcard so you'll know who sent it back to you.

- If you still don't hear back from the editor or reporter, try calling. Twice.
- If you're still stuck, find another reporter or editor at the same media outlet and start all over again with that person.
- If none of the above works, you might consider hiring a PR firm for a one-time job—to look over your press releases, who you're sending them to, and advise you on what changes you should make. Tell them you want to buy two hours of their time because it's all you can afford now. If it works, and your sales grow, you will probably be in the market for a PR firm on contract—and the firm who helped you would be at the top of your list for helping you now.

Hiring a PR Firm

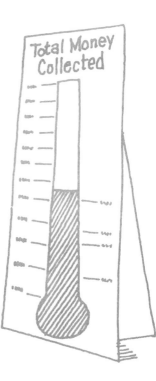

PR firms can help you grow profits—or they can be a complete waste of your money. Which result occurs depends more upon you than upon them. Here are some questions to ask yourself:

- Do I have a concrete plan for how to make money from people who read press about my company? Will I be getting a list of their names through, say, a free offer? Will readers be given the information they need in this publicity to easily reach my company? *If the answer is no to both of these questions, don't waste your money on a PR firm.*
- Will the publicity I can get from the media make people want to reach my company? *If not, skip the PR firm.*
- Is the type of material I could release from my company the type of material that gets substantial space in newspapers or trade magazines, or gets airtime on radio or TV? *If not, forget the PR firm. They can't do miracles. If you manufacture me-too buttons ("me-too" means copycat) then*

nobody—including magazines about button manufacturing—will be interested.

- Can I afford $2,000 a month in fees? (You might be able to get a local firm for less; many national firms will charge quite a bit more.) *If you can't afford a firm, you'll have to see what you can do on your own. Or, you could try to hire a local college student majoring in public relations, at a substantial discount, and see what he or she can do. If the student succeeds, it's great for you and it gives her career a boost to already have a real-world success story.*

If you have the money, the high-interest material, and the ability to make sales from publicity, then hiring a PR firm could be a big boost to your profits. Just make sure you get bids from at least two PR firms and that you get the following in writing:

1. Exactly what the firm will do for their fee
2. Exactly what expenses will be "extra" and billed to you on top of the fee
3. A list of current and past clients (insist on getting the names of two companies who no longer use them)

Publicity for Nationally Sold Products

Identifying Your Location

Publications usually identify a company by name only, regardless of the address or phone number you put in a press release. This isn't a problem for a local company appearing in a local publication because interested buyers can call local information and get your phone number.

However, if your company is based in Des Moines, Iowa, and your product is sold all over the U.S., you have a problem. A press release that gets picked up by a Nashville or a Detroit newspaper listing just your company or product name will be practically worthless to you. Actually, it used to be completely worthless, but now there are

Finding PR Firms

How do you find potential PR firms? Ask similar-sized companies (but not competitive with you) in your area what they know about the local PR firms. Have they worked with or known agencies they would recommend? How about ones to avoid? Also, if possible, get names at the firms they recommend. A firm might have one great PR person and a dud working for her. You want to increase your chances of getting the great one.

telephone services—though used by very few people—that will give you a telephone number for a company anywhere in the country.

You can get a toll-free number, but that isn't a complete solution, either. If someone calls 1-800-555-1212 for Information, they get 800-number listings. However, the 800 numbers are pretty well all gone, so you'll likely get an 888 number, or even something else.

Offer Something Free

If you are selling products through direct response (mail order, Web sites, telemarketing, e-mails, etc.) naturally you are trying to build a database (list of names, addresses, and interests) of potential buyers. Even if you're selling through retailers, most national brands today are trying to build up an affinity list (people who have bought their products). That's why car companies offer free magazines about their cars to buyers of those cars—to get the names in their database so they can try to make sure the next car those people buy is also from them.

Offering something free to people who write you is a great way to build up a database—and the best way of ensuring your address or phone number get into print.

Say your product is a unique garlic peeler. You could write a number of press releases on the product—each with a free offer for the publication's readers:

- Press release #1: Announces the new product with a photo of it.
- Press release #2: Announces the latest research on how garlic is beneficial to health. Offers "10 Great Garlic Recipes" free to everyone who sends a self-addressed, stamped envelope to your PO box. Included with the free recipes you send is an offer for your garlic peeler.
- Further press releases: Every second month you could send out a recipe using garlic to food editors, along with an offer to get nine more garlic recipes free by sending a self-addressed, stamped envelope to your PO box.

Say your product is a book for purchasing agents on how to negotiate better deals. You'll want to send press releases to the

business sections of newspapers around the country as well as to any newspapers or magazines or Web sites targeted to purchasing agents.

- Press release #1: Announces the book with a picture of it and who the publisher is (you). (Make sure you have deals with amazon.com and barnesandnoble.com, and that the books are already available through them before sending out the press release.)
- Press release #2: Announces some news item about purchasing agents (e.g., companies adding them, companies deleting the position, the rising importance of that position in companies, etc.). Offer "Five Negotiating Mistakes Made by Purchasing Agents" free to purchasing agents who enclose a business card. You send along with the "Five Mistakes" an offer to buy the book.
- Press release #3: Find some research on salaries for purchasing agents. If necessary, it may pay to do your own. Announce the U.S. numbers in a press release. Offer a free breakdown of how those salaries vary by geographic region to any purchasing agent sending you their business cards. Even though this has nothing to do with your book, it will be of the greatest interest to the potential buyers of your book. Send them the requested information along with a flyer for your book.
- Press release #4: You provide a negotiating tip used by purchasing agents. Offer five more free to any purchasing agent sending you his or her business card.

Offer a Column by a Company Expert

For business products, if you or one of your staff is a guru in your industry, offer the leading trade magazine in your industry a regular or occasional column on a topic related to the industry or product. If no one bites, offer it to the second leading publication. If they won't take it, offer it to the third . . . Although a catering service or food book publisher might talk some newspaper food editors into a regular recipes feature, etc., this gambit is likely to work only for business products.

Tip: Match the Phone Book

Make sure the name of the company or product you want publicized is the same as the name or names listed in the telephone book. You wouldn't believe how many people get publicity for a product their company makes with no mention of the company name. Of course, there will be no listing of the product name in the phone book—and you'll be out of luck.

If you can get paid for the column, great. If not, that's OK too. But in both cases, you get agreement for a tag line to your column, such as:

- Jane Doe is CEO of Mega-Corp Consulting Company in Park City, Utah.
- John Doe is the author of *Corporate Skiing*, a book on business and winter sport retreats, published by Mega-Corp Consulting Company in Park City, Utah.
- Jane Shaine is the owner of Jane's Restaurant on Main Street.

Marketing on the Internet

When you're planning your new business, take the time to think about how you could increase sales or cut costs by using the Internet. You might not launch that component of your plan at first, or, on the other hand, you might decide to launch *only* on the Internet. The Web offers many attractive selling features you can't get elsewhere.

By contrast, consider the costs of setting up a retail store. You have to pay rent and buy furnishings, fixtures, and display shelves or cases. On the Internet, you can do all that for a couple thousand dollars or less. Try beating that price with a physical store!

If your business is consulting or some other service, you can set up your own Web site for as little as $300 and a week's work.

Besides bringing in sales, you can cut costs substantially through the Internet. When Federal Express put its package-tracking information on the Web—where customers could track exactly where their packages were at any time—it saved the company millions of dollars a year in salaries of employees who no longer had to answer these questions for their customers.

Do you have plans for an expensive brochure about your company? If you send potential clients to your Web site, they can see your expensive brochure without it costing you a cent. And they can see it the second they want to see it, not a week or two later when it arrives in the mail.

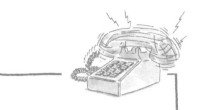

Research Your New Business Online

Even if you have no plans for an Internet component to your business, you absolutely must spend at least an afternoon on the Internet researching your potential competitors. If you've never surfed the Internet before, just go to your local library and throw yourself on the mercy of a librarian who will get you logged on and ready. Ask the librarian to show you how you enter a Web address into the browser.

The easiest way to get your first feel for the Internet is to go directly to a search engine. Simply type "www.altavista.com" into the browser your librarian showed you. That will take you to a site that is geared up to help you find different Web sites.

Say one of your potential competitors is named Jones & Warchawski. You can search for anything on the Internet with that name by typing in: "Jones & Warchawski." Include the quotation marks; otherwise the search will turn up anything that had either Jones or Warchawski in it. In that case, you'd probably have a million "hits"—a hit being a search engine find for a Web location where that word was found.

You can also search by topic area. If you offer a bookkeeping service, you could type in "bookkeeping" in the search engine; however, you'd probably get millions of hits. So try to narrow your search. Maybe you would type in: "bookkeeping AND San Francisco" (the all-caps AND links the two search phrases) so you'd only get bookkeeping services that also mentioned your business location of San Francisco. That would help you narrow it down to local competitors.

Each search takes a little finessing. If you try to search for your industry and get too many hits to even think about looking at, narrow down the list by adding another word. When "photography" gets too many hits to be worthwhile, try: "photography AND portraits" or "photography AND digital imaging" or whatever your particular niche is.

Surf for Competitors

If a search in AltaVista for a potential competitor doesn't net names you already know, try searching for them directly. In the

Search by Name

If you want to try something both amusing and a little scary, type in your own name, again using quotation marks so the search only turns up hits where your first and last name appear together.

I did this recently and found a site that quoted me about Billie Jean King (I used to publish *Sportswoman* magazine). I'd given the quote to a reporter back in 1973—back when there was no Internet—yet there it was! You can also use this feature to check on a potential client or employer by name.

browser area where you first typed in www.altavista.com instead type in the names of your potential competitors—using the prefix "www." in front of the business name and ".com" at the end. Eliminate any spacing between words. Thus you'd type "www.Jones&Warchawski.com" for our above example. If you don't find them that way, try "www.JonesandWarchawski.com."

Once you find a potential competitor, go through their entire Web site, seeing what they are offering and how they are set up.

Words that are highlighted and underlined on the Web are called "links." When you click on them with your computer mouse, they take you to a different "page" in the Web site that contains that information. If you find you've somehow gotten lost in a big complicated site, just look for the link that says "Home" and you'll be taken back to their home page (which is the entrance to their site). If you went to a page that didn't interest you, you can go right back to where you were by clicking a "back" arrow on your browser. It's usually at the top of your page. A helpful librarian or friend can show you simple ways to navigate.

Once you've researched your competitors, you'll have a much better idea of how important the World Wide Web will be to your business—in the short term. In the long term, almost everyone will want to be on the Web.

Creating Your Own Business Web Site

To set up your own basic Web site, you first need an ISP (Internet Service Provider). This is the company that sells you access time so you can get e-mail and visit Web sites. America Online is the easiest and most prevalent ISP, but EarthLink, Prodigy, Compuserve, and other national ISPs are available. Ask your friends which provider they use. You can find any of them by calling 800 number Information (1-800-555-1212).

Then you'll need a Web hosting service, which will carry your Web site on their computers full-time. For the greatest convenience, small companies will want it to be the same company as their ISP. America Online, for example, has an arrangement with a company

called Verio. Verio hosts business Web sites for America Online customers for a reasonable monthly fee.

Don't be waylaid by the free Web sites offered by most ISPs. Usually they are only a couple of pages, and—most damaging—you can't own your own domain name.

A domain name is your address on the Web. It's usually "www.yourname.com." The free Web sites offered by most ISPs are much more complicated. In addition, should you decide to change your ISP you would lose the address anyway. You do not want to invest your time and effort building up a Web site under an address (domain name) that you don't own.

Domain names cost about $80, a fee payable every couple of years to the national company that registers names (see page 152). You should try immediately to register one or more names you know you'll want to use to identify your company before someone else takes them. When I launched *Media Marketing* newsletter, I was distressed to learn a magazine company in Scandinavia had already taken www.mediamarketing.com.

What should this part of the start-up cost? The Web hosting company should have a package deal, where they get your domain name for you (about $80), set up your Web site location on their hosting computers (about $100), and maintain it and provide you with statistics on who is visiting your site (about $25 a month).

Designing the Site

Now all you have to do is develop your Web site. This will require a software program. I recommend Microsoft FrontPage 2000, but there are many other Web authoring programs available, including Adobe Page Mill, HomeSite, and—more advanced—Dreamweaver.

If you think you might be able to design your own site, but are terrified of trying it without more help than the manual that comes with the software package, look around for a class. Most medium- to large-sized cities have adult education programs that teach Web site design.

With great trepidation, I sat down one weekend with the Front Page program (which costs about $100) and tried to create my own Web site. To my relief and surprise, by Monday I had a fully functioning Web site of 29 different pages all linked to one another, with

Join the Fun!

Local autoparts stores are selling on the Internet. Local dry cleaners are on the Internet. Virtually any company selling nationally is on the Internet. Lots of international Web surfers are finding U.S. companies and placing orders; one newsletter publisher says 30% of the subscription orders that come in through their Web site are from companies outside the U.S.

an easy link to a pop-up e-mail form addressed to me, making it easy for visitors to contact my business.

It wasn't beautiful, but it wasn't ugly, either. It didn't have a shopping cart feature (where people can select and pay for products) or a registration feature (where you gather detailed information about the visitor), but both of those could be added. It had everything a consulting firm needed to sell itself and attract clients. Which it did.

Navigating Your Site

The best advice I can give you if you intend to create your own site is not to jump in directly with content. Instead, spend some time mapping out how visitors—your potential customers—will navigate your site.

The starting point on every Web site is the home page. It should present a sort of table of contents to the site. What different interests would first-time visitors have to your site? Make sure there are easy links for each on the home page. For example, people visiting the Newsletter Group's site get these links:

- Consumer newsletters
- B2B newsletters
- Launching new newsletters
- Fixing established newsletters
- Magazine companies launching newsletters
- About the Newsletter Group

Each of those links then leads to other links. "About the Newsletter Group," for instance, gives general information and links to contact us on the first link. Then you can go through more links to any of these sections:

- CEO bio
- Additional personnel bios
- Client list

Remember, the goal is to take visitors logically and quickly to the information they wish to see. Plus, give them links to jump to other sections quickly. Have an e-mail link on each page to contact someone at your company.

If, after seeing the site you designed, you believe you need better graphics and better design, you can hire a person to polish your site—doing it after the fact will cost far less than if you hired them to design it in the first place. They could do a lot for you with, say, five hours of their time.

Make sure, however, not to add too many graphics. Anything that takes more than five to 10 seconds to load (appear on the browser screen) can cause high percentages of visitors to move to a different site. Patience may be a virtue, but it is one almost universally lacking on the Internet.

Further, whether you or someone else designs your Web site, make sure it works using both the Microsoft Explorer browser and the Netscape browser. The more graphics you have the less likely it will look the same. Ask someone using the other kind of browser (check which browser your library uses) to see if your site works on it.

One more thing you need to know: metatags. Metatags are words that the Web site visitor cannot see, but which you add so that a search engine can determine how likely your site is to meet the criteria of someone searching. Look in your Web program's manual to learn how to add these tags to your site. For example, for the Newsletter Group site, I added these metatags: "newsletter, publishing, magazines, subscriptions."

Hiring Someone Else to Build Your Web Site

You can pay $1,000 for someone to design your site, or you can pay $500,000. That is not the problem. The problem is not knowing whether designers can do what they promise for the money they promise—and within the time frame they promise—or if they'll waste your time and your money.

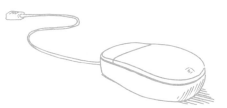

Before you contact anyone, choose several Web sites that look like the kind of site you want for your own company. Then contact the Webmasters of those sites. If you can't find them via the site, call the company and ask for the Webmaster running their site. Tell these people you're planning a similar site in structure to theirs (emphasize it will *not* be a competitive site).

Cyberspace Asset: Your Domain Name

As more people realized a domain name that was easy to remember and quick to find was a great way to promote a business, the cyberspace version of gold rush fever swept the land. Because each domain name has to be unique—even though many companies in the world may share the same name—the situation produced many bizarre twists.

Companies began suing other companies for real or imagined trademark infringement. Cyber squatters began grabbing domain names similar to names of big companies, itching to sell them at a profit. Obscure South Pacific islands began cashing in on the frenzy of the nameless, due to a quirk that some countries do not require that only their citizens be able to register a name under their country code. Companies began suing Network Solutions, which has operated the only registry in the world for top-level domain names since 1993, to express their fury. Some companies, known as domain name brokers, offered domain name registration to a public who was often unaware the firms simply registered the names with Network Solutions, charging extra for the privilege.

With over one million domain names registered by Network Solutions' InterNIC registry (*http://networksolutions.com*), in Herndon, Virginia, under a five-year contract with the National Science Foundation, a frequent grumble of Internet name-hunters is that all the good names are taken. After initially following a first-come, first-served policy, the company later adopted a policy protecting holders of federal trademarks obtained before a domain name was registered to thwart the efforts of name speculators.

"The IRS has even declared a domain name to be an *intangible* asset, seizing and auctioning off some domain names because people didn't pay their taxes," says David Graves, director of business affairs at Network Solutions. "We've also had causes of marriages or business partnerships which fell apart fighting over domain names because they were pieces of property." In such cases, the company asked the people to resolve the issue among themselves or get a court order, and deactivated the Web site in the meantime so nobody could reach it.

- Ask who designed their site.
- Ask about timeliness of delivery.
- Ask about any cost overruns.
- Ask for a rough total cost in design.
- Ask about anything they did that they'd recommend you *not* do.
- Ask what they'd do differently with their site if they were starting today.
- If you've gotten answers to all of the above, go for broke and ask if there's any company or companies they or someone they know has had bad experiences with.

Then, when you interview prospective site designers from their recommended designers, get references and grill those references with the same questions.

If you want a simple site, but are not willing to try it yourself, talk to someone who teaches Web design at a local adult education extension. Ask them if they are interested or if they know someone interested in developing a basic Web site for you. You can probably get it done for $1,000 to $2,000.

Getting Potential Customers to Your Web Site

The ironic thing about Web sites is that the technology that was to lead to a "paperless society" has generated more tons of paper than any other invention in recent history. It turns out that print—print ads, print notices, postcards, faxes, and printed stationery and business cards—plus some other old media—TV and radio—are exactly what you need to pull people to your Web site.

"If you build it, they will come," might apply to cornfields in the Midwest, but it doesn't apply to your Web site. Here's how you get the visitors you need to increase your Web site profits:

1. Put your Web site address on your business cards and stationery.

The Story of pokey.org

As a birthday gift from his father, a Bethlehem, Pennsylvania, boy named Chris Van Allen—whose nickname was "Pokey"—received a Web site with the domain name *www.pokey.org* in 1997. The twelve-year-old promptly posted photos of his puppy and pages on favorite games and pastimes. A few months later, lawyers for Prema Toy Co., makers of the toys Gumby and Pokey, sent a letter claming trademark infringement, and asked Chris to give up all rights to pokey.org.

(continued on next page)

2. Include your Web site address in any advertising you run (print or electronic). Companies that might be interested in your company can check out your Web site to see if they want to pursue that interest. It works like a charm for a consulting business, allowing skittish potential customers to feel more confident in contacting you.

3. Postcard campaigns are tactics that have worked well for many companies. Just remember that the goal of your postcard message is not to sell anything except a visit to your site. Once they're at the site, the site can sell them on your products.

4. Faxes promoting your site can only be sent legally to companies (or individuals) with whom you have a "prior business relationship." That does not mean they have to be paid customers. You have a "prior business relationship" with people who have requested your literature (via mail, in-person, by phone, or through your Web site). Faxes to such people work best when they are announcing something that fits within the "rushed message" image of faxes.

5. If you are speaking in front of any group, make sure your Web site is in your "speaker's bio."

6. Get listed in search engines. There is much advice available on the Web itself about how to get listed and there are books you can buy on how to increase your Web site traffic in one weekend. They list search engines for you to get listed with.

Your Web hosting company may well offer you something like mine did: "Get listed with the top 100 search engines for just $9.95." I did it, and you can as well, but these automated Web site listing tools are probably a waste of your money. Mostly they list you with companies that require you to receive sales messages from their service in order to continue being listed with them. I got a small boost in visitors to my Web site, which dropped off within a week. As far as I can ascertain they did nothing about getting my site into the leading search engines. Some free weekend I intend to read the book I got and figure out what the smart solution is.

If you are a B2B site, you can manage this on your own or with limited help. But if you're a consumer site, you will probably need to look into paid services offered by Yahoo!, AltaVista, and the other leading search sites. They sell banner ads (at this point in time they pull an average of only $1/2$ of 1 percent and even that response rate is falling) and some sell placement in searches. Thus you could pay to be in the first 10 listings for anyone who searches for your keyword—e.g., "cats" or "hair" or "blouses" or "carburetors."

The not-so-secret secret about search engines is that people using them seldom look beyond the first 20 "hits" that come up under the word searched.

Marketing Through Your Web Site

Web sites are actually catalogs for your company. The tactics needed to sell best are direct response tactics, which many dot-com companies learned too late for their survival. (Dot-com companies are companies based entirely or primarily on the Internet.)

Marketing a Service

Many Web sites function as a corporate brochure. It tells what services the company offers and how they can help other companies. It lets prospective clients research your company before actually talking to you, which some prospects strongly want to do. If they had to call you cold, having seen only your advertisement somewhere, some of them wouldn't. But being able to visit your Web site provides an additional level of comfort/ease about your company. And it presells prospective clients, so when they do call they have a better idea what they want from you.

Your service company Web site should also give some advice or valuable content free, rewarding someone for visiting the site. If the site only sells, it leaves a bad taste in visitors' mouths; there's a strong Internet culture that says sites should provide at least some free content. Think of what you could offer that:

- Demonstrates your expertise on your topic

The Story of pokey.org

(continued from previous page)

The lawyers also notified Network Solutions, which placed the domain on hold and gave Chris another site. Chris began to get thousands of supportive e-mails from all over the world as Internet users championed his case. His family hired trademark lawyers to fight.

But all's well that ends well. Art Clokey, the creator of Pokey—a toy rubber horse—probably sensing a public relations disaster in the making, finally wrote to and called Chris in 1998, apologizing for the mess and allowing the child to keep pokey.org.

- Is of value to potential clients visiting your site, but
- Doesn't give away too much of what clients should pay you for.

The Newsletter Group site provides names of the biggest consumer newsletters, with their subscription prices and estimated circulation sizes. Under the "magazines launching newsletter sites," it lists the four key reasons why magazines fail when they launch newsletters.

Marketing a Product

There are two kinds of products that can be marketed with the basic Web site already described:

1. Very expensive B2B (business-to-business) products, such as printing presses, car wash machines, etc. That is, any product where you solicit leads instead of sales. Where you ask potential customers to contact you "for further information." An easy e-mail link to the appropriate person at your company can accomplish the initial part of this sell.
2. Products generally sold by offering a "free trial." Here as well you can sell by having an e-mail link on your site where people can e-mail their name and address for their "free trial."

Other products sold via the Internet will need a "shopping cart" feature plus a secure ordering environment. Your hosting company can point you to software vendors who offer products compatible with their systems and with your Web authoring software.

At checkout, a Web site visitor can review all the items they wanted to purchase, and see the total price before shipping charges. They can delete items or increase quantities of the items selected. They can opt for overnight delivery or standard. They can have one or more items sent to a different person and address, with a gift card. Then, when the order is how they want it, they can enter their credit card and pay for it—or, for the cautious, they can call an 800 number and give their credit card over the telephone.

Don't imagine this shopping cart works only for small, relatively inexpensive items. I bought my last computer from Compaq through their Web site. You start with the model you want (based upon the specifications provided), then add all the features you want, such as a zip backup drive and a DVD player. Then you proceed to "checkout."

You can also buy a car the same way. I was interested in a Volkswagen EuroVan, and their site let me select all the options I wanted (such as the interior with a bed and a sink) and the color of the van and the upholstery, then proceed to checkout. (However, faced with a $40,000 price tag at checkout, I opted to cancel the order!)

Web Marketing Techniques

When you market your products on a Web site, you use many of the same techniques print catalog companies use, such as:

- Changing the positions of your products to feature those selling best.
- Removing poor sellers—since you don't have to pay for printing pages on a Web site, at least moving them away from the "high traffic" areas.
- Personalizing your catalog. Have you noticed many print catalogs have a picture of the company owner and/or the "friendly staff" at the company? It's usually on page 3 of the catalog and takes up at least $1/3$ page. Tests have shown that having such a section increases the sales of the other products more than enough to make up for the loss of products you could sell in that $1/3$ page.
- Making sure your order form is as simple as possible to use.
- Changing the home page layout frequently. Have you noticed that print catalogs often change only the cover and then remail that same catalog to you the next month? Web sites can do the same by featuring different products on their home pages (and the first page of each of their "departments"). This change keeps customers returning frequently. If a frequent shopper signs on to your site and sees the same products displayed in the first two screens (or even just the first one), he or she will decide there's "nothing new" and move on to a site that doesn't look so stale.

What Is a Shopping Cart?

A shopping cart feature allows visitors to browse your site and find products they might like to buy. When they see such a product, they can click on a button that says: "Add to your shopping cart (you can always remove it later)" When customers have finished shopping they click a button that says, "Proceed to checkout."

Using E-mail to Sell

There may be some fast-changing new laws regarding marketing through e-mail, so you will want to check with your industry association, or contact the Direct Marketing Association, before planning an e-mail marketing campaign.

Basically, e-mail marketing breaks down into two categories: bulk e-mailing, known pejoratively in cyberspace as "spam"; and permission marketing.

Spam is an e-mail marketing message sent to people who have not previously agreed to receive it. Most people will tell you that spam is bad and that only con-men send spam (I'm not exaggerating by much—there is a lot of heat generated by this topic). They'll say only *permission marketing*—in which people agree to receive e-mail marketing—is acceptable. I disagree, and you'll soon see why.

E-mail Name Lists

In order to market via e-mail, you need lists of names to which you can send your marketing messages. Those lists come in one of four forms:

1. **Directory names.** E-mail addresses compiled from directories and other sources.
2. **Opt-out lists.** These people have signed up for something (usually something free, such as a free e-mail newsletter). They are then sent e-mails promoting additional products and given the opportunity to "opt out" by telling the company to remove their name from the promotional list.
3. **Opt-in lists.** These are e-mail lists of people who have agreed to receive e-mail marketing messages, not by neglecting to change an already prechecked box, but by actively checking a box that gives their agreement.
4. **Double opt-in lists.** These people, after checking a box that says they'd like to receive e-mail marketing messages, are sent a confirmation e-mail by the company that requires them to confirm they are willing to receive e-mail marketing messages. If they don't confirm by reply e-mail,

E-mail Marketing to Consumers

When marketing via e-mail to consumers, do not spam. Not only will it annoy most of your recipients who actually see it (many have "spam filters" on their mailers that prevent your message from even getting through to them), but some of them will be annoyed enough to try to "get" you back electronically.

Also, for the health of the industry, broad bulk e-mailings to consumers is what will bring down federal regulatory wrath and put e-mail marketing into the limbo that fax marketing is today (it's illegal to fax a commercial message to anyone you aren't already doing business with).

their names won't be rented out. Thus these people have opted in twice.

E-mail lists cost much more than direct mail name lists. B2B names (executives at companies) cost about $200 per thousand plus a broadcasting charge of another $100 per thousand. If you wanted to rent those same names with street addresses for mailing an offer, you'd pay about $125/thousand total. However, you'd have to print up a piece and pay postage to get it in the mail, roughly another $350/thousand.

COSTS PER THOUSAND NAMES FOR DIRECT MARKETING

	E-mail Direct Marketing Costs	Print Direct Mail Costs
Lists of names	$200	$125
Broadcasting costs	100	0
Printing & postage	0	350
Total	$300	$475

E-mail Marketing to Businesses

Many marketers will tell you the rules are the same for B2B e-mail marketing. But that's not always the case:

1. Permission marketing may not work in B2B for finding new prospects.
2. Careful, conscientious "spam" to businesspeople is not as objectionable as it is to consumers.

Opt-in names (permission marketing) may not work for B2B.

There are certainly success stories in marketing through rented e-mail names. In the newsletter business, I've heard of good results for people marketing B2B products costing under $100. But here's a cautionary story for those marketing more expensive products.

One of my clients had a very successful newsletter. When e-mail marketed to its huge (60,000 names) house list (see sidebar), it got

The House List

The list of names of prospects and customers that you have collected yourself from various sources, such as advertisements, directories, customers, attendees at your conferences and conventions, and registered visitors to your Web site, is known as the *house list.*

A house list is one of your company's biggest assets. It represents people who have either bought from you or who at least know something about your company—usually from previous mailings you've made to them.

If you are direct marketing a product, your house list will have the best response of any list.

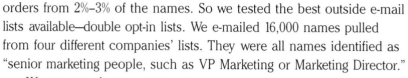

orders from 2%–3% of the names. So we tested the best outside e-mail lists available—double opt-in lists. We e-mailed 16,000 names pulled from four different companies' lists. They were all names identified as "senior marketing people, such as VP Marketing or Marketing Director."

We got exactly two responses.

You could hypothesize that the newsletter was only of interest to our house list, but that wasn't the case. Direct mail (via the post office) to VP Marketing and Marketing Director names pulled well for this client. So what was the problem? Let's look at the process.

In order to get into a double opt-in list, these marketing directors had to agree—twice!—to receive e-mail marketing pitches. Once they agreed, their names were rented out and they started getting two e-mail sales messages a day. If that annoyed them, they could cancel and get off the list.

I wondered, how many marketing directors are willing to get a couple of ads every day to their e-mail account without deciding enough is enough and getting off the list? My guess is, not very many. My further guess is that the people who remained might be in marketing, but they were junior level people—not top level.

List brokers who have rented out e-mail names for other clients have confirmed to me that the lists do work for some lower-priced B2B products. Unlike my client's product, which was $400.

Why would they have the wrong titles for these people? Because the best B2B lists right now come from business magazines that are sent free to qualified people in their industries. Thus, if you want to receive the magazine *Hotels* free, you have to fill out a card giving not only your name, company, and address, but also your company's number of employees. You also have to check off a box describing your position. Something such as:

❑ Senior marketing management (VP marketing, marketing director)
❑ Marketing (manager, account executive, associate)

The card you send in specifically says the free subscription is only for "qualified" people. Do some junior staff check off bigger titles than they actually have just to make sure they "qualify"? Of course they do. How prevalent is it? Nobody knows.

Bulk e-mailings may work with B2B lists.

How do you create careful, conscientious bulk e-mailings (spam) that won't upset its recipients? There are three essential rules:

1. **Always identify yourself, by name, company, and e-mail address.** It gives the appearance of being responsible (and it is). *(Bad spammers use dummy return e-mail addresses where you can't find them.)*

2. **Always give a way to get off your list.** Use strong words. My B2B e-mail says: "If you would prefer NOT to hear from us again, please hit the reply button and put "Do not e-mail" in the subject line. (Please also include the e-mail address at which you received this message—or we won't be able to find you to remove you!) <u>If you do this, you will never hear from us again</u>."

   NOTE: I had to add the second sentence when I discovered that the "Reply" button didn't always identify the responders by the e-mail address at which I contacted them.

3. **Give them something of value in the e-mail.** My B2B e-mail is for my newsletter titled *Media Marketing*. It helps magazine publishers and ad directors sell more advertising, by telling them tricks and tactics used by others. I used the subject line: "How *Audio* magazine increased ad pages by 143%." The body of the message starts out by giving the details of a program *Audio* used to sell 143% more ad pages. Then it says, "For more of these tips you might want to try a free trial subscription to *Media Marketing* newsletter, the only publication that . . ."

   The message closes with an e-mail link so the recipient can send me their name and address for the free 3-issue trial. It also says that if they find the newsletter isn't everything they think it should be they can just write "cancel" on the invoice and owe nothing.

Yes, this e-mail tactic is giving away free content—the very content the newsletter is trying to sell. But how is that different from giving a free trial subscription, which is how most B2B newsletters are sold?

Changes Ahead

Recent proposed legislation for e-mail marketing includes specific requirements for:

- Identifiable return e-mail address
- Easy way to get off the list

That's also giving away content. Both let potential buyers see that you really are worth the money (or if you are!).

Because everyone who reads this e-mail walks away with one idea on how to get advertisers to run catalog pages in the magazine, it gives them something valuable in exchange for their time. That's why the e-mail tactic works in B2B: everyone in my list is currently selling advertising and are thus interested in how to sell more ads. Their jobs depend on it. So they read the e-mail and don't automatically delete it as unwanted spam.

Consumer-directed e-mail doesn't—and can't—meet this urgency of interest or even the tight targeting, and thus it will always annoy. Just in case you aren't convinced, let's look at an example. Say you could get an e-mail list of cat owners. You want to e-mail them with news of your kitty litter liner product. All cats need kitty litter, you may reason, so it will be of interest to all of them.

Not so. Outside cats don't need kitty litter. Inside cats using clumping litter don't need your litter liners. And, of the remaining people who do use kitty litter liners, maybe half to 75% of them are quite satisfied with what they're using. They have no interest in hearing about something new on the subject, much less something not new but just selling. So your e-mail is unwanted, unneeded junk e-mail—bad spam.

Compare that to people whose jobs depend upon selling advertising. People who, even if they are already selling enough advertising to protect their jobs, get a commission (or bonus) based upon how many ads they sell. So my tip can directly put more money into their pockets.

Consumer e-mail that claims to offer ways to make more money doesn't have the same credibility or the same targeting. While all consumers might want more money, most are trying to earn it through their own jobs or their own companies and have no interest in even reading about the scams that are being sent out. And if yours isn't a scam? You'll be too closely identified with all the others that are, so you will lack the credibility.

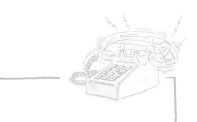

Marketing by Phone and Fax

If you get as annoyed by telephone sales calls as most people do, you may not have even considered this form of marketing as a potential source of revenue. However, telemarketing—and fax marketing—are two of the most powerful marketing tools in your arsenal.

The response rates on telephone and fax can be the highest of any direct response tool there is. Whereas direct mail generally produces in the 0.25% to 3% response rates and e-mail in the 1% to 4% range, telephone marketing can produce 2% to 10% and fax can produce 1% to 5%. Of course, these are norms, which means your response rates could be much lower—as in zero!—or much higher.

Both methods are effective where you have a limited number of prospects and your business plan requires you to introduce your new product and get a sampling of it from as many of those prospects as possible.

Legal Restrictions

Telemarketing

If you solicit customers by telephone or fax, you are required by law to create Do Not Call (DNC) or Do Not Solicit (DNS) lists. On those lists you must put the name of everyone who requests no phone/fax solicitation. If you telemarket to outside lists, you must have those lists checked against the national DNC list maintained by the Direct Marketing Association.

That being said, a large phone company repeatedly broke this law and, to my knowledge, never paid the consequences. Over a period of five years, I have received at least 20 telephone sales calls from this huge corporation trying to get me to change my service. With each call, I have told them to put me on the DNC list. In each case, they swore they would. When told of past noncompliance, they would pass the buck, saying that my DNC request must have gone to a different telemarketing center location.

However, this company has the lawyers to handle any lawsuits or regulatory notices that result from their actions. Unless you want to be tied up with lawyers and regulators, don't follow their example.

Open to Interpretation

Some mercenary lawyers have chosen to interpret the law so broadly that even the mention of your company name on a press release constitutes a "commercial message" because it promotes the name of your company. That allows these lawyers to threaten lawsuits against businesses who are sending faxes of this kind—*not* forbidden by the law—and demand financial payments to stop them from filing a lawsuit. A company might well win these cases in a courtroom, but most settle to avoid the legal expense.

Further, the bad will such actions create for the company can undermine your other forms of marketing for decades. This company could be selling eternal youth for $1, and I would never give them a cent of my money; and I'm not alone in this hostility.

Fax Marketing

Of all the forms of marketing, fax marketing has the most legal restrictions. Because an unsolicited fax can use up the recipients' fax paper, thus costing them out-of-pocket money—besides monopolizing the fax—laws were passed strictly limiting marketing by fax.

The law says you cannot send a commercial (advertising) fax to anyone with whom you do not have a "prior business relationship." Note the two parts of the restriction:

1. Commercial fax. In other words, noncommercial faxes are still permitted. You can send surveys, press releases, and anything else that will not generate money for you to anyone you want.
2. Prior business relationship. This is defined as any person or company who has contacted you in the past, or anyone you have contacted who responded. It does NOT require that they are, or ever were, a customer of yours. If they requested a free trial, or just more information, you have a prior business relationship with them.

Because only commercial faxes were banned to the general public, many marketers tried to create "two-step" programs that used faxes. A two-step program is a marketing plan that takes two steps. The first just pulls in a name, without even trying to make a sale, and the second step goes for the sale.

Marketers sent out questionnaires and at the bottom included the phrase "As a reward for filling out this questionnaire, we'll send you a free trial subscription to . . ." Or they sent out press releases about a topic in their newsletters, and added: "For more information and a free report on this topic, contact . . ." When these faxes attracted lawsuits, they lowered the commercial part of the fax to almost nonexistent status: A press release on a news item would be followed by a "For a free report on this topic, contact . . ."

Some companies still send unsolicited fax ads; I recommend you do not. Nor do I recommend you send press release faxes, even though they are supposed to be legal.

Faxing to Sell

Because fax marketing works so well when it's done legally, here are some ways you can use it:

- Test a fax offer to anyone who has ever contacted you or responded to you about anything. You can legally fax these people, and you will be glad you did.
- Offer a "Do not fax me" option on *all* faxes sent—allowing those people to be put on a list that you will never solicit by fax. This offer should be clear and at the end of your message. It can be a check box saying, "Please do not send me any further fax promotions or offers." List the phone number where the recipient should fax this request. The recipient of your fax should be able to simply check the box and fax it back to you to get off your list.
- If you find it hard to collect fax numbers in your other promotions, here's a short, easy way to collect a lot of them from businesspeople (it won't work as well with consumers). Send a free offer—"10 tips on picking quality clothing" or "five auto repairs NEVER to try by yourself"—by postcard. To get the free offer, recipients should fax the front of the card (with their name and address on it) to a number you provide. Because these people have requested information from you, you now have the legal right to fax them; and because they faxed the offer to you, you will have collected fax numbers on most of them from their fax machines.
- Make it readable and increase transmission speed. Don't use any type smaller than 11 point; 12 point is even better. If you fax on your letterhead, your address may be in smaller type

and become illegible. Fax it to a couple of friends first, and if it is even remotely hard to read, increase the type size. Don't use graphics or if necessary use minimal graphics. Never fax a black box with reverse type.

- If you are using a fax broadcast service—a company that sends out the faxes for you—know to shop around on price. At the time of this writing, telephone companies are offering deals that will pull your long distance costs to 10 cents a minute, but fax broadcasters are available at prices of 7 cents a minute up to 20 cents. If you question their price, most will offer you a lower number.

- Calculate your costs. A page without graphics and black boxes will go through in about a minute, so if you're sending a single-page fax, 10 cents a minute translates to 10 cents per person faxed.

- Limit your faxes. A single page is by far the best. If you're soliciting for a free trial or sample, you should never send more than a page. Two pages is the maximum for a solicitation.

- If you have fewer than a thousand people to solicit, you can do it yourself. Get WinFaxPro software (about $100) and spare yourself the agony of other software programs that are impossible to learn and can't be removed from your computer. I still have a fax program that I can't uninstall and that has created glitches in my computer. I'm going to have to wipe the entire hard drive to get rid of it.

- You can (from one computer attached to one phone line) send out about 400 one-page faxes a night. WinFaxPro will let you select the customer database to send to, address each fax to the appropriate name, and add the message you create (including your signature, if you scan it in with a scanner). Once you set the software, you push the button and go to sleep.

- Think Canada and the UK as faxing opportunities. You can fax offers to consumers and companies in these countries with impunity. In addition, Canadian laws allow unsolicited faxes as long as you offer a way for recipients to get off your list. Even then, Canadian law says that after two years you can fax them again to see if they've changed their minds.

Telemarketing Success Tips

- You can't sell something complicated on the phone. It has to be an easy-to-understand product and offer.
- And it almost has to be a "two-step" offer, meaning you solicit customers on the phone to receive free information or a free trial subscription or a free test drive, then you follow up after they receive their free offer to get them to buy more.
- Beware your natural tendency to describe your product too fully. It can actually hurt your response rates. A newsletter company built a line of 15 paid-subscription newsletters primarily by using the telephone. Their basic telephone offer is:

Hello, this is Jane Smith and I'm calling from Widgets *newsletter, the only newsletter that helps widget producers increase their sales.*

We're offering a free trial subscription, so you can see if Widgets *newsletter would be helpful to you in your job. You will receive three free issues. If you decide you don't like it, you just write "cancel" on the invoice and you'll owe nothing.*

Would you like to try it?

The president of that company told me that any time he tries to tell more about the newsletter in the call—more about what the newsletter contains, how it helps people, etc.—the lower the response rate goes.

Remember this lesson of brevity for any telephone marketing you do. As business owners, we are in love with our products, but others aren't. Tell consumers just enough to let them know your product can help them, then give them a way to sample it. Then take their name and get off the phone.

The Agony and Ecstasy of Telemarketing

There are two agonies associated with telephone marketing: the costs and the complaints.

Complaints should be few if you are careful. I recently tested 5,000 names for a client and only one called to complain. (Unfortunately, he called the company's president—which created some internal political heat!) The man told the telemarketer to put him on a DNS list and the telemarketer didn't know what he meant. Make sure your telemarketers understand that the acronyms DNS and DNC stand for "Do Not Solicit" and "Do Not Call." Double-check that they know you want to collect those phone numbers so you don't call those individuals ever again.

The ecstasy part of telemarketing is that for that 5,000 list, which produced one complaint, we got 241 orders for a trial subscription: a 5% response rate. Nothing else would have pulled that well.

Costs are substantial. Telemarketing firms charge $30–$40 per hour and reach, on average, six to seven people per hour. Most will recall numbers up to five times before giving up on them.

Telemarketing companies will tell you that their services are best for products that sell for at least $50. It's not cost effective for you to use telemarketing to sell products with lower prices.

CHAPTER EIGHT

Buying Advertising

Tracking Results

Traditional advertising can introduce your products or business to a large number of people and result in a lot of new sales—when it works. When it doesn't, you might as well take thousands of dollars—or millions!—and set them on fire.

Do you remember the Coca-Cola commercial with the little boy who hands a Coke to Mean Joe Green? It was widely promoted and even more widely loved by most of America. Until the marketing director at Coca-Cola killed it—because it wasn't increasing sales of Coke. Why not? Nobody knows. But if that marketing director wasn't watching closely, he could have blown millions more of Coke's money running an ad that didn't increase sales.

The cautionary message here is: Make sure you can track results of the advertising you place. Be wary of "image" ads that aren't directly selling a product—at least until you're big enough to have advertising money you can risk.

Discounted Advertising

Start Your Own Ad Agency

Publications pay 15% discounts to advertising agencies, so it makes sense to establish your own agency and save that 15%—unless you need the help a regular agency can provide in creating good ads.

All it takes to start an agency is some stationery and an extra phone line, which is always answered by the agency name. No need to lie, you can say yours is an in-house agency, which it is if you're creating and placing your own ads.

When you want to place an ad in a publication, you send an "insertion order," which comes with your agency name on it, lists your company as the client, and states what the order is for—e.g., a particular issue in a publication, a particular time slot on a radio program, etc.

P.I. Advertising—Great Deals, if You Can Get Them

For the entrepreneur on a budget—and other than a couple of dot-coms, who isn't?—P.I. ads can make a world of difference. P.I. stands

for "Per Inquiry." It means you don't pay for the advertising up front—you only pay per inquiry or per response.

For example, if *Ferret* magazine charges $1,000 for a four-color (which is full color) ad page; you might be able to negotiate that you don't pay the $1,000 four-color rate, but you pay them $10 for every order you get from your ad.

Sounds too good to be true? It is, because most magazines won't do P.I. deals. But, always a silver lining, some will. And if you position your offer to them correctly, more would.

Here's the little secret that makes this possible. A single sheet of paper has two sides; it cannot have only one side. Print publications can't add or subtract a single page from their publication. If they have enough ads and editorial material for three pages, they will have to deliver either two or four. So if the publication has the odd page available, you may have a P.I. deal.

Let's look at how different media handle P.I.'s.

Magazines

Most smaller magazines (under 500,000 copies) can't economically print less than an eight-page form—the sheet that is then cut up into separate pages—and the most economical for them are 32-page forms. Covers are usually printed separately as a four-page form. Large-circulation magazines often go up or down by four pages, and unless they are stapled sometimes go up or down by two pages.

Say that a magazine is 68 pages: a four-page cover and two 32-page forms. That is the perfect size for the number of editorial pages (the text of the magazine) they want to run and the number of ad pages they are getting. But, their ad pages are growing. There are only two ways to accept those additional ads: cut their editorial pages (which will hurt subscriptions), or add more pages to the magazine.

Let's say they need to add five more pages to the magazine to fit in the ads. But they're only 200,000 circulation and they can only afford to go up by eight-page forms. So, if they add eight pages, they will use five for the ads and have three left blank. What do they put on those three pages? Here are their choices:

1. Add more editorial pages. This is usually done, but the editorial is usually of little value to the readers: book

Get Your Mail Order Discount

If your ad solicits responses, either as sales or as leads for you to follow up, you are entitled to the "mail order" rate card from the publication. Most publications offer lower rates to advertisers soliciting direct responses. Sometimes the prices are as much as 40% less than the "regular" or "display" rates.

reviews, tidbits, stuff the editor hadn't planned to use but which he or she now has to dredge up to fill the pages.

2. "Smokey the Bear" ads. This term refers to free ads for charitable causes. This used to be a more popular choice, but now—with financial managers hovering over publishers and second-guessing their decisions—it is perceived as less fiscally responsible.

3. P.I. ads. Rather than get nothing for those three pages, why not put in ads that should make at least something from the per inquiry results it gets.

Newspapers

A paper can easily go up or down in size by two pages (a front and back). That gives them greater flexibility than all but the largest circulation magazines. However, newspaper pages are generally larger than magazine pages and thus require more to fill them up. Thus newspapers too are potential targets for ads that are less than full-page size. However, newspapers are not good direct marketing vehicles, except for FSIs (free-standing inserts). So your chances of success in a P.I. deal are much lower.

Local radio and TV stations

Though national TV spots are almost always sold out (and, if they aren't, the network uses them to promote their own programs), local stations will have some—or a lot—of unsold airtime. They're in

even worse a position than publications, because they can't cut their airtime at all. If a station can take eight ads in an hour and they've only sold six, those two empty ad slots are lost forever at the end of that hour. They might be very receptive to P.I. deals that include an 800 number, staffed by an outside 800-number service. Part of the deal could be that the outside service is instructed to send complete reports to both your company and the station, so the station can be sure they're getting their percentage of all sales.

How to Talk a Media Company into a P.I. Deal

To get a media company to seriously consider your P.I. offer, you must convince them:

1. That your company has strength and integrity. Media companies don't want even a hint of a shaky company that could go out of business and not fulfill the orders they get—or remit the percentage of the money due them.
2. That your product has a good chance of selling. It better be exactly the kind of thing that the media's readers/listeners/viewers are likely to buy.
3. That your product doesn't conflict with paid advertisers. Magazines almost never do P.I. deals with companies in the industry their main paid advertisers are in. They figure the information will get out to their paid advertisers and they'll lose money.
4. That you won't cheat them. You *may* need to have the money go to someone at the media company first, so they can be certain they're getting their share. Many media companies won't want to deal with that paperwork. So think of how else you can reassure them. For example, if your ad solicits calls to an 800 number, you can instruct the outside service that fields the calls to send complete reports to both you and the media company.
5. That your ad looks good or sounds good and won't hurt their image. (Even if they take ugly paid ads, they won't be receptive to an ugly P.I. ad.)
6. That running your ad won't cost them a cent. Tell the magazine they can run it whenever they have an extra page to fill. Any month. That gives them the flexibility they need to be interested at all. Tell the radio or TV station they can run the ad whenever they have holes. Of course, if your product is for the geriatric set and the "holes" the station has are at 2 A.M., you might question—and test!—whether that time slot will produce any orders.

Finding Media

Look for magazines that don't have a lot of ads; those magazines are a lot more willing to consider P.I. ads. Count the number of ads pages in the magazine. If they make up less than 50% of the pages, you have a good potential candidate.

For radio and local TV, count the number of ad spots in an hour on various stations. The number of ad spots they want to sell may vary depending on the hour of day. (Drive-time ads are almost always sold out for radio stations.) Contact the station that has fewer ads than its local competitors.

Filler Ads

Offer magazines and newspapers P.I. filler ads as well. Offer them your ad in $1/3$-page square size. It's the size most needed by magazines to fill holes. Offer it as well in $1/2$-page and $1/4$-page sizes.

When I was publisher of *Home Mechanix*, I never took P.I. deals, except once, when a reputable man from the industry, now with his own company, came to me with a full-page ad for a table. We weren't getting paid ads for furniture, only for furniture plans, so it didn't conflict with current advertisers. It also looked like the kind of furniture our readers liked to make—maybe they'd like to buy one instead. So we tried the ad three times and made a little money. However, that man got three full-color ads in a 1.6 million circulation magazine, basically for free.

There are companies who create full-page ads to run in filler space for magazines. They pay 20%–30% of the revenues they receive to the magazines for the space.

Bartering for Ad Space

If your company produces products or services that a magazine needs, you may be able to barter your products for ad space. Since your products cost you less than the "sticker price" of the ad, you'll come out ahead.

Magazines often barter with national hotel chains for rooms for their traveling sales force. Magazines and newspapers might be interested in bartering for computers, telephones—anything that they need in quantity.

A small publishing company in your market might be happy to barter for accounting services or graphics design. When I was publisher of *Audio*, I bartered an ad with Rolex. The watch we received was then used as a sales incentive to reward the ad salesperson who landed the most new accounts that year. Could your product be a "premium" used to reward a publisher's employees?

Also, don't limit yourself to ad space. Are there other products your company needs that you could barter for? It can't hurt to offer; if they turn you down, you've lost nothing. And they might say yes.

Great Places to Advertise

Yellow Pages

If you are a local business, the first ad you can afford should be in the Yellow Pages. However, think long and hard about the size of the ad you should buy.

Is your business visited many times a year by locals—a grocery store, hardware store, etc.? If so, when they want a hardware store, they're not likely to use the Yellow Pages. They'll go where they've always gone.

If the locals all know where you are, then the Yellow Pages will influence primarily out-of-towners and people new to your town. Because new people in town are critical to your business, you will want a Yellow Pages ad. But because they will come to know your company in other ways, such as driving past it, the ad need not be particularly big.

For nonlocals, consider whether they have characteristics that will make them better customers for you than locals. For example, if your business is selling souvenirs, out-of-towners may be much better customers than locals. Therefore, you might want a larger Yellow Pages ad.

On the other hand, a client of mine in the automobile towing business says that he runs small Yellow Pages ads, because the out-of-town business he gets is usually at automobile club rates and much less profitable. To attract local customers, they painted their tow trucks a flashy color with large lettering on the side. Locals see the trucks as they move from one job to another—and are likely to remember the name when they need towing themselves.

If yours is a business like reupholstering furniture, unless your shop is located on the main drag with a big sign, most locals will not know you exist or where you are. In that case, you'll want a Yellow Pages ad big enough to make you look like one of the top upholsterers in the area. Most locals will use the Yellow Pages when making a decision about a service business such as this.

You never need a Yellow Pages ad bigger than all your competition. If your important customers will be searching the Yellow Pages for your company, you'll want an ad roughly the same size as your biggest competitor—that is, unless you have a specialty that you can tout clearly in your smaller ad. If not so important customers—that is, nonlocals, etc.— will be finding you in the Yellow Pages, you'll need only a small ad— one large enough to get across your most important benefits message.

The Yellow Pages salesperson will of course tell you a bigger ad will increase your business—and it probably will. But the incremental dollars for the larger size might pull in twice as many extra customers if used elsewhere.

Flyers and Inserts

Flyers are a great way to sell something that is either new or on sale. Flyers have a sense of urgency that must work *with* your advertising message, not against it.

Flyers distributed locally

Local flyers are usually one sheet, printed on one side, which can be placed facing inside car windshields, under the wipers.

It's very important to check your town ordinances to see what, if any, laws control where flyers may be distributed. In general, you cannot distribute them on private property, such as a shopping mall parking lot. See what the penalties are. If it's a $150 fine, you might want to do it anyway and pay the fine—if the sales potential is great enough.

Flyers also work well when you are targeting a particular group of people who are attending an event:

- Say your best prospects are teens who go to the trendy new "in" spot in town. You can stand outside the doors and hand out flyers for your hot, trendy product.
- At a convention that has relevance for your produce or service, pay the organizers to be able to hand out your flyers to the attendees.

Flyers distributed nationally

One national media generally accepts flyers for distribution to its subscribers: newsletters. Preprinted flyers are then included inside the envelope in which the newsletter is sent. Prices run about $500 for 2,000 subscribers. You pay the printing cost.

These newsletters are mostly for businesspeople and usually targeted to very narrow niches. For example, though a business magazine might go to all sorts of corporate controllers, there are probably business newsletters targeted only to:

- Controllers in not-for-profit companies
- Controllers at companies generating at least $5 million/year
- Controllers at companies generating less than $1 million/year

Another way you could distribute flyers nationally is by direct mailing them yourself. However, if you're sending out direct mail, you might as well pay for a full package. The postage costs (your biggest cost component) would be the same, as long as you don't go over two ounces (bulk mail) or a half-ounce (first class) though your response rates should be much higher.

The only flyers that wouldn't do better packaged in an envelope are flyers soliciting attendees to a conference. These are generally sold by a four-page or more 8 $1/2$ x 11 flyer, folded once and wafered (a little glued circle that holds the ends together). Many companies have tried putting those same flyers in an envelope to mail, but it almost always cuts responses—often substantially.

Inserts

Usually single sheets of paper, printed on both sides, that are inserted into a publication. The only requirement is that their physical size cannot exceed that of the local or national publication they go into. Thus newspapers can take very large inserts, while most magazines can't take anything over 8 x 10.

With inserts, you pay for the printing. Then you pay a magazine or newspaper to insert them into their publication. Insert prices are highly negotiable. That's because they cost the publication very little.

Magazines do have additional postage costs, but not as much as you might think. If an insert increases the weight of the magazine by 1%, their postage costs don't raise 1%. That's because magazine postage is comprised of two parts: one part weight and one part a per magazine charge. Magazines also have to pay to insert the piece, and since it is usually bound into the magazine (instead of loose like in a newspaper) those costs are higher for the magazine than for a newspaper.

However, even with magazines, you can usually get your message delivered to prospects cheaper as a front-and-back single-page insert than as a paid one-page ad. That includes your costs of printing it.

Because inserts are usually on a slightly different paper—usually heavier—they get noticed more than regular magazine or newspaper pages.

Newsletter Directories

If your business product is essential for just a small group of businesses or businesspeople, check out a newsletter directory in your public library. It's likely you'll find one or more newsletters targeting exactly that group. Call to find out the details. Ask if their newsletter is delivered in an envelope. If it isn't, be leery; most important newsletters are mailed in envelopes; most freebie newsletters are not.

Ask if they accept paid ad flyers in their newsletter(s). Even if they haven't done it before, they have heard of the practice and may well decide to give it a try.

Creating Effective Advertising

If your product is national, with a big media buy, you'll want an ad agency to design the ads for you. Pick one that has previously worked for companies in your industry.

If you'll be creating your own advertising, you are advised to do three things:

1. **Go to school on your competitors' ads.** Pull together all the examples of your competitors' ads you can find. Pin them up on the walls and study them. Are there certain common characteristics they all have? If so, give your ads those same characteristics. I'm not advising you make your ad look like theirs at all. But if all your competitors' ads are discount ads, ask yourself if that's the only kind of advertising that might motivate your potential customers. At least consider that possibility before you commit your entire advertising budget to a different kind of advertising. (Also check where your competitors have placed the ads. They have probably tested other locations—and found those didn't work.)

2. **Get a designer for your logo.** This represents you to the world, and a poorly designed logo can sabotage your company from the beginning. Find a local person who has worked in commercial art. Maybe someone who designed ads for the local newspaper. You shouldn't have to pay too much, and it will be more than worth it. Make sure they give you five or six different options, and are willing to come up with a couple more, once you've seen the first pass. *(Example: For my newsletters and those of my clients, I found a great designer who had worked for a local magazine company. He was employed elsewhere and would freelance nameplate designs for me for $500–$1,000.)*

3. **Have a good designer design your first few ads.** They'll be night-and-day better than what you can come up with—unless you're a designer yourself. If you get them to supply the ads in a software program like Quark or Adobe PageMaker, you can then make small changes to the ads yourself without incurring additional costs. Quark and PageMaker are large and expensive page layout programs. If you do a lot of print advertising—and have plans to start your own in-house ad agency someday—investing in this software may be well worth it.

Weight Doesn't Matter

A newspaper doesn't pay more to distribute itself if it is heavier. Those kids on bicycles or contract delivery services charge per delivery and newspaper trucks are company-owned. The only costs are the costs of inserting the pieces into the newspaper.

PART III:

Structuring Your Business from the Inside Out

CHAPTER NINE

Choosing the Form for Your Business

Making It Legal

Your company can be structured legally in a number of ways. The most prevalent forms for small businesses are: sole proprietorships, partnerships, S Corporations, and, occasionally, C Corporations, which are regular corporations. Larger businesses consider C Corporations and LLCs, or Limited Liability Companies.

When You Need an Attorney

To set up a partnership, corporation, or LLC, you'll need an attorney with experience in the field.

For a corporation? Maybe. Your decision should be based on:

- Can you afford it? If so, always use an attorney.
- Will you be selling stock or soliciting investors? If so, you need an attorney to set up your corporation.

If you are planning a small corporation with no outside investors and you can't afford the costs of an attorney, take these steps:

- Buy a book on setting up your own corporation in your state (the laws are different for each state). You can find these books in most bookstores or at amazon.com. Read it. Reread it.
- Based upon what you have read, talk to a tax accountant who handles business returns. If you already have one for your personal returns, you may not be charged extra for this advice. Most of your choices (if you are not soliciting investors or selling stock) come down to which form would be best from a tax perspective.
- If, after reading the book and talking to a tax accountant, you are comfortable proceeding on your own, be cheered in knowing that many others have also set up a corporation without an attorney.

This worksheet will help steer you toward the appropriate legal form for your business. The column with the most Yes answers will guide your choice.

Who Takes the Fall?

One of the big benefits of incorporation, which will be discussed in this chapter, is limiting your personal liability. Thus, if the business fails and you can't pay your creditors, they can only go after the corporation's assets, not your personal ones. Be advised, however, that small corporations cannot generally borrow money from banks (or get investment capital) without a personal guarantee—which puts the liability right back on you personally. However, liability protection from other lawsuits, such as defamation or personal injury (someone slipped and fell on your premises), can still be a major reason for choosing to incorporate.

Choosing the Legal Form for Your Company

By answering the questions, you can determine which kind of legal structure would be best for your company. Boxes are blacked out when that choice is not good or not available for someone answering Yes to the question.

	Sole Proprietorship	Partnership	Limited Liability Company	Corporation — Sub-Chapter S	C Corporation
Do you require a partner for capital or for knowledge you're missing?	■				
If so, are you willing to be liable for everything this partner does?	■	■	■		
Is there any likelihood of someone suing your business? (Some businesses are more likely than others to be sued)	■	■			
Do you have substantial personal assets to protect? (House, cash in the bank, stocks, etc.)	■	■			
Will your business likely lose money for 2+ years?					■
Will being able to deduct medical, disability, and life insurance make a big financial impact on you?	■	■	■	■	
Will you have investors?	■				
Will you have more than 35 investors?	■			■	

Sole Proprietorship

Anyone can start a sole proprietorship just by taking in money for goods or services. A baby-sitter is in a sole proprietorship. So is a paper delivery boy. So are most small businesses in America.

Let's look at some of the advantages:

- Simple to quit: As long as you don't owe anyone money, just shut the doors and stop.
- Cheaper: You don't have to pay filing fees or attorney fees to set up a partnership, corporation, or LLC (Limited Liability Company). And you don't have to pay minimum fees each year as you do when filing state corporate returns.
- You can deduct most of your business losses from any other income (e.g., wages) that you or your spouse have that year. When a business is losing money, this deductibility is a key asset.
- You are not considered an employee of your business, so you don't have to pay unemployment taxes on your earnings from it.

But, there are also some disadvantages:

- No protection from liability: If you are sued successfully, they can take away your personal assets: your house, your cash in the bank, and probably your retirement plan.
- No tax deductions for generous medical, disability, and life insurance plans, such as you can make with a C Corporation.

Partnerships

Partnerships are much like sole proprietorships except that there are two or more owners. You can create one just as easily, just by starting up. The government requires no formal written documents for forming a partnership. However, you would be a tad crazy to do it that way.

Your partner(s) become like your spouse. If one of them defrauds someone, you're equally liable. If one of them runs up a huge debt on a fly fishing expedition with clients, you're equally liable. Even if your partner runs up *personal* debts he can't

pay, creditors can come after his interest in the partnership—which can seriously disrupt or even endanger your part of the business.

Further, ending a partnership can be extremely messy, expensive, and acrimonious.

Some of the items you'll want covered in a written agreement before forming a partnership are:

- What contribution each will make to the partnership, including cash, property, time, etc. Note that partnerships need not be *equal* partners, although that will be the assumption if there is no written agreement.
- How profits and losses will be divided among the partners.
- When and how profits will be taken out of the partnership.
- Compensation for future contributions to the partnership of services and/or cash.
- The duration of the partnership (in case one or more parties has a certain exit plan in mind).
- Who has the final word in the event of irreconcilable differences.
- How changes in ownership, death, or disability will be handled.

Limited Partnerships

This variation on the partnership format is used to raise capital. *Limited* partners get protection from liability—so they risk no more than their investment—as long as they are not involved in the business operations. The *general* partners are fully liable for all the business debts, including lawsuit judgments.

Both limited and general partners can deduct their share of partnership losses from their personal income tax returns.

Establishing limited partners does require paperwork—a written partnership agreement as well as some state forms that must be filed.

Corporations

The decision to incorporate is based upon many factors. As a rule, it probably won't pay off if you anticipate losses for a few years, although you could incorporate after that. But there are other reasons,

Plan Your Partnership

The key to a successful partnership is outlining the partnership agreement ahead of time. You and your partner(s) should get down on paper who is going to invest what, who will decide what, who will do what work, decide how and when profits will be divided, and how you will buy each other out in the future. It's always easier to decide these matters when the partners are in a good frame of mind—things get ugly if the finger pointing is done as the business founders.

If you're considering a partnership—even with a family member—sit down with a lawyer to formalize your agreement once you have the basics of your partnership worked out.

Tax Benefits of Incorporation

Insurance and medical expenses make up the bulk of tax benefits provided only to C Corporations.

Though insurance and medical expenses are tax deductible for S Corporations, a portion must then be reported as income to the recipient. Not so for C Corporation benefits.

If you have a C Corporation, you can establish a marvelous health plan for the benefit of your employees. That health plan might include some or all of the following:

- 100% coverage of all medical, dental, and eye expenses
- Gym or health club membership coverage

(continued on next page)

such as personal liability and the ability to sell stock, that may make incorporation desirable, even if early losses are expected.

The advantages of incorporation:

- Protection from personal liability
- Ability to sell stock to raise capital
- Deductibility of benefits not available to unincorporated businesses

The disadvantages of incorporation:

- The cost (at least $500 to $1,000) of original fees, plus maybe attorney fees, plus an annual minimum charged by many states. Also, if you are the sole employee, you will have to pay unemployment taxes as a corporation, which you would not have had to pay as an individual or a partnership. (Although that may be offset for some by the idea that if your corporation fails and you are therefore "fired," you can collect unemployment benefits.)
- The requirement that monies be put in the corporate bank account. If you have a corporation with too little capital matched against too much debt, the courts could decide it was a "thin" corporation, which would allow someone to "pierce the corporate veil." That means they could try to come after you personally for bad debts. This seldom happens, and many corporations live from client check to client check, but it is a possibility.
- The hassle of all the paperwork required: incorporation documents, minutes, resolutions, stock certificates, and (if you are the sole employee) the hassle of payroll reporting.
- The possibility of double taxation (for C Corporations only): This only happens when the corporation is making more profits than could "reasonably" be paid to the owner as salary. In that case, the corporation must pay taxes on its profits, then you pay taxes on the same money when it is issued to you as dividends. However, when you look at salaries paid many CEOs, there is a lot of room to grow your salary before this happens. And you can keep the capital in the business for future growth without

paying dividends (and thus double taxes). It is not an immediate concern for most business start-ups.

C Corporation vs. S Corporation

C Corporations are the norm for *large* businesses, and are sometimes preferred by *profitable, smaller* businesses. IBM, AT&T, and similar companies are all C Corporations.

S Corporations have a few key differences—some of which are advantages and some disadvantages:

Advantages of an S Corporation

- All losses—and all profits—are passed directly to the shareholders and thus appear on shareholders' personal tax returns. Losses can thus be deducted from other sources of personal income, reducing the taxes you must pay on those other income sources.
- Profits can be pocketed without being issued as dividends, which causes double taxation.
- If your personal tax rate is lower than the corporate tax rate, the pass-through of profits from your S Corporation will allow you to have that money taxed at a lower rate.

Disadvantages of an S Corporation

- You cannot have more than 35 shareholders. (Husbands and wives who each own stock are counted as one shareholder in this calculation.)
- Your shareholders cannot be corporations or partnerships, only individuals.
- None of your shareholders can be a nonresident alien.
- There are limits on the amount of "passive" income an S Corporation can earn. Passive income is income from passive sources, such as interest, dividends, rents, royalties, etc.
- Fringe benefits such as full medical coverage, disability, and life insurance are deductible for S Corporations, but are then taxable income for you, unlike C Corporation benefits, which are generally not taxable to you.

Tax Benefits of Incorporation

(continued from previous page)

- "Preventative Health" coverage, such as vitamins, minerals, and other supplements

These benefits are particularly attractive for corporations with only one employee (you) or two (your spouse as well). That's because these benefits must be made available to ALL employees in order for them to be both tax deductible for the corporation and not taxable income for employees. If you and your spouse are the sum total of all employees, you're set!

A further benefit for small businesses that have a C Corporation: You can set your fiscal year differently from the January–December tax year that is established for your personal income. Having a corporate year that ends in September instead of December can allow you to make strategic moves that can save you taxes (or delay them to another year). For example, you could pay yourself more in September and less in December. That would get your payroll expense up for the corporation's fiscal year (more deductions means less profit to report) and still provide yourself with the same annual salary. Talk to your tax accountant.

Limited Liability Companies (LLCs)

Think of an LLC as an S Corporation—with more options for selling stock.

- Like a corporation, an LLC protects the shareholders from personal liability.
- Like an S Corporation or a partnership, the business profits or losses flow through directly to the shareholders and are taxed on the shareholders' personal tax returns.

Unlike an S Corporation, an LLC:

- Places no limits on the number of shareholders
- Allows nonresident alien shareholders
- Allows corporate and partnership shareholders

Because LLCs are still relatively new (since 1988), you'll want to consult an attorney who has substantial experience in setting them up.

Also be warned that there are substantial costs in converting your business to an LLC from another legal form of business.

Retirement: No Longer Just for Corporations

You may have heard that the ability to set up a generous retirement plan is an advantage of incorporating. However, today even unincorporated business owners can set up generous retirement plans.

CHAPTER TEN

Hiring and Motivating Employees

Employees: Pros and Cons

So now you're doing well enough that you need more help. It's sage advice to think long and hard about it before you hire that first employee (other than family). Here are factors you should consider:

- You will have to cut back on the health benefits and insurance programs you may have established, so that they apply to all employees.
- Your time—which must be busy already or you wouldn't be thinking of hiring—will be further diverted into the hiring and then the training process.
- Employees will bring new personalities and politics into your operation.
- When money is tough, you'll still have to pay your workers—even if that means you don't get a paycheck.
- Firing employees can be a nightmare—and can include lawsuits.

Of course, employees also bring several great advantages to your company:

- A fresh point of view and different experiences may help your company move forward.
- You can better cover those areas where you are weakest, as well as those you neglect most.
- You'll need employees to grow.

So, before deciding to hire employees, you might consider one of the following alternatives:

1. Hiring temporary employees
2. Renting employees
3. Hiring independent contractors

Go Temp

Temps used to be clerical workers you'd hire in a pinch when your secretary (remember secretaries?) would go on vacation.

Today the temp world is much more sophisticated and diversified, and even more permanent. You'll find everyone from accountants to VP Marketing types all working for temporary agencies. Some are in jobs that last for six months—or longer. In the high-tech arena, $100,000 per year positions are regularly filled for six-month periods, then renewed. And renewed.

Maybe you only need help at year end and tax time. Maybe only for your Christmas rush season. But here's a tip: hiring temps to fill a position lets you evaluate a worker in that position. If you find someone wonderful, you might want to hire him or her full-time (even though you'll have to pay the agency a fee for that).

Rent-a-Worker

If you need someone throughout the year, but maybe only three to four hours a day, then renting an employee may be your best bet. The same may be true if you need only one or two employees.

There are thousands of employee-leasing companies in the United States. Look in the Yellow Pages, or call a temp agency. If the temp agency is not in the employee-renting business, they may be able to tell you who is.

Employers rent employees when they want to:

- Avoid payroll hassles (rented employees actually work for the leasing company, so it has all the headaches)
- Avoid hiring/firing hassles (getting rid of, or replacing, a rented employee is much simpler)
- Observe potential employees in operation before actually hiring staff

Employee-leasing firms do not charge the high premiums charged by temp agencies; usually their fees are just 2% to 9% of the wages. That means you can afford to use them on a more regular basis than you ever could with a temp agency.

The downside on renting employees:

- The 2% to 9% fee could instead be paying for other needed costs in your start-up.

> **Get IRS Advice**
>
> You can see the detailed IRS advice on independent contracting by logging on to their Web site at *www.ustreas.gov.* In their search box type in: "independent contractor" (use the quotes). IRS publication 15-A has more on this subject than you'd ever want to know.

- If the leasing company suddenly goes out of business, it could leave you stuck with a missing payroll. You sent it to them but they did not pay their employees. Check out the leasing company carefully. If you hear they have a "slow-pay" reputation, don't deal with them.

All about Independent Contractors

Independent contractors work for themselves, in their own businesses. Their business might be to supply bookkeeping services to companies such as yours, or to supply marketing help, write advertising copy, clean offices, and so on—just about anything.

Typically you can hire independent contractors for the same amount as an equivalent employee—often even less.

You know the contractor's skills, you set up an agreement as to what will be supplied, and you can terminate that agreement. He or she is actually a vendor—one who is supplying you advice or services instead of product.

If the person supplying the services is incorporated, you have no problem. If they are not, you may run into IRS and state taxation authorities, who all want to declare your independent contractor an employee because they think they can get more tax revenue if they do.

For example, editing a monthly, eight-page newsletter is usually a 20-hours-a-week job. Many newsletter companies seek freelance—independent contractor—editors. Those editors agree to create the copy for the newsletter and to meet established deadlines. They work out of their own homes, are free to schedule their own time, and they take other clients. Because editorial writing is considered the property of the person writing it unless otherwise specified, newsletters need to get a signed paper between them and the editor stating the work created is deemed "work for hire," and all the rights belong to the publisher.

The IRS looks at three areas to determine if the person is an employee or an independent contractor. They are:

1. **Behavioral control:** Does your business have the right to direct and control how the work is done, through instructions, training, or other means? If so, the person may be

an employee. Of course, a business is allowed to establish standards or guidelines of acceptable quality for work contracted out. This means you can tell the independent contractor what quality standards the work must meet, but you can't train him or her in how to meet them.

2. **Financial control:** Does the business control any of the following?

   - The extent to which the worker has unreimbursed business expenses
   - The extent of the worker's investment in the business
   - The extent to which the worker can realize a profit or incur a loss

   In practical matters, companies agree upon fees and, sometimes, timing of the fees (e.g., $1/3$ at signing, $1/3$ after completion of a specified portion, and $1/3$ upon final completion), but that is the extent of it. The IRS doesn't like employers paying expenses for independent contractors, but paying telephone and other out-of-pocket charges for consultants and other vendors is often standard practice.

3. **Other aspects of the relationship, including:**

   - Is there a written contract describing the relationship between parties? If yes, good.
   - To what extent is the worker available to perform services for other, similar businesses? If you use up 95% of the person's time, the IRS is more likely to consider the person an employee than if you use up just 25%.
   - Does the business provide employee-type benefits to the person, such as insurance, pension, vacation, or sick pay. If so, forget it—the person is an employee. Most businesses require independent contractors to sign a paper stating they are independent contractors and they recognize they are responsible for paying their own taxes, insurance, etc.

The Exception

California has decided that anyone creating "work for hire" is deemed an employee. The result? Newsletter companies based outside California won't hire California freelancers to edit their newsletters.

- To what extent is the relationship permanent? If it lasts a finite period of time (say three to six months), the IRS is less likely to consider it employment than if it has no termination in sight. However, many consultants and PR firms contract to provide x amount of advice per month without becoming employees.

Ten Tips on Hiring

If you're growing fast and need employees, here are some helpful general guidelines:

1. If you have fewer than four employees (counting yourself), most employment laws will not apply to you (except for some state differences). As you add more employees, you are required to meet more regulations.

2. Read about employment law. There are many things you cannot legally ask potential employees without risking a lawsuit. You can't, for example, ask if a woman has small children. But, if the job requires it, you can ask all applicants if they can travel overnight as frequently as the job requires it.

3. Create a written job description. You can't hire the perfect employee until you figure out that this employee will be doing. Writing the job description will help you focus on the tasks they'll do—and thus the kind of person you need. Example: You know you need help. But when you start figuring out exactly what kind of help you need, you realize you need someone to do the bookkeeping (which is about half a job) and someone to make cold call telephone solicitations to find you potential customers, which you will then follow up on. As you write out the description, you realize these are not the kind of skills that one person is likely to have: in fact, they're opposites. So you decide instead to hire an outside bookkeeping service and then hire a part-time marketer.

4. Get referrals from your current employees, friends, and business associates. These are usually your best applicants.

5. Evaluate applicants in the manner in which the job will dictate. Thus, if you're interviewing potential telemarketers, do it mostly over the telephone. If you're interviewing writers, get them to write for you. If you're interviewing salespeople, try to have them make a sales call on you. This may not always be possible, but it's a good interview technique.

6. Know what you want in this particular employee. Salespeople are different from accountants. Creative types are different from analysts. Sometimes the person you need will be very different from you, which worries many first-time employers. While you want someone that your gut says is trustworthy, don't look for a clone of yourself. Some degree of discomfort is fine—if they're bringing skills you lack.

7. If the employee will be working with a team, have the team interview him or her. There's nothing wrong with wanting help evaluating someone. Most interviews are way too short to tell you the kinds of things you really need to know, so adding interviewers cuts your risks. A client of mine who was staffing up for a new project asked me to sit in on second interviews with his top three candidates. He couldn't decide if one guy was incredibly great or just surface great, another guy he thought was top-notch, and a woman he thought was good but third of the group. Here's what I thought about them:

The first guy really was a worldbeater, but, in my opinion not somebody willing to get down in the trenches and do the grunt work that this project would require.

The second guy was very good, but I'd seen his type before. He was one of those people who lives in an open-ended world, where no decision is ever final and everything remains open to question. A good trait for an ongoing business where everything needs to be reexamined constantly to find small new opportunities, but a disaster

Quick Look: The Independent Contractor

Relatively strict IRS guidelines determine who is an employee and who is an independent contractor. The following are characteristics of the independent contractor:

- Determines how, when, or where to do the work.
- Determines what to charge for the work.
- Determines what tools or equipment to use.
- Determines what assistants to hire to help with the work.
- Determines where to purchase supplies.
- Is not reimbursed for most business expenses.
- Does not receive employee benefits.

in a new-project launch, where decisions not made can endanger the whole project.

The woman was not as good for an ongoing business, but much better for the launch my client was facing. She'd just come off launching a new division for a company that was incredibly hidebound and inflexible. She'd managed to move heaven and earth and launch—successfully—on schedule.

My added insights helped my client choose the woman candidate—who was every bit as successful for him as she had been for her previous boss.

8. Does the applicant *listen* to you? Or are some of the applicants so busy thinking what next to say that they miss what you're saying? People who don't listen well are a problem for almost any company. On the other hand, some people listen very well and respond quickly. Don't penalize someone for quick responses, as long as their words indicate they heard everything you were saying.

9. If you're hiring a management or salesperson, how well does each applicant research your company? Both types of employees need to do their homework and prepare well in order to do well in their jobs. If they didn't do it before meeting with you for a job application, they won't do it once they have the job.

10. Make sure you see the candidate in all situations he or she will be required to function in—*before* hiring them. That means if you're hiring a salesperson who will be required to take clients to lunch, don't hire anyone you haven't had lunch with. My ad director at *Audio* magazine hired a salesperson without doing that and found out that the guy had repulsive dining habits. He sucked on his teeth—often and noticeably. Clients mentioned it to the ad director, who then had to have an unpleasant discussion with the salesperson. The problem is with habits like these: The person will promise to change but may not be able to. And you're not there when they're entertaining your clients to keep an eye on them. Meanwhile, they can be reflecting poorly on your company.

How to Read a Resume

It's hard writing them—and it's sometimes hard to read them too. Resume reading requires a certain amount of decoding. Here are some guidelines for making sure you get the most from a person's resume:

1. Are there gaps in the dates? Unexplained periods of no job being listed? If so, it's a question to raise with the applicant. There may be logical reasons for it, or maybe—worst case scenario—the person was caught defrauding a company and went to prison, and have left that off the resume.

2. Is the person a job hopper? One year per job? Two years? Less than one year? In some industries, this is the norm, but in others it indicates a person who may not be worth the time to train. Make exceptions for job hopping if the person is in his or her early twenties. Also make exceptions for occasional fast changes spaced in between longer stints.

3. Call the references. That may sound like a no-brainer, but no brains is what a lot of employers exhibit by never calling references. Yes, many former employers won't say much these lawsuit-prone days, but they will say if the person didn't work there at all (then won't you be glad you called?). When telling you the person's strengths, they may clearly omit something critical for the job. You can creatively listen for silences. Also listen for voice tone. How does the former employer say the person was "good"? Does he sound enthusiastic or indifferent? Do you believe him?

4. Investigate the candidate's previous jobs for other people you can call. In your interviews, ask who he or she reported to at each job. Then call a couple of those people out of the blue and ask about your candidate.

5. Does the applicant claim a college degree? Call the university and ask. Faking degrees is not uncommon, and it will tell you a lot about the person (in most cases, it will tell you not to hire them!).

Protecting Yourself

There's a common believe that friends can be more dangerous to you than enemies, because you let the friends get close—where they can do more harm. This same principle holds true for employees. Because they are so close to your business—in fact, an integral part of it—they can do more damage.

However, there are measures you can take to protect yourself from some of the potential damage.

Noncompete Clauses

The biggest danger for small businesses with important clients is that an employee will steal away your clients and launch her own competing business. Noncompete clauses in employee contracts were designed to protect you from this. However, their protection is nowhere near as strong as it would seem on the surface.

Noncompete agreements usually specify that the employee will not compete with you for:

- A specific time period—usually one to two years; almost never three or more
- A specific locale (e.g., greater Cincinnati) or industry (women's apparel)
- A specific function (e.g., marketing or soliciting clients)

You must check with an attorney prior to drafting such an agreement; state laws vary widely. Some states take a hard line on any form of competition (such as the employee going to work for a competitor) and others practically ignore such agreements.

The problem with noncompete agreements is that few courts will allow you to prevent a person from making a living. If someone is a car salesman in Tulsa, a noncompete agreement will probably not be able to prevent him from selling cars at another dealership in Tulsa. But, if that person can make a living (and we don't mean they have to flip burgers at McDonald's) without competing, he can be required to do so.

When I took a job with a health company launching newsletters for the consumer health market, my noncompete agreement required me not to be involved with health newsletters targeting consumers for a two-year period after leaving. But I could work on other newsletters.

How to Find Good Employees

Source	Advantages	Disadvantages
Referrals	The referrer knows you and/or your company, so can refer better candidates.	From friends and employees, none, but watch out for acquaintances who refer someone working for them.
Ads in local paper	Fast and brings in a lot of candidates.	Candidates are not pre-screened, so check them out carefully. If they're actively looking, why do they want to leave their current job?
Postings on appropriate online sites	Very fast and brings in a lot of candidates.	Limited to certain types of jobs. Downloads of resumes may infect your computer with viruses, so ask them to copy their resumes into their e-mails.
Ads in an industry magazine or newspaper	Good positioning—will be read by your best candidates, including those not really looking.	Slow—many publications have monthly frequency.
Headhunters	Can find the best top-level people, including those not actively looking.	Expensive—will cost you 10%–20% of the hire's first-year salary.
Temp agencies	You can try out employees before deciding to hire one full-time.	Some people temp because they don't want full-time jobs. You'll have to pay a fee to the temp agency, on top of the higher wages you paid originally while the person was temping.
Independent contractors	More and more companies outsource with vendors. No employee hassles and opportunity to get high-quality help.	You control only the final product, with less control on the process. Not good for positions requiring a lot of client contact. If the person performing the work is not incorporated, IRS and state "independent contractor" regulations can be a problem.

Your marketing employee could be prohibited from marketing widgets (your product) for two years, but could be free to market other products. However, if marketing widgets is such a specialized niche that no other industry would hire a widget marketer, you wouldn't be able to make the prohibition stick.

If your employee will come into contact with your clients, add a nonsolicitation clause to the agreement, in which the employee agrees not to solicit your clients for a similar product/service for a fixed period of time after leaving.

Establishing Your Trade Secrets

Trade secrets are parts of your business that you keep secret and are important to your success. Famous examples of trade secrets are the formula for Coca-Cola and the seasoning mix for Kentucky Fried Chicken. But there are more general examples of trade secrets, such as:

- Subscriber lists for publications
- Customer lists for manufacturers, wholesalers, retailers, and service businesses
- Anything else that you want kept secret

You should do a couple of things in order to establish your trade secrets. Your reward is that former employees are not allowed to take these secrets to another company. If they do so, you can sue them and win substantial reimbursement. If the company they go to utilizes these secrets, you can sue that company as well. In 1997, Volkswagen had to pay $100 million to GM to settle a lawsuit. General Motors charged that their former employee Jose Ignacio Lopez de Arriortua stole trade secrets and took them to his new job with Volkswagen.

How do you "establish" trade secrets?

- **You keep them secret.** If you publish these secrets or make them easily available you lose your protection of them. Some things cannot be trade secrets because they are, by their very nature, public. For example, a magazine's lists of advertisers can't be a trade secret because anyone can see who the advertisers are in the pages of the magazine.

Job Interview Checklist

Qualities	Positive	Negative	Explanation
Candidate's Presentation			
Appearance: Neat? Appropriate?			"Creatives" won't dress like accountants, but all should be clean and neat.
At ease? Appears comfortable?			Important for client-contact positions, but not for others.
Makes you like/trust him or her?			Important for client-contact positions; less so for others.
Questions to Ask			
1. Give me a brief overview of your career— and what you've learned from it.			Does the candidate speak well extemporaneously? Did he organize his presentation?
2. What would you say was your greatest accomplishment on your last job?			Listen for specific ways she measures herself. Follow up to get more details.
3. Tell me about a failure you've faced, and what you've learned from it.			Be wary of a manager who has never faced failure; it means he hasn't learned the caution that comes with it.
4. (If the candidate can't recall a failure) Tell me about the most difficult job problem you've faced and what you did.			Look for how he thinks: Does he give up easily? Does he keep searching for new ways to overcome problems? Is he creative in his searches?
5. Everybody has strengths and weaknesses— what's your greatest strength? What are you best at?			How do these strengths fit in with you business's needs?
6. What would you say are your weaknesses? (If the candidate can't account for a weakness, try: What do you like to do the least? or What would former bosses say is your weakness?)			Don't expect people to tattle on themselves, but do expect to hear SOME weakness—or else it raises a trust question. This reminds the applicant you can ask for references; it may encourage candor.
7. Why did you leave your last job? (Or why are you considering leaving?)			Nobody's likely to tell you she's on the verge of getting fired, but you can still judge her responses.
Candidate's questions about the job to you:			
Does candidate ask about the challenges first? Or does he start with money?			Give him a chance to ask questions, so you can see what he thinks is most important.
Talk about the negatives of the job:			
Mostly number crunching? Mostly telephone? Fast paced? Late hours? Say so.			Tell her upfront about negative aspects of the job. You'll spare yourself having to train someone else after she quits or is fired.
If you are impressed:			
Talk about the positives of the job: Opportunity for promotion? Growth? Salary increases? Say so.			

References
* Call them! Ask them to tell you the candidate's strengths. Also ask for weaknesses, but if you don't get them, consider what was left out from their "strengths."
* Try to find others the candidate has worked for/with and call those people.

- **You tell employees what is secret.** Company policies that spell out confidential materials/practices that are not to be disclosed not only establish your trade secrets, but they also serve notice to employees that they will be judged on keeping them secret. For example, high-level corporate security companies warn all employees that their client names are to be kept completely confidential. (This same procedure cannot be used to protect illegal practices by your company.)

Dealing with Harassment and Discrimination

To protect yourself from lawsuits, any document you prepare for employees telling them about the company should include strong language on not tolerating sexual harassment as well as discrimination based on race, religion, or gender. It should also state that anyone feeling those policies are being violated should take their complaint directly to you. Or, if yours is a large company, to a designated person in human resources.

If an employee does complain, tell the person you will look into it and give a date when you will get back to him or her. If you haven't already talked to an attorney in drafting these regulations—and you should have!—call one who specializes in these kinds of cases and get advice on how to best respond. There are procedures that can give you the best chance of not being sued either by the person complaining or by the offender, should you decide that person's actions merit firing.

Monitoring Finances

There's no more potentially dangerous employee in the company than your controller and whoever opens the checks. There's no fool-proof way to be completely safe, because would-be thieves are incredibly inventive. The biggest mistake is assuming it can't happen to you. It happens to small and large business owners every day of the week.

Here are three things you absolutely must do to protect yourself:

1. Whoever prepares the deposit slips cannot be the same person who enters the payments into your company's

books. If you are too small to have two people in finance, but too large to be doing it yourself, take one of those jobs for yourself. Otherwise you're begging to be robbed.

2. The bank statements for your business should go to you *at home.* You should read them and flip through the checks. Look at each to make sure it's something you actually wrote and/or agreed to. One large newsletter publisher didn't do this and found out, after losing $50,000 to theft, that his controller was altering the bank statements to cover "bonus" checks to a phony company he set up.

3. Make sure your controller takes a two-week vacation. Controllers who won't take more than the occasional day off may have ulterior motives. And bring in an outside controller—a temp—for the time your controller is out. Consider it a mini-audit of the books.

Monetary Motivation

Don't take it on faith that your employees are motivated by the same goals as you are. You might be surprised to find out what their real motivations are.

As a junior executive, CBS sent me to their management school. Part of an exercise was to write out what I thought was going on in my department, while my staff, individually and anonymously, wrote out what they thought the "office culture" and staff motivations were. It was full of surprises. I had thought each of the four business managers under me were motivated by the chance to move up to my job—as I would have been—but only one of them felt that way. Two had already decided they would never get my job, including the person I thought was most likely. Their answers to several questions showed me that their biggest motivation was the sense of camaraderie in the department. They liked feeling that we were a team. A critical team doing critically important work. That's why they stayed and were happy with their jobs.

Nonmonetary factors can be a big part of an employee's motivation. It's important to feel appreciated, feel part of a team, and feel part of a growing success.

On the other hand, an employee who feels underpaid is often either underperforming—or out the door. At this writing, unemployment is extremely low. At times like these, employees move more often and for bigger jumps in salary.

Bonuses

Bonuses can't motivate employees if the employees can't control their own fate. Thus bonuses paid on whether the company makes a particular profit aren't strong motivators for anyone except the president or CEO. Others tend to shrug and believe the company's profits are out of their hands.

To strongly motivate marketers, bonuses should be paid on marketing results. To strongly motivate manufacturing employees, pay them bonuses based upon manufacturing results. What can you do with people who don't work in a profit center? Pay them bonuses based upon results they can control. For a PR department, bonuses could be paid upon the number of mentions they secure in designated press or, perhaps, the column inches they secure, which counts longer articles as more important than shorter ones.

That's not to say employees don't appreciate a $5,000 bonus payable if the company goes over its budget for the year. They appreciate it if they get it and are annoyed if they don't; but your office manager won't be working harder to try to get it, because he or she won't think their actions will make the difference.

Bonuses can also be two dinners at a local restaurant, an afternoon off, and an "Employee of the Month" parking space right by the door.

Other Motivation Tools

Motivation can also include the time you can spend with your employees, specifically:

- Telling them how smart/resourceful something they did was.
- Finding out what their career goals are, and seeing if you can help them move toward them by offering them additional training or letting them take over a new function.

Key to any feelings of satisfaction for an employee is knowing exactly what is expected of them. Not just for specific tasks, but also for the overall job. Don't think "performance evaluations" are only for large corporations. Everyone works better and happier when they know what they'll be judged on. Wouldn't you?

Set up the key responsibilities for each position, then talk with the employee to get agreement on specific ways of evaluating how well those goals are being achieved.

For higher-level employees, get them to draft their own goals and measurements, then review it and meet with them to iron out the differences. For those autocrats among us, it might sound crazy asking the person to be evaluated to set up the standards of the evaluation. But put aside your reservations and try it. If the person comes up with marshmallow goals, you can change them. Meanwhile, you've learned something valuable—and bad—about the person. Most people, however, will surprise you by coming up with pretty good goals and perhaps more strict measurements than you would have thought of yourself. Plus you'll find some goals or actions you might not have thought of. Employees will be less likely to resent goals they set for themselves—and more likely to achieve them.

Don't let an annual performance review keep you from giving periodic interim evaluations. If someone is not measuring up, don't spring it on them after months of seething. Nor should your delight in their performance be revealed only once a year.

Praise employees when their contributions are valuable. It is especially important for poorer performers to receive positive feedback for what they do that is good. People want to continue to please someone who is pleased with them. It makes them more open to problem solving with you on something that isn't working.

However, don't keep inefficient employees. If you can't fix them, you must get rid of them.

Employee Benefits

Most companies are lax in communicating all the benefits they provide employees—starting with the company's (involuntary) contribution to their Social Security accounts. (Companies have to match the amount of Social Security withholding from their employees.) When I worked at CBS, I was impressed with the annual benefits statement

Employee Rank

Here's a little psychological secret about employees: They each think they're really great, even those doing poorly. In tests where employees are asked to rank others in their group as to how capable and valuable each employee is, almost 90% of employees put themselves in the top 10%, including employees whom everyone else ranked in the bottom 10%. On the other hand, most employees (even those in the top 10%) don't feel appreciated enough. What does that mean for evaluating (and motivating) employees?

they sent to employees: it showed the dollar value of everything, including the Social Security payments, health insurance contributions, life insurance, 401(k) contributions—in short, you saw that the company was paying you about 30% more than your salary. Make sure your employees know how much extra you're paying to and for them.

Health Insurance

If you ask employees, the most important benefit they seek from a company is medical insurance. Thus, to attract and keep employees, medical should be the first benefit you offer. Many smaller companies pick up just half of the health insurance coverage, and ask employees to cover the other half.

If you're your only employee, you don't qualify for group health insurance; instead look for a personal policy. The National Association of Self-Employed Executives is primarily an association formed to sell its members health insurance. Check their rates. Many other trade-connected nonprofit organizations also offer group health insurance.

If you have two or more employees, get quotes from Blue Cross/Blue Shield and the larger HMOs in your area. Be willing to accept co-payments for HMOs—e.g., $10 or $15 per visit—which will lower the premiums, as will higher deductibles for non-HMO plans.

Ask other small business owners in your area what health plans they use. You can find a network of people to ask by attending the Lions Club or Rotary Club in your town.

Retirement Benefits
When you're the sole employee

If you are your only employee, you'll want to set up generous retirement benefits. Until you have a reliably profitable company, you'll want complete flexibility as to how much you do or do not contribute each year. The only plan that matches both those conditions is a SEP/IRA. With this plan, you the employer can contribute up to 15% of the salary you pay you the employee. But, in a bad year, you don't have to contribute anything at all. Another bonus is that there's next to no paperwork. Call a mutual fund like Vanguard, T. Rowe Price, or Fidelity and ask for a SEP/IRA form. Make sure to tell them if you will be contributing only as an individual or if your company will also be

The IRS Online

The IRS produces thousands of documents geared to helping you understand what to record, what to deduct, and what to pay. Most of these are now available on the Internet as well as in print. The online versions are to a certain extent searchable, which means that if you have a specific question, it might be easier to access the documents or specific answer by calling up www.irs.ustreas.gov. Printed versions of forms and publications can be acquired by calling 800-829-3676 (800-TAX-FORM).

contributing. They'll send you a simple form, which is the only thing you'll need to fill out; there's no annual reporting due to the IRS.

Once you're reliably profitable, talk to a tax accountant about Keogh plans. Some Keoughs will let you contribute more than $30,000 a year, but there is a tangle of rules and reporting required. You'll need expert advice.

When you have employees

Here's where a small business runs into additional costs—and another reason why you might want to rent employees instead of hiring them until your business has grown. You will naturally want to contribute fat retirement benefits to your own account. But you can't do it legally without including other employees in the same plan. Your only escape routes are:

- Hiring part-time employees who do not qualify (see a tax accountant about the number of hours someone can work and not be included)
- A waiting period, usually up to two or three years, before an employee qualifies for the plan

If employees would value your contributions to their retirement, you'd at least get their appreciation for the extra costs. Unfortunately, most employees under 40 couldn't care less about retirement benefits, so you won't even get much goodwill from them for your expensive contributions. However, by setting up the plans as SEP/IRAs, you will get more goodwill than from a vague pension plan. SEP/IRAs issue statements, so employees feel more that the money is theirs.

Stock Ownership Plans

Another way of attracting very good employees is to offer stock in the company, assuming you've selected a form for your business that allows stock ownership. But be advised to be leery of this idea. Here are just some of the things that can go wrong:

- People aren't impressed by 1% ownership, so you have to give more. Yet, if your company grows to a $100 million company, that 1% would have represented $1 million.

Phantom Stock

If offering stock is the only way to make a hire you desperately need, consider offering "phantom" stock. Phantom stock plans allow for someone to enjoy the benefits of stock ownership—that is, payouts when dividends are issued and a percentage of the sale price of the company—without having the legal standing of an official shareholder. If you give someone 5% of the company in phantom stock, they are entitled to 5% of the sale price if you sell the company. But they can't cause you some of the other troubles you could get from real shareholders. If you think this idea might help, talk to a tax accountant to get all the details of how it would work for your case.

Payroll Problems that Can Trip You Up

- Make sure your business account bank accepts payroll tax deposits; if it doesn't, get a different bank.
- When you report federal payroll taxes to the IRS, you don't send a check. Instead you have to make payments at your local bank along with Federal Tax Deposit Coupons. You will probably have to make monthly deposits at first, but if your taxes are large enough you will be required to make electronic deposits semiweekly.
- Watch out for look-alike state tax deposit requirements. By error I sent unemployment deposits to the state with-holding depository and it took a year to get the money back. (No, they wouldn't just transfer it themselves!)

(continued on next page)

- Because you have to give up more, you can lose control of the company if you have to seek outside capital. For example, suppose you give up 15% ownership to your VP Marketing. Then you need to raise outside capital. The venture capital firm won't accept less than 45% of the company. That would leave you with 40% in your own company. The venture capital firm would then have final control over your company.
- An official stockholder of your company, even if they own just 5% or 10%, can cause a lot of problems. What if you have to fire them? What if they leave you and go to a competitor? What if they file a lawsuit saying you're running the company poorly, causing their shares to degrade in value? Make sure you and any employee to whom you give stock sign a "buy/sell agreement," which spells out that departing shareholders have to sell back their stock and spells out how the price will be determined.

Payroll Taxes

Payroll taxes are a nightmare. Don't even *think* you can figure them out by reading books or IRS regulation pamphlets. I know two Mensa members (IQ in the top 2%) who own their own businesses. One just couldn't figure out the IRS regs and, especially, their state pamphlets. The other thought he had it figured out, but he kept getting notices from the state about missing or delinquent payments. Both finally gave up trying to do it themselves. One started using the payroll tax function from the financial software QuickBooks and the other hired a payroll tax service to handle it all.

Once you have an employee (even if it's only yourself), you should do one of the following:

- Use a computer bookkeeping program that calculates your payroll taxes—for both the IRS and your state—and prints out your forms 941 and 940.
- Use a bookkeeping or payroll–only service.

Computer bookkeeping programs get simpler every day. If you can write a check in your checkbook, you can do the same thing in the Quicken software package. At the end of the month, it will create great reports for you showing your expenses and revenues for the month. There are other programs, but not as good compared to Quicken. The cost is reasonable: in the $30–$40 range. You can start using it and move up to QuickBooks (their more advanced program for businesses) or you can take the plunge and start with QuickBooks. The advantage of QuickBooks is it has additional functions for inventory, for job estimating, and for payroll taxes and other things you might need. It will also create invoices for you and track accounts receivable (people who owe you money).

What I like best about QuickBooks is the payroll function. For about $60 a year, you get federal and state tax updates that automatically update your program. When you need to run payroll forms, it calculates everything for you—correctly—and prints out the appropriate forms.

Here's a tip: If you subscribe to the payroll service you may not need to keep buying the latest update of QuickBooks. I was using an old version of QuickBooks, which they apparently no longer wanted to support with their payroll software, so they sent me a newer version of QuickBooks in the mail, free.

Another tip: Before you decide on a method, look in your Yellow Pages and see if payroll services are listed. Call a couple and get a cost estimate. You may be surprised at how cheap it is to let someone else do it for you. You'll spare yourself a lot of grief that comes from dealing with payroll—even if you use a computer program.

By the way, those same services may be willing to handle your billing for you. Some karate schools and other small businesses subcontract out their monthly billing, so the business owners can spend their time on what they know and do best, instead of drowning in paperwork. However, I'd want some kind of lockbox or checking system on the money coming in—to make sure it all got into my account!

Payroll Problems that Can Trip You Up

(continued from previous page)

- Do not be late with any withholding deposits—not even by one day. And watch out for banks that close at 3 P.M. on the day you have to deposit.
- Pay your withholding taxes and unemployment taxes before you pay any other creditor. Pay them before buying food for your family. The penalties and fines for not doing so are ruinous—and you could go to jail for theft.

Firing Employees

I've personally fired six people in my life and I got sick before firing each one of them. Here are some things you can remind yourself, to make it easier:

- I've worked with him and advised him on how to change, but he can't or won't.
- I've warned her that her performance was unacceptable, but she hasn't changed.
- There must be another job where he can work satisfactorily, without the negative feedback he's getting in this one.
- Somewhere out there is a replacement employee who is dying for a chance to work hard and prove themselves with this job.
- I can't afford to have half (or a quarter or one-tenth) of my staff unproductive.
- It's bad for other employees' morale when they have to make up for the lack of performance of one of the team.

Further advice: Consult with an attorney before firing someone. This is essential if you are firing a woman, a minority, someone over age forty, or any other protected class. But it wouldn't hurt to consult an attorney even if the person is not in one of those categories.

CHAPTER ELEVEN

Secrets of Financial Success

First, Protect Your Cash

If you cut your arm and it started bleeding copiously, you'd try to stop the bleeding.

If you want your business to survive its first year, think of it as if it were your bleeding arm. Your business is bleeding every day—bleeding cash. Cash is going out for one thing after another. When the cash runs out your business is dead. Even if you could have turned the black-ink corner with just a little more time.

Protect your cash as if it were your blood. Do *anything* to avoid spending it. Here are some of the things you can do, depending upon your business:

- Work longer hours, to avoid hiring another employee.
- Buy an answering machine instead of a receptionist.
- Work out of your home at first, instead of getting an office.
- Use a personal checking account instead of a business one, which saves a couple of hundred dollars a year. (Not available for those who have incorporated.)
- Get needed work done by employees of other companies as outside freelance work. When salaried designers and writers freelance, you can usually get them cheaper than what their company would charge for them.
- Instead of launching with the whole business plan, start just a piece of your business first—the easiest piece to make money on. Then you can grow it into your full business plan.

The Magic in Cost Cutting

Let's look at Cash Management 101—a course that should be taught in schools. In this course you'd learn that most businesses have profit margins of 4%–8%. That means for every $100 they take in, they get to keep $4 to $8. Think about what that means if you are offered the following choice:

- A. $1,000 more revenue
- B. $100 cut from a vendor's bill

What's the correct choice? Unless you're a consultant, with little out-of-pocket costs per sale, the correct answer is B. The $1,000 in additional revenue will be eaten up by additional costs, leaving you with $40 to $80 in profits. Whereas the $100 savings on a bill goes straight to the bottom line.

What does this mean? A tight fist on the checkbook is your best source of profits; when launching a small business, it is often the difference between success and failure.

Most of us have a picture in our minds about us at the helm of our successful new business. That picture probably includes a nice office, nice furniture, a good car, and (for the bigger dreamers) a corporate membership at an exclusive golf club or even a corporate jet.

Those are great dreams and you should indulge yourself, *after* you become profitable and put away some serious cash reserves for unexpected problems. Before that, unless clients must come to your place of business, every cent you spend on furniture is a cent that might cost you your business.

How to Pay Less for Your Expenses

Some people are great cost cutters; they work hard to save the last nickel in any negotiation. The rest of us have to watch our natural tendency to think we've done "enough."

When I launched *Ancillary Profits* newsletter, I bid out the printing to three companies in the Yellow Pages and took the lowest bid. It was $1,100 for 1,000 copies of a two-color, eight-page newsletter. I figured I'd done "enough" to get a good price.

Boy, was I wrong. A little networking chitchat turned up someone who thought I was overpaying. She recommended I contact another printer—who bid on the job for $750. I was really impressed with my new "low" price. Then I joined the Newsletter Publishers Association. They published a list of printers recommended by members in their annual directory. I took the time to send a request for bids to three of them. The printer I ended up with charged me $450 for the same job I was originally paying $1,100 for—and gave me equal quality and better service!

Cost-Saving Techniques

There's almost no expense you're facing that couldn't be lowered. Here are some cost-saving tactics that will help you stanch the flow of blood (cash) from your company:

- **Bid out everything possible that you buy.** Do this at least annually. The point of a bid sheet is to make sure each of the vendors is bidding on the same job so you can compare apples to apples. (See the sample bid sheet page 215.)
- **Talk to your vendors.** Tell them you need to reduce costs. Ask them if there are charges included for items you may be able to do without. Maybe, in the case of a printer, their bill includes sending you a blueline (proof), when they could send you a fax instead and save you money. Maybe their bill includes services you don't need, or could do without. Maybe you could do part of the work yourself and thus lower your costs. Make the vendor your partner in figuring out how to lower their bill without cutting into their profit margin.
- **Barter for everything you can.** If you can provide services or products in return for needed items, you can conserve your cash.
- **Make your vendors your partners.** Sometimes you can get vendors to take a smaller fee up front in return for a larger bonus if there is a success. Some direct mail copywriters who charge $10,000 for a direct mail package are willing to take a few thousand less up front in return for a total of $15,000 if the package is successful.
- **Negotiate longer terms with vendors.** If you're buying products to sell, and you can get 90-day terms instead of 30-day terms, that gives you an extra 60 days to sell the item and get in the cash to pay for it. Longer terms are like cash in the bank for retailers.
- **Try to get bulk discounts.** If you have something you buy a lot of over the year, try to get an agreed-upon lower per-unit price in return for a commitment to buy x number over the year. You can often do this *without* paying for all of them up front.

Bid Sheet for Printing Vendors

Specification	Explanation
Quantity to be printed	How many do you need?
Flat size	11 x 17 (flat size for a folded 8 $\frac{1}{2}$ x 11 booklet)
Actual size	8 $\frac{1}{2}$ x 11
Folded size	Folded to fit in #10 envelope
Type of fold	Accordion fold, overlap fold, etc.
Number of pages	At actual size
Coloration	Black is one color; 2C is two ink colors, usually including black.
Paper weight	60# is normal typing/printer paper. 50# is lighter (and black ink more likely to show through).
Paper type	Offset is normal typing/printer paper. Fancier papers are available for fancier prices.
How material supplied	On disk? E-mailed to them? Camera ready?
Number of halftones	If you do not scan in your own pictures, you'll have to pay the printer to do it.
Blueline required?	This is a proof, which they will charge you for. Small, uncomplicated jobs can be proofed via fax.
Product delivered to where?	Will you pick it up? Must they ship it to some other location?

Using Financial Ratios to Stay on Track

Every industry has established simple financial ratios that can help you recognize when your business is spending too much in a particular area. Almost every industry tracks the following:

- **Profit margin.** The return on sales—how much of each dollar you bring in you get to keep
- **Sales per employee.** If the norms in your industry are $500,000 per employee and you're at $100,000 per employee, that's a good clue you are overstaffed. Although you might want to be at first—to grow fast. But you'll want to watch that ratio carefully to make sure it's moving in the right direction—to more sales per employee.
- **Sales per product line.** Define "product line" in whichever way it makes the most sense for your industry. For example, in apparel, product lines might include blouses, suits, vests, pants, etc.
- **Sales per "X."** Auto repair businesses track sales per garage bay (work area). Towing businesses track sales per tow truck. Is there something similar to track in your industry?
- **Employees per product line.** Another measurement that may be valuable for your industry. Newsletters, for example, average 2.3 employees per newsletter. That tells you that if your newsletter has four employees you'd better have double the revenues of most newsletters to make up for it. Even then you may be overstaffed.
- **COGS expenses as a percent of revenue.** Does your industry typically spend 40% of revenue on COGS (Cost of Goods Sold)? Or is it closer to 50% (as it is for the magazine industry)? Whatever the number is, you need to know it—and to track whether your own expenses are out of line.
- **Selling expenses as a percent of revenue.** How much are you spending to bring in your revenue? Some industries spend 15%–20% (like the magazine industry). Others spend 35% (like the newsletter industry). You not only want to make sure you aren't spending *more* than the norms, but it's equally good to

make sure you're not spending *less*. Why worry if you are spending less on marketing? Because that means your sales are—or will be—slipping relative to your competitors.

- **G&A (General & Administrative) expenses as a percent of total expenses.** Here's one area where spending less than the competition would be great. G&A expenses are a necessary evil, but an evil nonetheless. They're the only expenses that aren't advancing your company. COGS expenses are creating the products you sell and selling expenses are selling your products, but G&A expenses result in neither products to sell nor sales. The lower you can keep G&A, the better. Some industries have G&A at 6% of total expenses. Some have it higher and some lower. Try to keep yours lower.

Setting Up Financial Systems

People without a financial background can be intimidated by the mere idea of setting up systems for accounting and financial reporting. But if you're one, don't worry. If you can balance your bank book you can keep track of your finances—that is, with a little additional help from an accountant or from the manual or Help screens of a software program like QuickBooks. Many small business owners do their own books, then have an accountant or bookkeeper review them once a month at first, then once a quarter.

The Parts of Financial Reporting

Financial reporting consists of the following elements:

- **Key statistics.** Things you need to know to evaluate parts of your business, such as number of sales, average amount of each sale, cost per product, etc.
- **Cash flow statements.** The easiest of all to understand, and the most important for the new business. They consist of three items:

  1. Cash receipts: the money you receive.
  2. Cash disbursements: the money you spend.

Best Sources for Industry Ratios

The most valuable financial ratios are available only in confidential membership studies from trade associations.

Many industry associations poll members once a year, getting their financial ratios. That information is sent anonymously (usually to a third party) and compiled into a report. That report is usually made available only to the people who participated in the study. (New members can usually talk the association into giving them the study their first membership year.)

Contact the association(s) in your industry and ask if they do that type of financial research of members. If so, it will probably be worth the cost of membership to join the association in order to get the study. If they don't do it, many industry publications will pull together as many of the ratios for their industry as they can find.

3. Net cash flow: the difference between the two. This figure can be positive (congratulations!) or negative.

- **Profit & Loss statements.** Can be virtually identical to the cash flow statements, or they can differ substantially. Profit & Loss statements (P&Ls) differ when one of the following situations exists:

  - Your business buys a lot of products and inventories them.
  - Your revenues from products come in primarily before (or after) your expenses to buy or deliver those products.

- **Balance sheets.** Show whether your assets (cash in the bank and money due from customers) are more than your liabilities (loans and money owed to vendors). Many businesses can safely ignore these (except when their accountant prepares one for them each quarter) as long as they keep close tabs on their cash flow statements.

Charting Your Accounts

You will need to set up a "chart of accounts," which are accounts that track the key revenue and expense items for your type of business. If you're using a software package, it comes with a sample chart of accounts. You can either use it and modify them as desired or, from the basic accounts listed below, modify your charts to your needs.

Revenue accounts: If you only have one source of revenue (e.g., consulting income) you may only need one account to put it in. However, if you have a clothing store, you may want separate accounts for clothing, belts, jewelry, and hats, so you can track how well each of those categories pays you.

COGS accounts: COGS (Cost of Goods Sold) are the actual costs of creating and delivering the product. If you buy the products you sell, COGS is what you pay for them. If you make your products,

COGS is the cost of what goes into the products. For example, COGS for a magazine includes the expenses for editor salaries, editor telephone, articles, photographs, typesetting, printing, and postage to mail the issues. For a Bagel Shop, it would be flour, raisins, poppy seeds, and the cost of the employee who cooks the bagels. For a clothing manufacturer, it would be fabric, thread, zippers/buttons, and the cost of production.

Selling accounts: These are the costs to sell your product. They would include salesperson salaries, advertising expenses, direct mail to customers, the cost of your Web site, commissions, etc.

G&A accounts: General and Administrative (G&A) expenses are the overhead costs at your company. They include rent, electricity, equipment, stationery, telephone, your office manager, and your receptionist.

Asset accounts: These are your assets, including cash in the bank, equipment and furniture, and accounts receivable (the amount of money due from customers that you haven't yet received).

Liability accounts: These are your debts, including invoices you owe but haven't yet paid, loans you've taken out, money borrowed from your parents, etc. Liabilities also include items you have yet to deliver for which you've already received payment.

Owners equity: The difference between your assets and your liabilities. It's like owning a home: if you owe more on it than its current market value, then you have negative equity. Similarly with a business, if your cash and accounts receivable are less than your debts, you have negative equity. If the opposite, you have positive equity. This can be a great account for your business, but probably not for a few years.

Jones & Smith
CORPORATION

Financial Accounts Chart

Here is a sample chart of accounts. See which categories work for you and customize a chart for your business. Note that they fall into one of four types:

- Assets
- Liabilities
- Income
- Expense

Account type	Account	Explanation
Asset	Bank account	If you have two or more, have separate accounts for each.
Asset	Accounts receivable	Not needed if people pay you immediately. Also not needed if you have only a few clients: you can book sales when you get the cash and ignore this account.
Liability	Loans payable	Money you owe banks, friends, or even yourself.
Liability	Deferred liability	Money you've received for products/services you will not immediately send/fulfill.
Income	Sales	Create as many sales accounts as you need to track important differences. You may only need one.
Income	Interest received	Interest you receive on your business bank account(s).
COGS (Cost of Goods Sold)	Cost of product	One account if you buy the products you sell; more if you create the products. For example, fabric, thread, buttons, and production might all be accounts under COGS for an apparel manufacturer.
COGS	Cost of product delivery	Packaging & shipping costs for the products you sell.
Expense	Selling expenses	Include salaries, bonuses, commissions, and the telephone and postage costs for your salespeople.
Expense	Advertising	Include ads, direct mail campaigns, telemarketing, your Web site and any other promotional sales costs.
Expense	G&A (General & Administrative)	You'll want separate accounts for your rent, utilities, equipment rentals, office supplies, administrative salaries (including office manager, receptionist, etc.), your health plan, tax accountant, lawyer, and other similar expenses.

Evaluating a Plan

If you've seen business plans with cash flow statements, you've probably wondered how to evaluate such a plan. Lots of revenues are coming in and lots of costs are going out. How does anyone know if the numbers make sense? Can one just plug any number in there? Is there some trick to understanding the numbers?

The answer is a page called Key Assumptions. This is probably the most important page in any business plan. Without it, all the financial statement numbers are as meaningless to investment bankers as they may be to you.

When I was head of development for CBS Magazines, lots of potential entrepreneurs would send me their business plans hoping to get CBS to fund their start-up idea. Here's how I evaluated them, and how other sophisticated potential investors will evaluate your plan.

1. How was the idea? Did anything immediately make me think it wouldn't work?
2. What were the assumptions in the plan? How reasonable were they? (Almost all plans submitted died right at this step, since I could see immediately that something was wrong.)
3. If the assumptions were reasonable, how much money would the product make? Was that enough money to interest CBS? (NOTE: The above three steps took maybe between five and 20 minutes on my part.)
4. If the idea passed the first three steps, then I'd read the entire plan. And my real goal in reading the plan was to get an idea about what kind of person the entrepreneur was. How smart, how well thought out was the plan? Was this somebody winging it, or had she really thought out the potential problems and upsides? How strong was her background in this industry? What specialized skills did the entrepreneur lack? And had she brought in someone else to compensate for her weaknesses?

Important!

The most important thing to consider in making revenue assumptions is to be *conservative.* That means you underestimate the amount of revenues you really think you'll get.

Key Revenue

Estimating your future revenues is the hardest part of budgeting. Once you get this, everything else is much easier. Here's where you'll need the market and competitive research you did in Part 1 of this book.

All revenue assumptions can be broken into at least two different measurements:

1. Units sold
2. Average revenue per unit

Obviously average revenue per unit is an estimate. If your business is a store selling items from $29 to $129, your average will be more likely in the lower range. Once your store is up and running, you will want to track the actual average each month to keep an eye on the mix of your sales.

Following are sample worksheets for estimating revenues for different kinds of businesses.

REVENUE ESTIMATES

For manufacturers and (non-walk-in) service businesses

	1st year	2nd year	3rd year	4th year	5th year
A. Estimated units sold					
B. Average revenue per unit	$	$	$	$	$
Total (A x B)	$	$	$	$	$

If you have two or three distinctly different products, with very different potentials, you should do an estimate for each of the products.

REVENUE ESTIMATES

For stores and storefront businesses

	1st year	2nd year	3rd year	4th year	5th year
A. Estimated monthly traffic					
B. Estimated average sales per customer	$	$	$	$	$
Total (A x B)	$	$	$	$	$

For this estimate in your business plan you'll need the competitive information gained on traffic in stores near your proposed location and of the same type as your store (see Chapter 4). Your sales estimate here will only be as good as your estimate of potential traffic.

Retail stores should do a further estimate to establish the industry norm in sales:

INDUSTRY NORM REVENUES FOR STORES

A. Square footage for the store you plan to lease or build	
B. Average sales per square foot (based on figures from your industry's associations and/or trade magazines)	$
C. Industry norm sales for your proposed storefront (A x B)	$

Reality check: In the fifth year of your plan, have you projected less or more sales than in C above? If less, congratulations! If more, your plan may be too optimistic. Why would your store generate more sales than is normal for your industry? You'll need concrete reasons.

Your Maximum Revenue Potential

If you are able to calculate the potential size of your market (see Chapter 3), here's an additional quick reality check on your revenue estimates.

If the potential universe of names you can easily find and promote to is, for example, 100,000 names, then follow this calculation, using only the column that pertains to the type of products you will sell.

(Not sure whether your products are sold to consumers or businesses? The defining difference is: Who pays for the product? Does the individual pay? Or does his or her company pay—or reimburse—the buyer? If the company pays or reimburses, you're selling to businesses.)

| | Products Sold to | | |
	Consumers	Businesses	Explanation
A. Estimated number of potential buyers available (based on estimate made in Chapter 3)			Put your estimate in the appropriate column.
B. Lowest norm of market penetration	0.02 (2%)	0.08 (8%)	
C. Low estimate of potential buyers			Multiply your estimate A by the number in B (0.02 or 0.08, depending on which column applies)
D. Number of units you estimated you would sell in 5th year of your plan			Put your estimate in the appropriate column.
E. Average number of products your customers are likely to buy in one year			

1. <u>Where E is greater than 1</u>: Multiply E times C. Is the number greater than D?
2. <u>Where E is 1 or less</u>: Is C greater than D?

If D is lower: Are your estimated sales numbers for the fifth year lower than the estimated norm for penetration rates? If so, that's terrific. In your plan, you'll want to use language like this: "In the fifth year, we estimate sales of XX units, which are only X% of the total universe of potential prospects." (You fill in the XX and X numbers.) This phrasing will help persuade readers of your plan (and potential investors) that:

- You are savvy about realistic marketing goals.
- Your plan is conservative in your market estimations, so you're more likely to actually make your numbers than someone who is estimating a high percentage of the market as customers.

If D is higher: If your estimated sales are higher than the norms for market penetration, you may have unrealistically high ideas about the amount of sales you can achieve in your marketplace. Try using lower sales numbers and see if you can still make money with your plan. If not, can you raise prices and then make money? If you can't do either, think long and hard before launching with this plan.

Your Key COGS (Cost of Goods Sold)

If your business is consulting, you will have little to do concerning COGS, unless you hire employees or outside consultants to fulfill part of your consulting work. If it's only you, you can list any research you have to buy to create your report(s), the costs of binders (for the reports you issue), and perhaps overheads or slides for your presentations.

For every other type of business, Cost of Goods Sold (COGS) expenses fall into two different types: 1) variable; and 2) fixed.

Variable costs are those that change with the number of units you sell. For example, if you're selling model trains, your variable costs are: the motor, wheels, carriage, and anything else that includes the physical cost of the train, plus the costs of someone to assemble it.

Fixed costs are those that will not go up or down depending on the number of products you create. For example, if you have a loom used to knit the sweaters you sell, your maintenance for that loom and your depreciation of it will not change, regardless of whether you make one sweater or 1,000.

When you list your key statistics on your business plan, you should list as many of the following COGS assumptions as fit your particular type of product:

- Units created (manufactured)
- Units sold (estimate)

- Fixed costs (manufacturing equipment you rent or have purchased)
- Variable costs/unit (the costs to manufacture a single unit, *excluding* fixed costs)

For manufactured products, you may also wish to include what the main components are in your product costs. This could include:

- Costs per unit of each of your materials included in the finished product
- Costs per unit of distributing your product to its end customers
- Other costs of creating and distributing your product to customers

The worksheet on page 227 will help you estimate COGS expenses per year. Expanding your COGS expenses for a five-year projection is simple once you've calculated the number of products you estimate you can sell in each year (based on your revenue assumptions).

Your Key Selling Costs

Next to estimate are your selling costs. Selling costs are everything involved in selling your product/service, including salespeople, advertising, expenses for sales calls, telephone for salespeople, postage for salespeople, etc.

If your company is starting small, don't bother to break out telephone, postage, and similar expenses into selling, COGS, and administrative expenses, unless these expenses are significantly high in any of these categories. Instead, just lump all telephone, postage, utilities, etc., under G&A (General & Administrative), which we will get to next in this chapter.

Some of your selling costs may be variable costs, depending on the number of items sold. You usually find variable selling costs when you pay commissions on your sales to salespeople. If so, just put commissions on a separate line from salaries and (if you are using a spreadsheet) make the software calculate it automatically as a percent of sales or as a fixed amount per unit sold.

Cost of Goods Sold (COGS) Expenses

	PER UNIT costs	PER YEAR costs
Variable Costs (per item)		
A. Actual costs of products you buy to resell, OR		
B. Costs of components that make up your product		
C. Actual costs to distribute your product (e.g., postage, UPS)		
D. Any labor costs to create your product(s) that are on a per-piece basis		
E. TOTAL VARIABLE COSTS (Add either A & C or B, C, & D)		
Fixed Costs (per year)		
F. Depreciation of machinery used to create your products		
G. Utilities, oil, supplies used to create your products—that do not go up or down depending on sales		
H. Labor costs of people creating your products—that do not go up or down depending on sales		
I. TOTAL FIXED COSTS		
Total COGS for 1 unit		(Add E and J)
Total COGS for 100 units		(Add E x 100 plus J)
Total COGS for 1,000 units		(Add E x 1,000 plus J)
Total COGS for 10,000 units		(Add E x 10,000 plus J)

Note: Your per-unit variable costs will be lower when you create larger quantities. Adjust them to account for this in the totals.

Your total COGS per unit will go down as the units rise, because your fixed costs are being spread over more units.

Use the worksheet on page 229 to estimate selling costs.

Your Key G&A (General & Administrative) Expenses

Here's where you put all expenses that are not directly tied to creating a product or selling it. These expenses include:

- Employee salaries (the president, the receptionist, the controller, etc.)
- Extra facility costs (rent or mortgage, utilities, etc., of a separate office). If you're using a portion of your home or apartment, save that calculation for the tax benefits section that follows.
- General office expense costs (office supplies, pizza delivered free to employees on Fridays, etc.)
- Professional costs (taxes, accounting, legal, etc.)
- Equipment costs (equipment rental, purchased equipment under $5,000 that you expense directly)
- Dues, fees, subscriptions, research
- Taxes

IRS Caution

If your product is something you, yourself, might consume—e.g., milk, bicycles, apparel, etc.—the IRS will expect you to keep track of how much you use. You must then report it as a deduction to COGS on your income tax.

The Key Assumptions Statement

Page 231 is an example of a Key Assumptions page from a business plan that included a newsletter, directory and Web site all targeting a single industry. You can see that it provides answers to the key questions you would need in order to ascertain if the numbers are reasonable. Think of the key statistics for your business.

Selling Costs Estimate

	1st year	2nd year	3rd year	4th year	5th year
A. Salespeople's salaries	$	$	$	$	$
B. Salespeople's benefits (Add 14% to their salaries for your contribution to FICA, plus any medical/insurance/ 401(k) benefits.)	$	$	$	$	$
C. Bonuses/commissions: % (% = percentage of sales)	%	%	%	%	%
D. Bonuses/commissions: $$ (C times your estimated sales for each year)	$	$	$	$	$
E. Office expenses for sales-people (Only if substantial; otherwise put it in G&A)	$	$	$	$	$
F. Advertising expenses	$	$	$	$	$
G. Direct mail promotion expenses	$	$	$	$	$
H. Telemarketing expenses	$	$	$	$	$
I. Web site marketing expenses	$	$	$	$	$
J. Fax marketing expenses	$	$	$	$	$
K. Conference/convention/trade show expenses	$	$	$	$	$
TOTAL (Add up all rows except C)	$	$	$	$	$

G&A (General & Administrative) Expenses

	1st year	2nd year	3rd year	4th year	5th year
A. Number of employees					
B. G&A employee salaries	$	$	$	$	$
C. G&A employee benefits *(Note: Add 14% to their salaries for your contribution to FICA, plus any medical/ insurance/401(k) benefits)*	$	$	$	$	$
D. Office supplies	$	$	$	$	$
E. Postage	$	$	$	$	$
F. Telephone	$	$	$	$	$
G. Office rent or mortgage *(Only out-of-pocket costs, not a % of your home or apartment)*	$	$	$	$	$
H. Utilities *(Only out-of-pocket costs)*	$	$	$	$	$
I. Office cleaning	$	$	$	$	$
J. Tax/legal/accounting services	$	$	$	$	$
K. Dues, subscriptions, research, Internet hookup	$	$	$	$	$
L. Equipment rental/equipment purchases	$	$	$	$	$
M. Taxes	$	$	$	$	$
TOTAL *(Add up all rows except A)*	$	$	$	$	$

Key Assumptions Statement

Key Assumptions for Newsletter, Directory, and Web Site

	1996	1997	1998	1999	2000
Newsletter					
DM* quantity mailed	440,000	1,500,000	2,400,000	3,300,000	4,100,000
Issues per year/price	10/$39.95	10/$39.95	10/$39.95	10/$39.95	10/$39.95
Direct mail/cost/thousand	$544	$400	$400	$400	$400
Additional cost/subscription	$2.10	$2.10	$2.10	$2.10	$2.10
Net response (no bill-me's)	2.5%	2.2%	1.3%	1.0%	1.0%
New DM subscribers	11,000	32,250	31,000	33,000	41,000
Conversion rate	40%	40%	40%	40%	40%
Renewal rate	60%	60%	60%	60%	60%
Conversion/renewal price	10/$49.95	10/$49.95	10/$49.95	10/$49.95	10/$49.95
Cost/expire	$3.10	$3.10	$3.10	$3.10	$3.10
Average subscriber file	4,896	24,708	44,633	49,382	61,303
DM cost per new subscriber	$23.86	$20.70	$33.07	$42.10	$42.10
Av. promo cost/subscriber	$45.16	$26.48	$24.51	$29.93	$29.85
Issues/year	6	10	10	10	10
Pages/year	48	80	80	80	80
Print order—subscriptions	29,375	247,075	446,330	493,820	613,030
Print order—other	12,000	20,000	20,000	20,000	20,000
Total print order	41,375	267,075	466,330	513,820	633,030
Mfg. & dist./issue	$0.78	$0.75	$0.75	$0.75	$0.75
Directory					
Cover price	$9.95	$9.95	$12.95	$12.95	$12.95
Wholesaler discount	40%	40%	40%	40%	40%
Sell-through	45%	50%	55%	60%	65%
Print order	200,000	200,000	200,000	200,000	200,000
Book size	200	240	264	290	319
1,000 printed pgs. (MPP**)	40,000	48,000	52,800	58,080	63,888
Mfg. & dist./MPP	$4.65	$4.65	$4.65	$4.65	$4.65

Key Assumptions Statement

	1996	1997	1998	1999	2000
Web Site					
Monthly maintenance costs	$5,000	$6,000	$6,000	$6,000	$6,000
Full-Time Staff Detail					
Publisher	$64,000	$90,000	$120,000	$150,000	$200,000
Marketing dir./general mgr.	60,000	72,000	72,000	72,000	72,000
Telemarketing manager	28,194	35,000	35,000	35,000	35,000
Telemarketer	20,139	25,000	25,000	25,000	25,000
Telemarketer	0	25,000	25,000	25,000	25,000
Office mgr/bookkeeper	23,750	30,000	30,000	30,000	30,000
Production/database manager	19,792	25,000	25,000	25,000	25,000
Database maintenance asst.	0	12,000	12,000	12,000	12,000
Total full-time salaries	$215,875	$314,000	$344,000	$374,000	$424,000
Head count	6.0	7.5	7.5	7.5	7.5
Payroll tax/benefits/% of sal.	20%	20%	20%	20%	20%

*DM stands for Direct Mail.

**Thousand Printed Pages (MPP) is a statistic used to figure printing costs. It allows for more or fewer publication pages and more or fewer quantities of issues printed—coming up with a number (MPP) that allows you to see how good a printing price you have.

CHAPTER TWELVE

Moving Forward: Strategy and Tactics

Your Cash Flow Analysis

Now is the point when all your hard work researching your business will come down to the bottom line. Will your new business have a chance of success—or should you forget it and save yourself the money and aggravation? You'll know the answer by analyzing your cash flow.

Take the numbers you came up with in the previous chapter's worksheets and enter them into this template:

CASH FLOW

	1st year	2nd year	3rd year	4th year	5th year
A. Revenues (Cash Coming In) *(From Revenues worksheet)*	$	$	$	$	$
B. Cost of Goods Sold (COGS) *(From COGS worksheet)*	$	$	$	$	$
C. Selling Costs *(From Selling Costs worksheet)*	$	$	$	$	$
D. G&A (General & Admin.) Expenses *(From G&A Expenses worksheet)*	$	$	$	$	$
E. NET CASH FLOW (Subtract B, C, D and from A. Put loss numbers in parentheses.)	$	$	$	$	$
G. Return on Sales (ROS) (Only if E is a positive number) (Divide E by A. Shows what percentage you keep of each dollar you take in.)	%	%	%	%	%

Tax Adjustments to Cash Flow

	1st year	2nd year	3rd year	4th year	5th year
A. Net Cash Flow *(From E in preceding worksheet)*	$	$	$	$	$
B. Home/Rent deduction for office in the home *(Based on the % of your home used for your office)*	$	$	$	$	$
C. Utilities for home office *(Use same % of expenses as above)*	$	$	$	$	$
D. Cleaning of home office *(Use same % of expenses as above)*	$	$	$	$	$
E. Medical premiums not deductible previously, but which your company can deduct	$	$	$	$	$
F. Glasses, dentist, contacts, prescriptions, office visits *(Unless you were able to deduct these anyway last year.)*	$	$	$	$	$
G. Life insurance premiums you already pay, but which the company can take over paying	$	$	$	$	$
H. Depreciation of equipment you already own that can be turned into business assets (e.g., computers, car) and which you have not already deducted as an expense on your taxes	$	$	$	$	$
I. TOTAL TAX ITEMS *(Add B through H)*	$	$	$	$	$
J. Your highest tax rate paid *(From your last tax return. State it as a %.)*	%	%	%	%	%
K. Tax benefit to you of tax items *(Multiply I by the percentage in J. 21% = 0.21 and 30% = 0.3)*	$	$	$	$	$
NET CASH FLOW—ADJUSTED FOR TAX BENEFITS (Add A and K)	$	$	$	$	$

If You Are Losing Money

Know that most businesses lose money in the first year, except for consulting businesses that don't count the owner's salary. Many businesses lose money the next two years as well. There are spectacular examples of businesses that lost money for seven or more years (like *Sports Illustrated* magazine) and then turned the corner. But they're the exception, not the rule. I, personally, would never launch a business if I couldn't be making money by the third year. For B2B newsletters, I want to turn the profit corner after eight months, or I won't launch.

Adjusting Cash Flow for Tax Benefits

If you want to see what your cash flow would look like after adjusting it for tax benefits, the next worksheet will take you through this exercise.

If you want to play hooky from some numbers, you can skip this and go directly to the following section on "How to Analyze Your Numbers."

Note that many tax benefits are available only to businesses that are formed as C Corporations (see Chapter 9). Make sure you're not counting anything that won't apply to your legal form of business.

How to Analyze Your Numbers
If You Show a Cash Flow Loss

The first thing to remember is that the numbers you just ran are not written in stone. They are directly the result of the cash assumptions you estimated in the previous chapter. If you don't like the results you're seeing, go back and look at your assumptions.

Revisiting your assumptions is critical. By analyzing your assumptions in relation to the results they produce, you will make great—*informed*—decisions that will increase your chances of success. For example:

- You might decide to delay hiring some people, in order to save money.
- You might decide you can't succeed with the price you planned to charge. Raise it and see what the change does to your profits.
- You might decide you have to sell more items/services. What can you do to achieve that? Can you increase your advertising? Can you hire another salesperson?
- You might decide to eliminate rent and a lot of other expenses by starting the business in your home.
- You might decide to start the business part-time until you can land enough clients to enable you to pursue it full-time.

These are exactly the kind of practical, hard-nosed decisions that people without a business plan never realize are needed. Don't despair at a loss; here's where your creativity can come in.

If you make all the tough decisions you can and your business still looks as if it will lose money forever, don't launch it.

Abandoning an idea that won't work doesn't mean you're giving up your dream of your own business. Instead, spend the next year or two saving money and thinking about other ideas. If you've had one business idea, you're bound to have more. Don't waste your money, your time, and your youth on an idea that has little chance of paying off. Save it for the better idea that's just around the corner. That idea will have an even better chance of success because you'll be better funded from the money you're going to start saving.

If You Show a Cash Flow Profit

Are you all excited because your numbers show a huge profit? Let's hope all your numbers are right! In fact, calm down, because there could be some errors. Look for these profit danger signs:

- **The business ROS (return on sales) is 20% or greater.** (Occasionally businesses have this kind of ROS, but it is rare. The norm for businesses is in the 5%–8% ROS.)
- **You show a profit in year one.** (This is extremely rare—unless you are a consultant and you aren't counting your own salary.)
- **You show a little loss in year one and big profits after that.** (This could be accurate; but recheck your numbers using the guidelines below.)

Here are some reality checks to use on your numbers. Everyone should consider them; if your numbers reflect any of the warning signs above, it's essential.

1. Go back over your COGS expenses. Often there are additional charges that vendors add on to their quotes. Have they (and thus you) excluded any of the following?

   - Shipping costs to get the products to you

A Mouse Click Away

If you use an accounting software program and regularly input bills, payments, invoices, and checks as they're received, you're only a few mouse clicks away from an up-to-date picture of your current finances. With QuickBooks, for example, a pull-down report menu will not only lead you to a P&L, balance sheet, and cash flow statement for any accounting period you choose, but also to reports detailing accounts receivable and payable, sales, and inventory, among others. This can be extremely helpful when cash flow is tight, for example.

Lifeline: Your Accountant

Sometimes you're just too close to your plan to see exactly what the problem might be. There's nothing wrong with calling in an outsider.

Your accountant can be invaluable in helping you understand what's really happening in your business plan. Use him or her, especially if divining profit and loss statements is not your strong suit. Accountants are particularly good at foreseeing financial struggles. If you work with your accountant to determine typical financial ratios within your trade, he or she can help you measure your own business against the norm and identify trouble spots.

(continued on next page)

- Warehousing charges (in case you don't want the product all at once)
- Other add-on costs, such as wrapping, packaging, etc.

2. If you will make your own products, have you added in money for:

- Spoilage of items sitting in your warehouse waiting to be used in your products?
- Waste—normal in creating products—such as print over-runs, end-of-fabric bolts, fish that die before they can be sold, etc.?
- Staff time (or extra help) to count and handle inventory?
- Staff time needed to explain procedures, to traffic items to and from vendors, etc.?

3. Go back over your Selling expenses. Make sure your numbers allow for:

- Training time to get new salespeople up to speed (they may have to tag along for a couple of months before they can handle their own accounts).
- Advertising/direct mail/telemarketing results that aren't always as strong as you've budgeted. Be conservative: Results that come in better will be wonderful, but results that come in worse can threaten your business.

4. Go back over your G&A expenses. See if there's anything you may have missed, such as:

- Planned postage increases. Postal rate increases are usually announced several months ahead of time. Ask the post office if a new one has been announced and for when.
- Telephone monthly fees that enable you to "qualify" for reduced rate plans.
- The expiration of lease agreements. If your rental lease is almost up, what kind of price increase will you be

facing? How about your equipment rentals? Are you leasing your car?

- A couple hundred dollars a month (for a small operation) listed as "Miscellaneous." You'll be astonished at all the expenses that will come up that you forgot to plan for.

Are you still showing a fat profit? Again, reserve your excitement. Can you find an accountant familiar with your industry? It will be worth your money to hire her to spend one or two hours looking at your assumptions and cash flow plan to see if she can find any holes in it.

When I evaluated business plans for CBS, I would frequently see plans that looked incredibly good because the entrepreneur forgot to include at least one very big expense. Usually, for magazines, they forgot to include all the expenses related to people who order magazines then don't pay. These people require issues sent to them, plus all the billing costs associated with them.

An accountant familiar with your industry can give you excellent insights that will help you adjust your plan so that it dramatically increases your chances of success.

Once your cash flow analysis has passed an industry accountant, and it still shows a nice profit—well then, Congratulations!

Now, all you have to do is make it happen—and not be cowed by the setbacks and new problems that could and probably will arise.

Monthly Tracking—Finding Your Break-Even Point

Once you have a plan that works on a five-year basis—meaning it will generate enough cash for you to be willing to risk the launch—it's time to work on the next year's numbers. You need to break them out by month so you can see how much cash you'll need immediately.

For example, your first year might lose $50,000. But, how do you get to that number? Will you lose an even $4,170 per month? Or might you lose $100,000 in the first four months, then make enough revenue so that at the end of the year you're down only $50,000?

Lifeline: Your Accountant

(continued from previous page)

A word of caution, however. At the risk of unfairly generalizing an entire group of professionals, remember that accountants deal in realities. Theirs is a world of hard numbers—one and one always equal two. Entrepreneurs often find success by figuring out some seemingly impossible way to make one and one into three. Listen to your accountant in order to understand clearly what is going on in your business, but don't be afraid to trust your own instincts as well. Have your accountant show you what you have done so far, but make up your own mind about what can be done in the future.

You need to know what the maximum amount of money is that you'll be down before your revenues start equaling or bettering your expenses.

If your first year does not show a positive (profitable) cash flow, copy the Monthly Cash Flow worksheet and do one for the next year as well. Even if the full second year is profitable, it is possible you will need some additional cash early in the year before you pass the break-even point.

Your Final Decision: Should You Launch?

After this exercise, you may need to reevaluate once again. Will you have enough money to invest in the business before it breaks even? What if something in your calculations goes wrong? Will you have an extra cushion to cover it?

I'm sorry to report that of all the business plans I've looked at, only a few beat their original start-up figures. It seems it is easier to include in the plan all the positive things that could happen. Somehow we don't think as easily of all the negatives that could happen.

Sometimes that's a good thing—or it might paralyze you into inaction.

Are you faced with a good plan that requires more cash than you can afford? What can you do?

- Be conservative: Kill the plan.
- Be conservative: Find a way to launch the plan while still holding a job or bringing in some other source of money to protect yourself.
- Be moderately risky: Launch but set yourself specific goals. If you aren't meeting x amount of sales by (date), you'll stop and get a job. (This sounds like the best plan, but I can tell you that most people will not have the fortitude to stop if they haven't met a particular goal.)
- Be highly risky: Launch anyway, without a safety net, and believe you can find a way to make it work.

Monthly Cash Flow

	Jan	Feb	Mar	Apr	May	Jun	Jul	Aug	Sep	Oct	Nov	Dec	YEAR
Cash Receipts													
COGS (Cost of Goods Sold)													
*													
*													
Total COGS													
Selling Expenses													
*													
*													
*													
Total Selling Expenses													
G&A (Gen. & Administrative)													
*													
*													
*													
*													
*													
Total G&A													
Net Cash Flow													

(continued on next page)

A Tale of Forgotten Inventory

When I was a business manager at CBS Magazines, we had a direct marketing division that sold products in filler space. The first year they booked $250,000 in profits in that division. The second year it was $100,000. Then one day I got a call from the warehouse, located in a different state. They were rearranging offices and wanted to know what we wanted done with the pile of stuff in one of the rooms. What pile of stuff? All the unsold products the director of that division had bought.

What's the best advice? Launch from the safety of a job—at least a part-time one. If you can't do that, then the decision is only yours to make. There have certainly been people who launched when the numbers said they shouldn't, and made a success. There are, however, many more people who launched into that situation and failed.

Deciding whether to launch is one of the toughest decisions you'll ever make, but it's also one of the most exciting.

Preparing P&Ls

If your cash flow projections are satisfactory, you may need to prepare Profit & Loss statements—P&Ls—as well. P&Ls are particularly needed in the following situations:

- You're seeking investors.
- You have an inventory of items you sell for profit.
- You have large expenses in one calendar period while the revenues for those expenses will come mostly in a different period.
- You have cash sales for products you deliver spread out over time (such as a magazine subscription).

However, creating profit and loss projections can help you improve your business model and your chances of growing and maximizing your profits for any business.

If You're Seeking Investors

If you only fit the first qualification—seeking investors—but none of the rest, you can easily create P&Ls by taking your cash flow numbers and adding in depreciation expenses. And, if you have a fat, one-time payment to launch the business, you can spread it out by dividing it by 12 (for one year) or 24 (for two years) and expensing that piece of it each month until it's gone. That's called amortization. That's all you'll need to do for P&Ls.

If You Have Inventory

Inventory is handled by setting up an asset account called "Inventory." All items you buy for sale go into this account. When

you buy inventory, it does not appear on your P&L, only on your cash flow reports.

When you sell your inventory, you expense the cost of the items at the same time you book the revenue for them.

Say that on January 1 you buy 1,000 items for resale at $10 each. The $10,000 you paid comes out of cash (paid by your check) and goes into inventory—which now shows a balance of $10,000. Then, on March 8, you sell 15 items for $20 each. You book $300 in revenue (it will show up in your cash flow and P&L reports). You take $150 (15 items times $10 each) out of inventory and book it as COGS expense.

If you will have inventory, and you won't have an outside service doing your books, have someone either set up a QuickBooks account for you, or set it up yourself and have someone make sure it's right. Then you don't have to worry about where each item goes and which report each item should appear on—the computer will do it for you. The program remembers where things go.

A word of warning about inventory: Nothing can torpedo a business's earnings faster than unsold inventory. Particularly because—due to P&L bookkeeping—you can easily forget it's there. Since you only book the costs of your inventory when you book the sales, it's easy to forget you've got $100,000 tied up in that inventory—$83,000 of which has not been expensed.

Seasonability and the P&L

Suppose you do a big advertising campaign each year for Father's Day. All your expenses come in May, but your sales come in June. Well, your P&L can defer those expenses until June, by putting them in a Prepaid Expenses asset account until you are ready to "recognize" them on your P&L.

Suppose you buy a book from an author. You pay the author $15,000. After printing the book, you plan to sell it for the next two years. You can divide the $15,000 by 24 months, and expense $625 each month. Or, you could decide that most of the sales will come in the first year and smaller sales for the second year. So you might divide $10,000 by 12 and expense $833/month for the first year. In the second, you'd divide $5,000 by 12 and expense $417/month.

A Tale of Forgotten Inventory

(continued from previous page)

Here's what the "stuff" was:

- Products he overbought to get a better per-unit price
- Products that sold at first and then stopped selling
- Products that never sold as he thought they would

Because of the P&L inventory booking system, we had $400,000 worth of products that had never been expensed. When we wrote them off as a loss, it wiped out all the profits that division had ever produced.

In each of these cases, you used the P&L to tie particular revenues to the expenses that generated them. This is the value of a P&L over a cash flow.

Delayed Product Deliveries

When you receive the cash up front but deliver the product over time, such as a magazine subscription, the IRS says you have to recognize the revenue spread out over the life of the delivery.

If QuickBooks sells someone their payroll service, they get a check from that person for $60. In return, they have to send out updates when the tax laws change, usually three or four times a year. They put the $60 into a Deferred Liability account—it's considered a liability because if you don't deliver it the customer could get the unserved part of their money back. In other words, the money isn't technically yours until you've completed the year's worth of service.

So, QuickBooks' cash flow would show the $60 in the month they receive it. Their P&L would show only the amount that corresponds to their first month of service: one-twelfth of $60, or $5 as revenue. The next month would show an additional $5. After those two months, the amount still in the Deferred Liability account would be $60 minus $10 or $50.

"Present Value" and Inflation

Many business plans make assumptions about inflation over the five-year period, and put those assumptions into the plans. Or they make "present value" calculations about how much revenue five years from today is worth in today's dollars. Voice of experience: skip this.

I have yet to hear of a bank or investor who won't accept instead a simple statement in your plan that says:

Inflation assumptions in this plan: This plan assumes that prices will be able to rise sufficiently to cover inflationary increases in expenses.

P&L (Profit & Loss)

	1st Year	2nd Year	3rd Year	4th Year	5th Year
Revenues					
*					
*					
Total Revenues					
COGS (Cost of Goods Sold)					
*					
*					
*					
Total COGS					
Gross Profit *(Revenue minus COGS)*					
Selling Expenses					
*					
*					
*					
Total Selling Expenses					
G&A (General & Administrative)					
*					
*					
*					
*					
*					
Total G&A Expenses					
Total of Selling + G&A					
Profit/(Loss) *(Gross profit minus Selling & G&A)*					

Unless there is some reason why your costs (the per-unit price you pay for required items) should raise substantially, this statement should be sufficient.

If there is a large planned postage increase, for example, and your business plan depends upon a lot of direct mail, you might amend the statement as follows:

Inflation assumptions in this plan: This plan assumes that prices will be able to rise sufficiently to cover inflationary increases in expenses—except for next year's 14% increase in postage. That increase has been included in the financial projections of this plan.

Your Risk Level

There are a lot of potential sources of funds for your business, but only a few that will apply to you. Potential investors have different categories for business investments, which are based upon how much risk your investment represents. Following are five general categories of risk and their chances of attracting financing.

1. Low risk—Your company is already profitable.

If your business is already established, and you are firmly profitable, you'll have very little trouble raising capital—unless your industry is perceived as being on the decline. Your best sources of capital are bank loans, because you won't have to give away equity. Which is especially important because you *are* profitable.

Further, banks will lend money to you because of your profitable status. The old saying that "Banks will only lend money to people who don't need it" has a lot of truth in it.

2. Medium risk—Your company isn't yet profitable, but it's growing rapidly.

Some companies are growing so fast that every dollar that comes in the door must be used to fund more products to fill the demand.

This is not to be mistaken for the situation of some of the now dead dot-com companies, where the only things rising were expenses and expectations without much, if any, sales.

As long as you have sales and they are growing rapidly, you should be able to get bank funding for your growth. You could probably also get some investors, but why? Again, never give away equity if you don't have to.

3. Medium risk—Your company is a store or storefront.

Banks feel more comfortable investing in stores and storefront businesses (such as a quick-print storefront, an auto repair shop, etc.).

If you have read the material in this book to prepare a strong business plan, it should give you all the ammunition you need to go to local banks and interest them in your company.

Plus, if your business needs particular equipment (e.g., auto paint machines, bakery equipment, restaurant equipment, etc.) banks are comfortable lending a big piece of the equipment price, because they can resell the equipment if you go under.

Banks also lend money to buy inventory because, again, the inventory is their collateral against your default.

4. Medium-high risk—Your company is a launch, with test results.

Although most banks won't lend you money at this high-risk stage, you have a good chance of interesting venture capitalists if the following exist:

- A strong business plan that shows venture capitalists will be able to double their money in three to four years.
- A business plan that shows your business will soon generate enough revenues to pass a "minimum." Each venture capital firm has established a minimum amount of money an investment must be able to return in order for them to be interested. After all, it will take as much of their time and effort to oversee a $100,000 company as a $10 million company.

Definition: Depreciation

Say you buy a printing press to create your own books. It costs you $50,000. At some point in the future, that printing press will fail and no longer be repairable, so you'll need another one. Depreciation allows you to recognize that each year the printing press is older and closer to failing.

The IRS allows a fixed period of "life" for each piece of equipment. Let's say for this printing press that the life allowed was 10 years. Each year, you can *depreciate* your printing press for $5,000 ($50,000 divided by 10 years). That means you can take a tax deduction each year of $5,000!

Depreciation of this kind is called "straight line" depreciation. Your tax accountant is well versed in all forms of depreciation and can recommend the best one for you to use given your tax situation.

- Test-market results that validate the sales projections in the business plan.
- A strong management team for the business that includes people with strong expertise in every factor of the industry, from marketing to manufacturing to financial management.
- Your industry is interesting to venture capitalists. Don't laugh, but this is a real factor. Venture capitalists put together funds of investors and those investors want not only to make a lot of money, but also want to have something to talk about with their friends. Picture an investor chatting up the mayor of his town, or the president of his alma mater. Now picture that man talking about his investments in . . . a hog farm? Probably not. A new high-tech gizmo? You bet.
- The market hasn't just tanked. When the dot-com stocks fell, a lot of venture capitalists found themselves left with 30% of the funds they had before the fall. Those people were no longer interested in high-risk investments. If you were trying to get funding then, you'd have found it much more difficult.

5. High (and highly risky) risk: Your company is a launch with no test results.

A launch without any kind of testing is the kind of start-up that can't raise capital from banks or, usually, venture capitalists. Although venture capitalists threw caution to the wind with the dot-coms for a couple of years, they have come back down to earth. Even if you could get venture capital money for this stage, they'd want 40%–60% of the company for as little as $30,000 (more money for seductive high-tech plans).

This kind of plan—where there's nothing whatsoever to prove that the would-be entrepreneur wasn't dreaming when he or she wrote it—is usually limited to the following sources of capital:

- Your savings
- Your parents
- Your spouse

- Your best friends
- A second mortgage on your house
- Personal loans (get them *before* you quit your job to launch the company)
- Credit cards (at ridiculously high rates, the worst choice but one used by more than one entrepreneur—including a *few* that miraculously didn't go belly up)

First Spend Money to Get Test Results

If you can't self-fund your own launch, and you're not a store or storefront, you'll want to spend your first money to get some proof that your plan will generate sales as you say it will in the plan. Proving you can actually sell the products you plan to sell goes a very long way toward convincing people and banks to lend you money or invest in your company.

If your business will sell by direct marketing—either over the Internet or by direct mail, e-mail, or the telephone—you can raise a small amount of capital for a simple but convincing test. Companies targeting businesses via direct marketing can be tested for as low as $500, on up to $10,000 to $20,000. Companies that target consumers usually require more money for testing as the pool of potential buyers is larger and thus a larger test is needed to show solid results. (See Chapter 5, which discusses in depth the types of testing you can do.)

If your business depends upon face-to-face sales, make the first sales calls yourself and line up the clients. A solid business plan, accompanied by signed sales contracts for 20% of the sales projected in the first year, makes the plan look much less risky.

Be Ready for Change

Watch out for complacency. Once you've started your business, and you start making a profit, it is easy to forget the changeable nature of business. Any of these things could change:

- The sales you're getting
- The response rates to mailings

Choose Investors Wisely

At first glance, pulling in your family and friends as investors may seem ideal; however, consider it carefully. If your business goes under, and your family and friends were investors, who will give you a shoulder to cry on or a kindly pat on the back? Or, who will still be speaking to you when you lose their money?

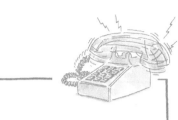

- The number of customers who walk in the door every day
- The number of potential clients who respond to your ads

And they could change in a couple of months. Those nice numbers you're tracking can go south quickly. Sales can drop by 10%, 20%, 30%, or even more due to unpredictable trends:

- The nursing shortage you counted on for clients has turned into a nursing glut.
- Your dot-com company clients, who were rolling in money, are going under left and right.
- The hot new toys to buy are computers and peripherals, and your primary market is now spending their extra cash in that industry instead of audio speakers. Your sales drop by 40%, even though there's no recession.

How to Bulletproof Your Company

New business owners who haven't experienced a recession are in particular danger from bad times. Only painful experience can tell you how bad business can suddenly be.

Starting a new business is an act of courage. Bringing it to profitability is a tribute to your brains, your strength of will, and your street smarts. Losing it after all that effort would be a terrible waste.

Many entrepreneurs aren't looking to start a mega-company; they really just want a job for themselves that they control. When those entrepreneurs reach a level of financial comfort with their company, there's a tendency to relax, to treat it more like a job instead of a business. They put in the hours more mechanically—without spending the time necessary worrying about the future.

Here's the problem with getting too comfortable. In a recession—either a general economic one, or a downtown that affects only your industry—a big company may keep its employees even though its profits nosedive. However, if the profits on a small business nosedive, they can become big losses. Losses can kill the company. If you're spending what your company earns, you're endangering your family's future. Trust me on this: One day your business will desperately need that money to stay alive.

Finding Venture Capital

Where can you find venture capitalists? There are books and lists of them published, but they are pretty much worthless. A plan submitted to a name on a list is unlikely to attract someone. You'll need to work as hard finding money—or harder—than you'll need to work in your business (which is another reason to avoid seeking outside money if at all possible).

Three good sources of venture capital are, however, available to you:

1. Through your alma mater or through a local business college. Many business school alumni groups have periodic "New Venture" meetings where would-be entrepreneurs present before a group of potential investors. You might interest someone in the audience. But you'll learn a lot in the presentation and the questions asked afterward that will help you prepare for one-on-one meetings in the future.
2. Through your local bank. Your local bank manager should know who the local investors are who would be interested in the type of business you are proposing. Get names and any information that can be provided, particularly the type of deals these investors typically do and the industries that interest them.
3. Many venture capitalist firms specialize in particular industries. You need to uncover which are the top ones in your industry. That can take some digging—via Internet research and through back issues of your industry's trade publications. If you are a member of your industry's association, your association director can steer you toward the better firms in your industry. You can find out names by networking with similar businesses in your industry. Even competitors may be willing to tell you who the heavy hitters venture firms are in your industry.

If your company is too small to interest the venture capitalists, then your potential sources are:

1. Enlightened banks—that can recognize a good plan and the good test-marketing results
2. Unenlightened banks—that will invest money for particular pieces of equipment you need, in return for having a lien on the equipment
3. Friends and neighbors
4. Former business associates who know what you can do and are willing to bet on you, given the good test results
5. Personal loans
6. Second mortgages
7. Partners you bring in to supply the needed money and some expertise

Here's the solution: Once you're making money, put off getting comfortable for just a little longer. Recession-proof your company by building up a bad-times nest egg. Wait to relax until you have a full year's operating expenses in the bank. Then go to the Bahamas!

How to Anticipate Change

One of the best reasons for tracking the different financial ratios explained in Chapter 11 is to help you spot changes before it's too late. Here are two examples of how you can use ratios to spot changes and react to those changes before they do serious damage.

Change Alert 1: Sales per Salesperson Drop

Suppose your revenues last year were $500,000 and this year they're $700,000. You're doing great, right?

Well, further suppose that last year you had two salespeople and this year you have three. Your profits per salesperson have dropped from $250,000 to $233,000: a warning sign and a clue that you need to investigate further. Here are two scenarios you might encounter:

Scenario 1: Your first two salespeople are doing $300,000 each this year ($50,000 better than last year) and the new salesperson—assigned to completely new accounts—is doing $100,000. You decide:

- That is fine, because those new accounts were going to be hard to land, OR
- The new salesperson may not be working out.

Scenario 2: Your first two salespeople are doing $200,000 each this year ($50,000 *less* than last year) and the new salesperson—assigned to completely new accounts—is doing $300,000. You decide:

- Maybe both your established salespeople are going soft at the same time, OR
- Maybe the market is declining—a sign of trouble ahead

How could that be when the new salesperson is doing $300,000? Well, maybe the new clients he or she is covering are in a segment of your market that is growing while the established segment is shrinking. This raises a lot of questions about your future:

- Should you stop or slow down creating new products for the older (declining) segment and create more for the new (increasing) segment?
- Should you change where you're putting your advertising money?
- Should you go on sales calls with your established salespeople and find out more about why their sales are declining?

Your answers may be yes to some or all of the above.

Change Alert 2:
The Mix of Clients Changes

Nursing88 magazine was doing wonderful business. Our ad pages had grown at least 10% a year for the past two years. Profits were at an all-time high. There was a big nursing shortage, which caused hospitals to run recruitment ads in *Nursing88*.

When we looked at the advertising "mix" ratios (which *types* of ads we had), recruitment ads had jumped from 50% of the total mix to 70%. That was a little disturbing—our success was strongly due to the nursing shortage. That meant that whenever the shortage was over (and nursing shortages seem to be cyclical)—our ad pages were going to go down fast.

An investigation gave us even more reason to worry. Not only had the *percentage* of nonrecruitment ads gone down, so had the actual number of ad *pages*. We now had fewer pages of nonrecruitment ads than we had two years previously. So when the shortage eased, we were going to be worse off than we were before.

Knowledge like this—that lets you glimpse into the future—is priceless. It led us to divert some of the profits we were currently making into new research that would help us sell nonrecruitment ads.

Too Much Money

A small group of entrepreneurs—certainly not most—feel a little embarrassed by profits. They worry about taking more than their "fair share" of the spoils of business. If that's you, waiting until you have a year's worth of operating expenses in the bank before indulging yourself should make the difference.

Guarding Against Recessions

A recession is on and your business hasn't seen any drop in sales. Are you safe? Probably not. No *immediate* changes doesn't mean you're safe.

Some industries have peculiar responses to recessions. For example, newcomers to the magazine industry can get blindsided by a peculiarity of the industry. When a recession starts, magazines don't feel it. Other company's sales are declining but magazine sales are staying comfortable. If you didn't know the industry, you might think you were going to be just fine. However, three months after the general economy goes into recession, it suddenly hits the magazine industry.

And, when the general economy comes out of a recession, it takes the magazine industry three to four months longer before it starts recovering.

Prospering in Hard Times

Prospering in a recession depends on how good you were about putting away money for just such a cause. If your sales drop by 25% (as my subscription sales did to *Sportswoman* magazine in 1973), and you do not have a substantial financial cushion, you'll be scrambling and cutting back everywhere just to stay afloat.

However, there are some opportunities to be exploited for the brave business owner—with cash reserves—in a recession. Here are some of the opportunities to profit:

- When people are scared financially, they do more than just stop spending. They actually *increase* spending on certain kinds of items—items to help them in a recession. Thus books, magazines, and newsletters that provide information on coping with a recession can all experience sales growth. Financial planners can jump in sales. Items that help people save money can also jump, for instance, vacuum cleaners for those considering dropping their cleaning service and mowers for those considering dropping their gardening service.
- Advertising clutter (the loud noise of millions of ad messages all screaming at a potential customer at the same time) is substantially reduced during recessions, because most companies cut their ad budgets. Some advertisers believe that a recession is

exactly the time to keep spending—so you can take share of market from your retrenching competitors. That's a great idea—*if* your advertising spending is still bringing in enough customers to cover the ad costs, plus the product and delivery costs. Otherwise each dollar you spend is digging a deeper financial hole for you.

- Recessions are great times to buy out your competitors. If a competitor wasn't smart like you and doesn't have a cash reserve, they could find themselves in trouble in a recession—and likely to listen to buy-out offers. Some companies, instead of buying out their competitors, hope for them to fail so they can save their money. The danger in that strategy is that another of your competitors could buy them out and emerge from the recession as a bigger, stronger competitor than either were before.

- The more you help your clients during a recession, the better positioned you are to reap the fruits of that partnership when the economy improves. Here are some ideas on how you could help your clients/customers during a recession. Remember that these tips apply to general recessions as well as to industry-specific recessions.

1. **Flexible payment plans.** For consumers, this might mean a small monthly charge to a credit card instead of the full price up front. For businesses, this might mean allowing them to pay for November and December purchases the following January (on next year's budget)

2. **Smaller-sized packaging.** Can you deliver half the goods for half the price? For 55% of the price?

3. **Valuable add-ons.** Can you add something to your product that makes it better for your customers in any of these ways?

   - Makes it more valuable to them
   - Helps them save money
   - Helps them look smart, which could help them keep their job
   - Offers them better service

4. **Personal help.** If any of your clients lose their jobs, keep a job-search ear out for them. Most people stay within the

Economic Downturns

Listen to the general economic news to anticipate downturns:

- When the stock market falls, people feel less flush, which will probably mean they'll be cutting back on their overall purchases.
- When the economy goes into recession, people lose their jobs. Naturally, those people stop buying. But so do others—seeing their workmates get laid off strikes fear in the hearts of even the biggest spenders.

same industry. If you can point them to a new job—great! But even if you can't help them, when they do get a new job they'll remember that you tried.

Using the Internet

We covered a lot about Internet marketing in Chapter 7, but this chapter will address those of you who think your business has nothing to do with the Internet. There's probably not a business in America that won't be affected—powerfully—by the Internet over the next five to ten years.

Who's using the Web right now? All the national companies you'd expect, plus a lot of local ones:

- Beauty salons—sites give hours, prices, credentials of their stylists, and travel directions
- Auto body shops—specialties, references, travel directions
- Car dealerships—an Internet boom area
- Pet stores—who can resist those kitten pictures?
- Restaurants—catch their guided video tour showing great seats, cozy hearths, and great views
- Real estate brokers—video tours of houses or offices

Et cetera, et cetera . . . And these are only a fraction of the ways the Internet is changing business as we know it.

Brilliant for Business Research

You haven't seen anything until you do business research on the Internet. If your business doesn't harness this powerful tool, you'll be bested by competitors who have and are using it.

Here is a sampling of the things you can do in just an hour or two on the Internet:

- Find new competitors you didn't even know you had.
- See what your competitors are selling—and what's selling best. (The best-selling items are brought to the "front" of the Web site, just like prime space in a bricks and mortar business are near the entrance by the cash register.)
- See what prices your competitors are charging.

- Get quick Dun & Bradstreet financial reports on your competitors—and on potential clients! (I had a client once who raised my warning signals; for $100, I got an instant, and very detailed, credit report on him that reassured me.)
- Find out what information is "out there" about you, personally, and about your company.
    - What are the credit bureaus saying about your company?
    - If a potential client does a search under your name, what comes up? Is there a business with your name? A crook with the same name who has bilked investors? Have you posted anything risqué in an Internet newsgroup that might be available to the eyes of anyone researching *your* name?
- Become an expert on an obscure topic. Is a potential client into dog racing? Learn the best tracks, the fastest dogs. Is a biotech company willing to listen to your insurance proposal? Learn about the area of biotech they're into. There's no faster way to learn than to research it on the Internet. In 15 minutes, you can find:
    - The hot issues currently facing an industry.
    - Printouts of major articles on a topic and/or its key companies.
    - A list of the top 15 books on the topic, and which companies are buying which books. (And, if you wish, order those books for guaranteed delivery the next day.)

Online Dogcatchers

In talking to Internet-adverse clients, I used to joke and say that only dogcatchers could escape the Internet future. Now I know that dogcatchers won't escape at all. They are going to have to deal with Internet databanks of lost pets in their local areas. They'll be posting pictures of dogs captured for anxious pet owners to view. And, for unclaimed dogs, the postings of them on the Internet will become a new way would-be pet owners can be tempted without having to get in the car and come over when they might be disappointed.

Too much to read to stay current in your industry? If you're worried about missing important information, you can get your own "Personal News Agents." They will roam the Internet looking for anything they can find that has your chosen key words in it, deliver the gathered information to your e-mail box at whatever time of the day or night you desire. Daily. Weekly. Even hourly. Free. America Online has a limited one. Yahoo (*www.yahoo.com*) has a better one. So do other ISPs. Just look for "personal news." The *Wall Street Journal* has a good one for information on publicly traded companies.

The Web as Customer Magnet

Even if you think your current customers are completely satisfied without a Web offering, you're missing sales from potential customers.

This is the biggest surprise for most companies that go onto the Web. Some find their sales go up by 10% or 15%—from overseas customers. Others find that same increase with customers from the U.S.

Even businesses selling to businesses find there are companies buying from them that they never knew existed before.

Just as you may prefer to deal with vendors over the telephone or in person, there is a large—and growing—group of managers who prefer to find their vendors over the Internet. If your company isn't there, you may not even be considered for their business.

The Web as Money-Saver

Savings from using the Internet come in two primary areas: promotional cost savings and savings in customer service.

Promotional Cost Savings

1. Savings from the promotional pieces you send out. No more four-color printing of expensive brochures and high postage charges. Also, no more instant obsolescence of your promotional materials requiring you to go back to press to get up to date.

If you now print a fat catalog showing your products, you will certainly be able to print less copies if you have a Web presence. Companies selling to business will probably be able to drop the printed version of their catalogs completely in the near future—saving tens of thousands (or hundreds of thousands) of dollars a year.

2. Savings from more expensive forms of direct marketing. There's nothing that will make a quicker believer out of you than doing a promotional campaign to your prospects for the grand total expense of . . . nothing!

You can send customers a message—with no printing and no postage costs. That message will include a link that customers click on to be taken right to a Web page with pretty color pictures of your product(s) and all the sales information you want to convey about it. Because you're not paying for printing the information, you can include all the detail any customer might want before making a buying decision.

Then you can take orders without paying a single order taker—orders and credit card information will be transmitted electronically so it's entered automatically in your database. And, since you've set up an "autoresponder," it immediately—within 10 seconds of receiving the order—sends the customer an acknowledgment that spells out the details of the order, including cost and when the customer can expect to receive the order—and thanks them for their business.

Meanwhile, the three people who were annoyed by receiving direct marketing promotional materials from you didn't call and take up customer service time. They hit a "Get me off this list" button that automatically removed them from the list and put them on a "Do not e-mail" list.

Look ma, no hands! It's all taking care of itself!

Customer Service Savings

If you have a database of products, the Internet will be a big cost saver for you. No longer do you have to worry about keeping two databases current—the one you use to control your business and the one you use to solicit sales. Now you simply update the one database and it—or the parts of it you designate—is automatically on the Web where your clients can use it to plan purchases.

You'll also be able to provide your customers with 24-hour service: a Web site is available any time they want it. No charges for overtime!

Plus, clients won't have to call your customer service to ask questions like:

- Is this particular product in stock?
- When is the fastest I can get it?
- What else do you carry in the same style?

Your clients can go online whenever they want, see everything you have in current stock, check the shipping as to how fast they can get something, place an order, and go about their life.

Promoting Your Site

Your own e-mail newsletter, which people register to get free, is probably the most effective promotional device these days. Dr. Koop's newsletter on America Online has six or more one-paragraph items, each with a link to a full article on his main site. It would be hard to just read the newsletter and not click through to the main site, where products and health-related services are sold.

Getting Customers to Your Site

Of course, it's not all a bed of roses in cyberspace. A potential is the imminent proliferation of new rules and regulations regarding e-commerce. For instance, currently no sales tax is charged if the sale is to an out-of-state customer. States are losing millions in tax revenue as a result and are lobbying to change the tax regulations. You'll have to keep current on what is and what is not allowed.

The second problem is how to get prospects to your Web site.

Your established customers who want to order from you can find you easily—and they will. But how do you get everyone else to find you?

Entire books have been written on how to lure customers to your site. New ideas are being invented as we speak. Here are some general guidelines at this point in time:

- Turning up on the fifteenth page of someone's search for your product is probably worthless; most people look at the first three screens and never look at the next 100. What *is* currently working is paying for position. Thus you pay one of the top search engines (e.g., Yahoo! or AltaVista) a fee so that when someone searches for "rap music" your band shows up on the first page of 10 hits.
- Banner ads are not worth it. They're pulling very low numbers of people who click on them to get more information. However, expect new ideas for banners in the future that may increase their response rate.
- Advertising in e-mail newsletters related to your product or service is, at this time, pulling relatively well. The trick is finding a very targeted newsletter, whose topic will be of great interest to exactly your potential targets. Each issue of the newsletter usually carries two advertisers who get one paragraph of sales copy and a link where readers can click through to their site.
- Mailing postcards to your database touting something special on your Web site works.

Appendix 1:
Plan for a Product Sales Business

Rainbow Kites, Inc.

SUMMARY

Business Concept

The kite industry has expanded rapidly in the past several years and growth is expected to continue at a strong pace in the foreseeable future. This offers excellent opportunities for new companies to enter this market. We intend to address the needs of customers in this market who seek higher-quality, higher-priced kites. We will address this need by importing, selling, and distributing higher-end kites in the U.S. and Canada. Distinguishing characteristics of our business will be top-quality products, special emphasis on higher-end independent retailers, and a high level of service.

Current Situation

We are a start-up, incorporated in 1999 in the State of California. The principal owner is Tom Anderson, whose title is President and who has many years of experience in the toy industry. Other key personnel include Nancy Anderson, his spouse, who has experience in customer service, bookkeeping, and office work. At this time we are seeking additional equity capital to complement our own equity investment and seeking to arrange a bank line for inventory and receivables financing. We have firm commitments to distribute several highly sought-after overseas kite manufacturers and have verbal commitments from independent retailers primarily along the West Coast to stock our products. We hope to ship our first products within six months of finalizing financing arrangements.

Key Success Factors

The success of our business will be largely a result of superior products, superior service, extra attention to detail throughout our operation, personnel, and our high level of experience in the industry. In particular what really sets us apart from the competition is that we are *only* going to sell high-end kites and we are *only* going to sell to higher-end outlets. This will allow us to give absolutely top service and product selection for these accounts without getting distracted from the very different product and service demands of the more mass market outlets.

Financial Situations/Needs

In order to effectively launch the business, we project a total need for $300,000 in equity financing. Principal uses of the funds will be to finance operations until cash flow becomes positive and to create a stronger balance sheet in order to help secure additional bank lending to finance inventory and receivables. To date we have raised $132,000 from founders Tom and Nancy Anderson, and their relatives. We project that the company will be profitable within two years. We project that within three years of reaching break-even, this new investment could be cashed out by either the founding partners purchasing this investment stake or by replacing the investment stake with additional bank financing.

VISION

Vision Statement

Our vision of what our company will become in the future is to have developed relationships with key retailers so strong that they will view us more as indispensable partners than as just another supplier. We will work closely with each retailer we serve to recommend product assortment unique for their customer base, appropriate stocking levels, pricing, and display assortments. We will constantly seek out and work with the manufacturers we represent to deliver the most innovative and exciting products possible to the retailers we serve.

Milestones

1. Overseas manufacturers agreements in place . . . done.
2. Verbal commitments from many West Coast retailers . . . done.
3. Presentation to potential investors . . . underway now.
4. Presentation to potential banks for inventory and receivable financing . . . underway now.
5. Financing commitments in place . . . 60 days.
6. Product catalog completed . . . 30 days.
7. Additional sales reps being recruited . . . underway now.
8. Sales rep selection finalized . . . 60 days.
9. Warehouse lease signed . . . 90 days.
10. First written orders from retailers . . . 75 days.
11. First orders to manufacturers . . . 110 days.
12. First shipments from our warehouse . . . 160 days.

MARKET ANALYSIS

The Overall Market

The overall size of the industry is currently $150 million in the U.S. and Canada. Because the industry includes a very diverse group of product types with significantly different characteristics, it is more meaningful to break out analysis of the industry into roughly two groups. The first group and by far the larger unit volume is lower-end kites sold primarily through mass market outlets such as discount department stores. The second group is higher-end kites that are sold largely at independent and specialty chain stores. While the unit volume is much less, the dollar volume is approximately the same ($75 million) as that for lower-end kites because the average price point is much higher.

Changes in the Market

The most significant development in this marketplace over the past decade has been the shift in the toy and kite business away from independent stores to national mass marketers. However, recently this trend has slowed as independent toy and novelty retailers have become better at differentiating themselves and their product selections from those offered by national mass marketers.

Market Segments

The market is primarily segmented by distribution channel. The mass market retailers are looking for low-priced products and a high percentage of their products are licensed merchandise, for example, based upon kid's cartoon characters. Independent specialty retailers, however, are trying increasingly to be as different from the mass merchants as possible and are generally selling much higher-priced products and seldom want merchandise based upon licensed cartoon characters.

It should be pointed out that there are few stores that sell just kite merchandise—even among independent specialty stores, most of the volume in kites is sold at stores that sell a wide assortment of other merchandise, such as toys or other novelty items.

Target Market and Customers

Our target market is independent and small chain merchants that are committed to selling higher-end kite products. We particularly want to focus on accounts that just sell higher-end kite products and that are committed to stocking a selection of at least a dozen different kite products. These accounts we feel offer the best growth potential and will benefit the most by the help we can bring to them in selecting and displaying our higher-end merchandise.

Customer Needs

The basic need of target retail customers is to differentiate their store from mass market stores and give customers a reason for shopping their store and paying significant premiums for their products instead of getting a low-end product at a discount department store.

These stores really appreciate stocking a line that is not sold at mass market accounts. They also appreciate dealing with an importer who is committed to specialty stores exclusively, not mass market accounts.

Customer Buying Decisions

The buying decision is almost always made at an in-person sales presentation. The personal touch appears to be essential for moving buyers to action for this product because these high-end retailers are very demanding about the product quality being stocked in their stores. They insist upon seeing finished products, not just mock-ups or catalog pages. Some purchases are made at trade shows, but only a small percentage.

COMPETITIVE ANALYSIS

Industry Overview

Across the U.S. and Canada there are many companies that distribute kites. The vast majority, however, distribute only one or two low-end kites as a very small part of their overall distribution business.

There are several distribution firms that offer between a dozen and as many as one hundred kite products. These firms represent many different products and the sale of kites represents a very small fraction of their business. These firms also sell to a wide variety of outlets including mass merchant accounts.

Changes in the Industry

The big change in the kite industry over the last few years has been the concentration of lower-end kite sales in mass market accounts, along with a strengthening market for higher-end kites in upscale specialty accounts.

Current distributors representing larger kite product lines, while still selling to a wide variety of outlets, have tended to focus most of their efforts on selling lower-end products to mass market type accounts—where their revenue is much greater.

Opportunities

While the competition for this product is well established in—and gives a lot of focus to—current major markets, they are much less aggressively pursuing the higher-end kite market. This market offers terrific potential because it has significant growth potential, and the competition is not well entrenched here. Furthermore, this market differs from the other markets in many important ways. While this market may not be the largest, it appears a very solid opportunity for a newer competitor.

Threats and Risks

Because we are a small firm, we do not anticipate a meaningful or prompt reaction to our market entrance from our larger and more established competitors. We think a strong reaction from existing distribution firms is particularly unlikely because the primary competitors derive only a very small percentage of their business from kite sales, and even that revenue is largely from mass market accounts that we plan on avoiding. However, we have developed contingency plans for certain reactions that competitors may make. If a competitor lowers their prices on the exact same product we are offering, we will match their price on that product. But we intend as much as possible to emphasize products that our competitors are not selling to begin with.

STRATEGY

Key Competitive Capabilities

We are better positioned than our main competitors to take advantage of the increasing demands of upscale independent specialty stores, to sharply differentiate their kite selection from those of mass merchants. Because we are going to focus exclusively on importing higher-end kites for independent specialty stores we will be much better able to serve their needs than current distributors, who handle many items other than kites and also give their primary attention to larger mass merchandise customers.

Tom Anderson's extensive experience in the toy business and his solid knowledge of the kite market in North America, his personal contacts at independent retailers on the West Coast, and his contacts at overseas suppliers give us a strong competitive advantage.

Nancy Anderson's background in running offices and handling customer service issues will give us a strong service advantage.

Key Competitive Weaknesses

Our primary weakness is that we are a new business competing largely against established firms. To significantly build sales, we must not just find new customers—we must take customers away from existing firms. However, by offering a superior selection of kites and focusing exclusively on upscale independent stores we feel we can quickly open accounts at many retailers and build strong relationships. Cofounder Tom Anderson has had many discussion, with owners and buyers at retailers that confirm this opinion.

Another disadvantage we have is stronger personal ties with accounts on the West Coast of the U.S. and Canada than in other parts of these countries. We plan on offsetting this weakness by hiring experienced commission reps for other territories. We have already had preliminary discussions with several highly successful reps and these reps have shown interest in continuing discussions with us.

Financially we do need additional funding. But after the targeted funding is in place we will have ample financing for the foreseeable future.

Strategy

Our strategy is to focus 100% of our efforts on the market for upscale kites. By focusing all of our effort and energy on this particular niche, we expect to quickly develop and maintain a leadership position. While other firms try to be all things to all people, we believe that our singular focus will give us significant advantages. Most of the firms serving this niche now also serve much larger markets and give only secondary attention to the upscale. On the other hand, our firm will give our total focus to this niche; our key people will stay in personal touch with customers in this niche; and we will be able to respond to changes in this market much faster than our competitors.

We will offer the best, most highly personalized service in the marketplace we serve. Being a very small, owner-operated company, we especially intend to use this to our advantage to be absolutely certain that every one of our customers receives excellent service.

We will go out of our way to make sure that our customers know that they truly matter to us. For example, we will carefully recommend seasonal inventory plans for each store that reflects the customer traffic that the store receives. We will also make display suggestions and create a number of displays that can be adopted to the needs of particular stores. Sales reps and in-house employees who deal with customers will be carefully trained and will be given wide latitude for ensuring that customers are always satisfied.

PRODUCTS/SERVICES

Product/Service Description

Our underlying philosophy in selecting products has been to choose lines that will bring excitement, surprise, and satisfaction to demanding higher-end customers. We personally test each individual product. Special attention is given to ease of assembly, durability, and general overall attraction.

We prefer to choose lines that we can represent exclusively, but because our first priority is on representing top-of-the-line merchandise, we have agreed to take on two leading lines on a nonexclusive basis.

A complete draft copy of our first catalog detailing our initial product lines and products is available upon request.

An important component of our business is not just our products but our service.

These are some of the important service elements we offer:
- Stocking of all products offered in our West Coast warehouse, avoiding long waits to fill orders from overseas
- Detailed advice on inventory planning and sales forecasting for individual stores
- Display fixtures custom-built to suit the needs of our customers
- Full returnability for any product defects
- Coordination of cooperative advertising programs with manufacturers

Positioning of Products/Services

We intend to position our business not just as a distributor of products, but as a partner bringing a high level of service to the stores that we enter into business with.

We will work with stores through merchandise selection and display options to significantly increase the sales and profitability of their kite business. By doing this we expect to develop a strong loyalty among our customers.

SALES AND MARKETING

Marketing Strategy

Our basic marketing strategy is to work with our retailers on a one-to-one basis to develop unique marketing programs for them. Especially because we want to develop close working relationships with our customers, we want to establish accounts in as personal a way as possible. Hence we will overwhelmingly emphasize in-person sales calls to build accounts.

We will closely integrate all of our marketing and sales efforts to project a consistent image of our company and a consistent positioning of our products or services. We will build this image around our name, "Rainbow Kites, Inc.," and will emphasize to retailers the wonderful color and excitement that a well-done display of top-quality kites can add to their store.

Although we will attend some trade shows and produce a color catalog, these marketing initiatives are seen as supporting, not competing with, our independent sales representatives.

Sales Tactics

Our primary sales method is face-to-face selling by independent reps. A particularly important aspect of our sales process is that we will fly all of our independent reps to our West Coast office to extensively train them in our product line, in building displays, and in building a bigger kite business for our customers.

We will insist that our independent reps represent only noncompeting, nonkite lines. We will stay in close phone contact with our reps in addition to having sales meetings with them at least four times per year, usually at major trade shows.

We will pay our reps on a "ledger" basis, giving them commission on all sales in their exclusive territories even if the account phoned the order in directly to our main office.

Advertising

We will have a small advertising budget, devoted exclusively to trade publications designed to reach buyers and owners of upscale independent stores. The objective of our trade advertising will be limited to reinforcing the image of our company and the excitement of stocking upscale kites. All ads will be four-color and between $1/8$ and $1/4$ page in size. Each ad will prominently feature our logo and a bright, colorful, changing display of upscale kites.

We will also work with our retailers to obtain co-op advertising funds for their own local advertising. Currently very little co-op money is being provided by kite manufacturers, but we believe that we can make more funds available especially if we work with a U.S. ad agency to develop effective advertising layouts and copy that our retailers could use.

Publicity

Our publicity effort will be three-fold. For one, we will send news releases to trade magazines, to try to get product or company feature coverage in front of the eyes of retailers. Second, we will produce a few generic press releases about kites that our retailers can use to try to obtain publicity coverage for their stores in local publications. Third, we shall have a quarterly newsletter for retailers that we are currently serving or hope to be serving. We anticipate sending 1,000 copies of the news release out our first year and gradually increase to 2,000 copies by our third year. In the newsletter we will highlight not just our products but also display ideas and success stories of stores that increased their kite sales.

Trade Shows et al.

We will have a small booth or tabletop display at four national conventions each year, including the National Toy Show in February in New York, the Toy and Hobby Show in April in Toronto, the International Gift Show in Las Vegas, and the West Coast Toy and Gift Fair in May. We will emphasize not just our products but the custom-built displays that we are producing for retailers.

We will also provide limited funds for display space for our independent reps at regional trade shows that they attend. Typically we will pay for one tabletop display.

OPERATIONS

Key Personnel

The Company will be managed by the two founding partners, whose individual areas of expertise covers many of the functional aspects of the business. Tom Anderson will serve as the President of the Company, and will be responsible for Product Selection and Sales & Marketing. Nancy Anderson will be the Vice President, in charge of Administration. She will be responsible for customer service, accounting, shipping, and the general administration of the business.

Tom Anderson has a long history of experience in the toy business and specifically in kites. For several years he grew the kite business at Ocean Gifts and Toys in Los Angeles into one of the largest and most profitable kite stores in the country. Tom has many industry contacts and an in-depth knowledge of the kite and toy business. See Tom's resume for further details.

Nancy Anderson directed a staff of twelve as the manager of customer service for LA Selections, a major local jobber of novelty goods. She has also held a wide variety of other inside business and operations positions. See Nancy's resume for further details.

Organizational Structure

The organizational structure is very simple. The independent commissioned reps will report to Tom Anderson. Support staff at the office and warehouse will report to Nancy. Because Tom will frequently go on buying trips to the Far East or be on the road selling, Nancy will be able to support any day-to-day needs that the reps may have. However, even when Tom is on the road he will be in constant touch by computer or phone.

Product/Service Delivery

In order to deliver high-quality, personalized service we will carefully select all employees—especially sales reps, and customer service representatives who deal directly with customers. Tom is currently interviewing candidates for sales reps. We will carefully review references not from past employers or manufacturers but from retailers that these sales reps have served. We will also make sure that each employee understands our way of delivering quality service to each customer. We will have immediate backup support available by phone from our office for more difficult service issues. And we will give employees enough latitude so that they can respond immediately to almost all customer requests or complaints—which in this industry usually means granting prompt credit for damaged merchandise.

Customer Service/Support

We intend to prioritize customer service and make it a key component of our marketing programs. We believe that providing our customers with what they want, when and how they want it, is the key to repeat business and to word-of-mouth advertising. Not only will we train our employees to deliver excellent service, we will give them the flexibility to respond creatively to client requests. In addition, we will continually monitor our clients' level of satisfaction with our service through surveys and other convenient feedback opportunities.

Initially we expect to have few enough accounts so that Nancy and one additional employee can handle all customer service issues. Having just one employee to train should help ensure that Nancy can help make the new hire a top performer. As our business grows we intend to hire additional customer service people one at a time and pay a premium over market labor rates to attract and retain quality help.

Shipping problems are a huge issue with the firms that we compete with, largely because they insist on using surface shipping methods to keep their costs down to charge low prices to keep their mass merchant accounts happy.

We intend to use air freight to import our kites from the Far East. This will add to our costs slightly. But because all of our products are more expensive, it makes more sense for us. It will also allow us to have much thinner inventories in our warehouse without risking stocking out.

Our relatively high cost of shipping has put us at a competitive disadvantage. We are attempting to reduce the current cost of shipping for an average order by 10%. We intend to achieve this cost reduction by putting our overall shipping requirements out to bid.

Facilities

We plan to lease approximately 10,000 square feet of space as soon as our financing is finalized. We have a specific property in mind and have a tentative agreement with the landlord's agent. This building, located near LAX airport, has 8,500 feet of warehouse space and a small 850-square-foot office. The lease rate is $6.35 per foot triple net for a two-year lease with the option for two additional years at an increase of 5.9% per year.

The building is located in a busy industrial neighborhood, but because we do not intend to have customers visit us we have decided we are better off with a lower-rent location than a location that could double as a fancy showroom.

Appendix 2:
Plan for a Service Business

Lawn Masters of Newton

Business Concept

Lawn Masters of Newton is part of the lawn maintenance industry. Our target market is homeowners in the Newton, Massachusetts, community. Our principal service is lawn care, including seeding, fertilizing, mowing, and shrubbery and tree care. Our service differs from competitors in that we offer a complete set of services offered on an a la carte basis. Our intention is that the company will become the leading provider of lawn maintenance services in Newton.

We have been successful in providing lawn maintenance services, with a special emphasis on one-stop shopping. We have an excellent reputation and are best known for our customer service and flexibility, which differentiates us from our competitors. The company is profitable and has great potential for growth and for becoming a leader in the local market area. To best take advantage of our growth opportunities, the company would like to purchase new maintenance equipment and move to a larger facility. These expenditures will allow us to finance and support our planned growth, without sacrificing the quality of service that we are known for.

Current Situation

The company was founded as a corporation in the Commonwealth of Massachusetts on April 1, 1986. Currently the company is well established in its market, with sales in our past fiscal year reaching $1,350,000. In recent years our sales have been growing steadily. The major challenge the firm is facing at this point is expansion in order to increase market share. It intends to respond to this challenge by purchasing new equipment so that we are able to put more teams in the field, by moving to a larger facility, and by launching several innovative marketing and publicity efforts.

In the next few years, it is estimated that lawn maintenance services in Newton, Massachusetts, will grow by at least 10%–20%. This growth will be driven by the aging of the population base, the increasing value of residential property in Newton, and the robust overall economic situation in New England. We know that we are not the only company to see the business opportunities created by this expected growth, but we do feel that our one-stop, menu-oriented service structure is a unique response to the situation that will help us stand out in what will be a crowded marketplace.

Key Success Factors

The success of our business has been and will continue to be largely a result of our ability to deliver dependable, high-quality lawn maintenance services custom-tailored to each customer's needs.

More specifically, the key factors that can be identified as being particularly important in our firm's ability to succeed are:

1. A comprehensive set of lawn maintenance services—we can do it all
2. A very flexible, menu-oriented system for choosing services
3. An especially well-trained staff, able to deal professionally with customers
4. A very well-organized set of operating procedures that guarantees our dependability

Another major asset is our highly talented and experienced management team. The three key individuals complement each other well, combining backgrounds in diverse areas. Jack Duffy brings expertise in finance and management; Ed Davis brings expertise in lawn maintenance techniques and operations; and Janice Kendall brings expertise in sales and marketing. Together, these strengths cover all of the major aspects of the business with solid experience and a proven record of success.

We are, above all, very customer-focused, committed to solving all of our related customer's needs and doing everything we possibly can to keep them satisfied. This approach will ensure that we retain a highly satisfied clientele and get referrals.

Financial Situation/Needs

At this time we are seeking $30,000 in a credit line and $180,000 in an asset-backed loan. The credit line will be used for moving expenses, improvements to the new facility, and early season advertising expenditures. The loan will be used to purchase equipment (utility truck and associated tools) for the ten new crews that will be needed to service our expanded customer base. We will be able to pay down the loan completely in 18 months, a process we will begin in August 2000. The credit line will be cleared before the end of 2000.

GOALS

Vision Statement

Highly personalized service has always been the hallmark of Lawn Masters of Newton. As a very small, owner-operated company, we are able to be very flexible in the way we provide yard maintenance services and do whatever we can to accommodate our customer's needs—from mowing and pruning to fertilizing, mulching, and weed control.

Now we intend to be a standout even more as the best managed and most professionally operated firm operating in the City of Newton, Massachusetts. In a field filled with small "mom and pop" operators who run their businesses by the seat of their pants, we intend to distinguish ourselves by planning our services and operations carefully; having rigorous hiring and training programs; having specific policies and standards for serving customers; and carefully monitoring the quality of our service. We are also going to carefully communicate to our customers the key differences and advantages in doing business with us so our target customers know that choosing us as a supplier is the safe choice for consistent, high-quality service. These steps, we believe, will allow Lawn Masters of Newton to double our sales revenue during 2000.

Milestones

Important milestones for our business the upcoming year are:

Move to new facility	1/15/00
Obtaining financing for new equipment	2/01/00
Launching an upgrade of our services	3/01/00

The Total Lawn Maintenance Package:

Launching a new advertising campaign	3/01/00
Adding local cable television advertising to our sales effort	3/01/00
Launching a web site	3/01/00
Achieving sales of $2.2M	9/15/01

MARKET ANALYSIS

The Overall Market

We estimate the total current market for residential yard maintenance services in Newton, Massachusetts, at about $12.5 million. We have derived this number by estimating the percentage of Newton homeowners (20%) who contract for these services and multiplying that number of customers (25,000 occupied housing units x 20% = 5,000) times an average annual fee for mowing, pruning, and Spring and Fall cleanup ($2,500).

The current market for this service appears to be growing because several more companies offering these services just opened their doors in the last two years and all of the firms appear to be prospering.

Furthermore, as discussed in the customer needs section of this plan, the overall market may be able to grow further if a new business can offer new service dimensions that meet needs not currently being served by existing competitors.

Changes in the Market

As the market for yard maintenance services continues to mature, buyers have become increasingly discerning and increasingly aware of and interested in the key feature/benefit differences from one competitor's offering to the next. As a result many, but not all, buyers are placing much added importance on features and performance, and how well the service appears to serve their needs, and are placing less emphasis on price. We believe, for instance, that it will be to our competitive advantage to offer a full range of services—from mowing and pruning to seeding, weeding, and insect control—so that customers will not have to contract a variety of different firms to accomplish all of their needs.

Market Segments

The market can be broken into a basic three segments: the full-service segment for consumers who are more interested in a comprehensive approach and are less concerned with price; the midrange segment for consumers who want more than a bare bones package; and the economy segment for consumers who are most concerned with price. While some yard maintenance companies are on the borderline between these groupings, this segmentation applies to most service offerings, and most potential consumers are generally likely to only consider options within one segment at any one time.

Target Market and Customers

We intend to direct all of our effort within the City of Newton, Massachusetts. To reach our sales goals, we estimate that we will need to achieve about 20% market share—not enough to provoke an aggressive competitive response.

Although we could easily travel to surrounding towns to provide yard maintenance services, we feel that from a marketing standpoint we are much better off focusing on Newton. One advantage is that we will be able to build sales momentum more easily by purchasing larger ads in one local newspaper. We feel that we will also be able to quickly build a word-of-mouth reputation. The demographics of Newton, of course, are particularly good for our business.

Customer Characteristics

All of our prospective customers share the need for professional yard maintenance services. Most of them have the following characteristics: two-income homeowners; own at least quarter-acre lots with lawns, shrubs, and trees; college-educated; concerned with the environment and the proper use of pesticides and other chemical treatments. Many, but not all, of our target customers are middle-aged or elderly.

Customer Needs

Even within the market segment that we are targeting, customer needs vary significantly from one buyer to the next. Most companies are currently dealing with this broad range of market demands by specializing in servicing a narrow portion of the market segment; i.e., just offering lawn mowing, or focusing exclusively on re-seeding and fertilizing services. We intend to take a "menu" approach, in which customers can pick and choose any level of services they need.

Customer Buying Decisions

The buying decision is almost always made at an in-person sales presentation. The personal touch appears to be essential for moving buyers to action for yard maintenance services because homeowners in Newton feel very protective and proprietary about their property. To support the sales presentation, pricing incentives are not very important in closing the sale—but testimonials, especially from nearby neighbors, are.

Buyers in this market tend to put a lot of weight on the company rather than just on the particular merits of the product or service being offered. We intend to make this work to our advantage by carefully developing a very specific and favorable image for ourselves.

When we sell to married couples, both the husband and the wife play a role in the decision making. Usually the husband plays the key decision-making role, but the other spouse must at least acquiesce for the purchase decision to move ahead. For this reason, we have found that it is highly desirable to be able to make the sales presentation when both spouses are home.

COMPETITIVE ANALYSIS

Industry Overview

Competition in the yard maintenance field is highly limited by locality. Customers are reluctant to use service providers based in distant locations and even tend to do business with a service organization that specifically focuses on their city or town. As a result, in our target market of Newton, Massachusetts, there are only eight significant direct competitors. Because these companies are private, exact sales information is not available, but based on their number of employees, we estimate that no one competitor dominates, and that the market share for each firm ranges between 10% and 15%.

The actual competition in this industry is rather mild. Customers do not to switch firms very often and do not tend to carefully comparison shop before making buying decisions. Market shares have tended to be relatively stable. Competitors do not make aggressive marketing moves, such as running predatory or comparative advertising campaigns. There is little competition on price, and price incentives or promotions are rare. Relationships are of primary importance. Customers tend not to seriously consider unsolicited overtures from new vendors, and it takes a strong reason for them to specifically request a presentation from a new vendor.

The industry obviously has pronounced seasonal swings. The first quarter tends to account for less than 10% of sales. The second and third quarters represent the vast majority, over 80%, of sales. Some Fall cleanup work extends into the fourth quarter, bringing in, like the first quarter, about 10% of the annual revenue. Seasonality in this industry has important implications—because the billings have to take place during the Spring and Summer months, it is essential to carry out any sales or marketing activities during the late Winter, so that customers can be signed up and ready by late March or early April.

Ease of entry in this industry can be characterized as moderately difficult. Barriers do not involve capital requirements or staffing issues, but rather the difficulty of developing a customer base from scratch.

Most firms in this industry are sole proprietorships, or closely held corporations. These ownership patterns have been relatively steady for years. Debt loads in the industry tend to be relatively marginal, in the range of 20% of total capitalization.

Nature of Competition

Competition focuses on the quality of service, particularly on reliability. Price is seldom emphasized and tends not to vary much between most firms. Instead firms try to emphasize to their customers how their service is better than that of their competitors. For example, they might mention in their advertising or sales pitches the number of years in service in Newton and the guaranteed availability of crews and equipment.

Companies strive not only to build relationships with their current customers, but also to emphasize to new customers how strong and beneficial a long-term relationship with them will be. The emphasis is on selling not a particular product or service, but the whole company. Often extra intangibles, such as direct knowledge of an established customer's specific landscaping situation, are emphasized to show that the value of the whole relationship is greater than the sum of the actual services that are being sold.

Changes in the Industry

The industry is currently experiencing a period of moderate growth caused by the aging of the population base, the increasing value of residential property in Newton, and the robust economy. In the years ahead, this trend is expected to continue. We believe that there will be more and more customers, and that they will be looking for one single source for their yard maintenance needs. This gives a huge advantage to firms that offer an extremely flexible and broad array of services, and a disadvantage to those that don't.

Direct Competitors

Our #1 competitor is Green Lawns, Inc. They compete largely by being a full-service provider. Their major competitive strength is their years of full-service delivery in Newton. They have succeeded in the market because they have a local focus and they will agree to do just about anything.

Our #2 competitor is Total Lawn. They compete largely by being a full-service provider. Their major competitive strength is their large client base and the economies of scale that offers them. They have succeeded in the market because they operate in several communities and offer a wide range of services.

Our #3 competitor is Landscaping Specialists. They compete largely by emphasizing quality and the most up-to-date equipment. Their major competitive strength is their professionalism They have succeeded in the market because they dominate the profitable commercial services sector.

PRIMARY COMPETITORS

Name	Green Lawns, Inc.
Location	123 Washington Street Newton, MA
Sales	$1.3 million (est.)
Profitability	?
Number of employees	50 (peak)
Years in business	30
Strategy	Full service
Competitive strengths	Large client base. Offers wide range of services
Competitive weaknesses	Lack of modern management
Other pertinent info	

Name	Total Lawn
Location	88 Mt Auburn Street Watertown, MA
Sales	$2 million (est.)
Profitability	?
Number of employees	70 (peak)
Years in business	25
Strategy	Full service
Competitive strengths	Large client base. Offer wide range of services
Competitive weaknesses	Lack of modern management. Not focused in Newton
Other pertinent info	

Name	Landscaping Specialists
Location	78 Boylston Street Newton, MA
Sales	?
Profitability	?
Number of employees	65 (est.)
Years in business	About 20
Strategy	Commercial and residential
Competitive strengths	Modern equipment; offers top-quality commercial services
Competitive weaknesses	Perceived to be oriented toward businesses
Other pertinent info	Owned by holding company with several other similar businesses operating in different parts of Greater Boston

MAIN COMPETITORS

	Green Lawns	Lawn Total	Landscaping Specialists
Industry rank	3	2	1
Overall competitiveness	1	2	3
Estimated sales	$1.2M	$2M	$2M+
Sales trend	Up	Steady	Up
Estimated profits	?	?	?
Financial strength	High	?	High
Apparent strategy	Full-service	Full-service	Full-service, res. and com.
Seen by customers as	Familiar	Outsiders	Business-oriented
Loyalty of customers	High	Medium	?
Quality reputation	Medium	Medium	High
Sales strength	Medium	Medium	High
Advertising strength	Low	Low	High
Use of promotions	Low	Low	Medium
#1 Strength	Service range	Service range	High-quality work
#1 Weakness	Disorganized	Disorganized	Nonresidential focus

Our #1 competitor is Green Lawns, Inc. They compete largely by being a full-service provider. Their major competitive strength is their years of full-service delivery in Newton. They have succeeded in the market because they have a local focus and they will agree to do just about anything.

Our #2 competitor is Total Lawn. They compete largely by being a full-service provider. Their major competitive strength is their large client base and the economies of scale that offers them. They have suc-ceeded in the market because they operate in several communities and offer a wide range of services.

Our #3 competitor is Landscaping Specialists. They compete largely by emphasizing quality and the most up-to-date equipment. Their major competitive strength is their professionalism They have succeeded in the market because they dominate the profitable commercial services sector.

COMPETITIVE PRODUCTS/SERVICES

Service	Complete lawn maintenance
Competitor	Green Lawns, Inc.
Dollar sales	$1.3M
Sales trend	Up
Profitability estimate	$300K
Price	$2495
Target buyers	Newton homeowners
Primary positioning	Full service
Features/attributes most emphasized in ads/sales pitches or packaging	1. Full service 2. Local experience
Sales methods	Flyers, telephone
Advertising budget	Minimal
Advertising themes	?
Promotional/incentive programs	Referral incentive ($100 off)
Competitive strengths	Full service; track record
Competitive weaknesses	Not well managed
Other pertinent info	Crews often appear and act unprofessionally

Service	Complete lawn maintenance
Competitor	Total Lawn
Dollar sales	$2M
Sales trend	Steady
Profitability estimate	$400K
Price	$2295
Target Buyers	Homeowners in MetroWest area
Primary positioning	Full service
Features/attributes most emphasized in ads/sales pitches or packaging	1. Full service 2. Reliable
Sales methods	Telemarketing
Advertising budget	None
Advertising themes	?
Promotional/incentive programs	?
Competitive strengths	Full service; well established
Competitive weaknesses	Lack of professionalism; lack of community focus

Service	Complete lawn maintenance
Competitor	Landscaping Specialists
Dollar sales	$2M–$3M
Sales trend	Up
Profitability estimate	$500K+
Price	$2,750
Target Buyers	Homeowners in Greater Boston
Primary positioning	Modern and professional
Features/attributes most emphasized in ads/sales pitches or packaging	1. Up-to-date equipment and techniques 2. Broad range of experience
Sales methods	Telemarketing; door-to-door; direct mail; newspaper
Advertising budget	>$200K
Advertising themes	The best and most up-to-date
Promotional/incentive programs	Referral incentives; start early, save money
Competitive strengths	Well capitalized; well managed
Competitive weaknesses	Not focused on residential services

Opportunities

An examination of the competitive offerings finds several weaknesses. The most critical weakness is the fragmentation of services offered. Some firms only mow lawns and prune shrubs. Others only do re-seeding and care for new lawns. Still others specialize in weed and pest control. Such fragmentation makes one-stop shopping difficult if not impossible. This weakness is particularly important because it is of major concern to many buyers—they want one company to do exactly what they need, no more, no less. That is the role we intend to play.

In addition, we do not feel that most of our competitors run their businesses as efficiently as possible. We will be the only service organization in Newton, for instance, to schedule crews by computer, to communicate with the field via mobile communications technologies, to have serious staff training programs, and to offer customer feedback and evaluation through our Internet Web page.

Threats & Risks

We do not anticipate a meaningful or prompt reaction to our marketing initiatives from our competitors. However, we have developed contingency plans for certain reactions that competitors may make. If competitors lower their price, we will match their move. We plan to watch for other competitive actions, such as special offers or service changes, and we plan to react swiftly to any competitive move. Reacting to competitive moves will in the short run hurt our profit margins, but will in the long run preserve our market share.

STRATEGY

Key Competitive Capabilities

We have a strong competitive advantage in our superior ability in overall management. Important differences between our capabilities and those of our main competitors are: vastly superior scheduling, staff training, and customer feedback systems. We believe that our highly visible management differences will help make us appear in the consumer's mind to be a more reliable service provider.

Another key competitive advantage lies in the flexibility of our service concept. Potential customers can literally select from a menu of options that covers every aspect of lawn maintenance. There is no dimension of the service we will not provide—none of our competitors can make that claim. Other firms give lip service to the importance of their customers, but leave a lot to be desired in how far they go to serving them. We will definitely go the extra mile in serving and responding to our customers' needs.

Key Competitive Weaknesses

Being a small, locally owned firm we have several inherent advantages in facing large, national competitors—but there are some disadvantages as well. The larger competitors have economies of scale, large buying power, and a brand-name identity. None of them have successfully penetrated our target market community yet, but they could. The professionalism and flexible service package that currently distinguishes us could be matched by a larger, well-funded national company. If a competitor like this does emerge, we will attempt to overcome them by dramatically increasing our local advertising and stressing our local ties, our in-depth knowledge of the Newton community—and all of the good works we participate in as a member of this community.

Main Strategy

Our strategy will be to offer the best, most highly personalized service in the marketplace we serve. Especially being a very small, owner-operated company, we intend to use this to our advantage to be absolutely certain that every one of our customers receives excellent service. We will go out of our way to make sure our customers know that they truly matter to us. We intend to be very flexible in the way we provide service, and to do whatever we can to accommodate our customers' needs. Employees who deal with customers will be carefully trained and will be given wide latitude for insuring that customers are always satisfied.

Implementing this strategy means building a broad line of services to meet a broad range of needs for our customers. The market trend is toward one-stop shopping. Currently customers are increasingly giving a larger share of their business to vendors who provide multiple services. Vendors who have the broadest product lines have the most advantage in working with customers in the lawn maintenance field. This strategy is also one of the fastest and strongest ways that we can differentiate our company from the competition.

We understand that we will be setting a new standard of customer service. We are going to go well beyond the definitions of old and take customer service to a new level. In addition to just plain treating customers well and being responsive to their needs, we are going to provide additional services to customers. Initially these new services are going to include online feedback and scheduling of special services via our Web site, and a completely nontoxic, nonchemical option to weed treatment problems.

Positioning of Products/Services

We will position ourselves as providing highly customized solutions to customers with particularly demanding or specific requirements—and in our community, almost every homeowner believes that they have particularly demanding or specific requirements. We will be highly flexible and responsive in adapting our services to the needs of consumers in Newton. The types of buyers who are most likely to benefit from our approach will be single-family homeowners with full acre lots and plenty of trees and shrubs.

Product/Service Description

Essentially we provide one comprehensive lawn maintenance service, but we offer many different options, including:

- Spring cleanup
- Tree and shrub trimming
- Fertilizing
- Mulching
- Weed control
- Insect control
- Mowing
- Leaf removal
- Winter prep
- Seeding
- Sodding

Our underlying philosophy in developing this spectrum of services has been to present ourselves as the one-stop solution for all lawn maintenance needs. Important objectives are to manage each account carefully to lead to profitability and repeat business. We ensure that we achieve these objectives by following up frequently to see that every customer is satisfied, and to give them a feedback/evaluation and special services request vehicle at our Web site.

Our revenue breakout (FY '99) by service is:

Product/Service:	Unit Sales	Revenue	Percent of Total
1. Spring cleanup	300	$ 90,000	6.6%
2. Fertilizing & mulching	150	150,000	11.1%
3. Trimming	200	75,000	5.5%
4. Weed control	150	75,000	5.5%
5. Insect control	60	50,000	3.7%
6. Seeding	200	200,000	14.8%
7. Sodding	125	200,000	14.8%
8. Mowing	300	300,000	22.2%
9. Leaf removal	400	120,000	8.8%
10. Winter prep	300	90,000	6.6%
TOTAL		$1,350,000	

Future Products/Services

We are planning a new service, to be launched next year (2001), which can be described as a local supply and support center for homeowners who wish to do some of their own yard work. Specialized tools and equipment will be available for purchase or rental. Top soil, fertilizer, sand, and stones of various sorts will also be available. This support center will complete our goal of offering some product or service for every aspect of lawn maintenance, including the do-it-yourselfers.

Marketing Strategy

Our marketing program will support our overall company strategy by emphasizing the flexibility and comprehensiveness of our service offerings, as well as the efficiency and professionalism with which we work. This will be reflected in all of our marketing, including our sales presentations, our advertising, and our literature.

Our marketing objective is to increase sales to $2.5M by 9/15/00, the end of this season. We want to increase our customer base to approximately 1000 homeowners, which would bring our market share to about 20%.

Our marketing strategy will be based around an aggressive sales effort. In-person sales presentations, scheduled at the potential customer's home on the weekends or in the evenings, will be the core of our selling effort. Other marketing activities, including advertising and publicity, will be geared to increasing the receptiveness of potential customers to agreeing to meet with our salespeople.

This strategy will be supported by advertising in the local newspapers, The *Tab*, the *Graphic*, and the *Chronicle*. Our selling effort will consist, in part, of responding to and selling inquiries generated by this advertising.

Our marketing program will have three major components, focused on developing qualified leads for sales presentations and on strengthening our image as the most professional lawn maintenance organization operating in the City of Newton.

- **Program 1:** A Referral Incentive program, in which current customers who refer a potential new account receive a rebate on their annual service bill equal to 10% of the annual service bill of the referred account.
- **Program 2:** A Free Service Consultation, which is how the at-home sales presentations will be represented. A well-trained and professionally attired consultant will inspect the potential customer's grounds, give an expert opinion as to any unusual needs, and make an overall recommendation as to an annual service plan.
- **Program 3:** A well-publicized effort to support and work with the Newton Community Gardening organization at Nahanton Park as a gesture of goodwill of contribution to the community.

Sales Tactics

Our sales process begins when the potential customer responds to our advertising by telephoning us for more information. We have found that rather than providing more information over the phone, our best chance of closing the sale is to arrange an appointment to visit the prospect in person. We have found it is fairly easy to persuade potential customers to agree to see a representative of our company in person. The most difficult part of the sales process, however, is closing the sale. Closing the sale requires not only knowledge of the service but also strong sales skills. We have found that the unique advantages of our service that are important to emphasize in sales calls are our flexibility and professionalism.

An important part of our sales process is uncovering the key concerns and needs of the buyer—which often differ from one customer to the next. Because of this, it is important to have bright and engaging salespeople who can think on their feet and who are also effective in establishing a rapport with their customers.

Senior people in the company will do most of this sales work. This is an important competitive element because customers prefer to deal with the management and be sure that the company will do everything possible to land the sale and keep the customer happy.

We will support our sales effort with the following collateral: brochures, flyers, and testimonial sheets.

Advertising

Although our service has several strong, unique competitive advantages, we will focus on just one in our advertising in order to more clearly distinguish ourselves from the competition in a meaningful way—rather than confuse consumers with multiple messages. The benefit we will focus on is our flexibility; that is, the customizable nature of our service offerings. We have developed the following unique selling proposition that will be an important focus of all our advertising: "Whatever It Takes to Let You Enjoy Your Yard This Summer."

The purpose of our advertising is to support our sales efforts. It will do this by increasing awareness of our company and its services. This in turn will make it easier for salespeople to get appointments with buyers and achieve their sales goals.

We will advertise in the following local newspapers: The *Tab*, the *Graphic*, and the *Chronicle*. This will allow us to zero in on the Newton market, and help position our firm as being closer to the local community than firms that advertise in more broadly circulated media.

We will also experiment with cable television advertising, featuring short interviews with satisfied customers recorded in their own yards.

Finally, we intend to employ the following low-cost advertising techniques: delivering leaflets door to door, putting flyers on car windshields, leaving flyers at other businesses, and car/truck advertising.

We will run our advertising daily during early Spring (March and April) and start to scale it back gradually throughout the Summer. Another daily push will start after Labor Day and run through September, focusing on leaf removal and Winter preparation services.

Promotions/Incentives

We will run one major sales promotion as an early sign-up discount during the month of March. Discounts off of standard pricing will typically run about 5% to 10%. We will promote this sales incentive with coupons and flyers, mailings to current customers, and newspaper and radio advertising.

We will also use giveaways to attract new customers and to build loyalty with current customers. We will give away items that depend on a good lawn—such as croquet sets and badminton games.

We see our World Wide Web site playing primarily an operations support role—but it will also have some promotional role. On the site we will offer service information, basic information about lawn maintenance, suggestions on how to use our service more effectively, links to related sites, discount coupons that may be printed out, and information on how to reach us. We will promote our Web site on all our literature, by listing our Web address everywhere our street address is listed, such as on business cards and on our stationery, and in our advertising.

We will offer free estimates and evaluations without any obligation. We will use this free offer as an opportunity to familiarize the prospect with our business, emphasize our competitive advantages, and try to close the sale.

Publicity

The main purpose of our publicity is to increase the general awareness of our services. Our publicity is also intended to emphasize our commitment to Newton and to inform customers and potential customers of new developments concerning our services.

Our publicity campaign will emphasize our involvement with the Community Gardeners of Newton by sending press releases and videotapes, and arranging media interviews. We will target local newspapers, radio stations, and cable television shows.

We will produce and send a newsletter every month to promote our company and our services. We will send approximately 500 copies to current customers, and another 1,000 or more to prospects. In the newsletter we will highlight items of interest to people who care about lawn maintenance. There will be an editorial column by the President of the company, a Q&A feature, tips, short anecdotes drawn from actual experiences in Newton, and updates on our involvement with the Newton Community Gardeners.

Trade Shows, Business-to-Business Shows, Consumer Shows

The City of Newton sponsors several events that are appropriate for our participation, including a Spring Festival, a July 4th event, and an Octoberfest. All of these events are held on the grounds of the City Hall, and local businesses are invited to rent booth space and exhibit. Our objective in attending these events is to get names of possible leads, build relationships with current customers, emphasize our

unique services, and portray our firm as a major player in business in the Newton community.

We will make an effort to gather names of prospects at the show by having a drawing and a guest book. We will follow up with attendees after the show by phoning to arrange a face-to-face meeting.

OPERATIONS

Key Personnel

The company has three employees who are considered to be key. Jack Duffy, President and CEO, is responsible for management, finances, accounting, and other administration issues. He has been with Lawn Masters of Newton for over ten years, and previously held the position of Regional Manager for Home Depot in New England. Ed Davis, Vice President, will be responsible for services and overall operations, including training and supervision of all the work crews. He has been with Lawn Masters of Newton for five years, and has a degree in environmental studies from the University of Massachusetts. Janice Kendall will be responsible for sales, marketing, and customer relations. She is new to our company, and was most recently an Assistant Director for Publicity with the Massachusetts Audubon Society.

The compensation and incentives plan offered to key personnel is designed to give these individuals a significant stake in the company's success as a way of encouraging top performance and of retaining them in their positions. In addition to salaries, compensation for key personnel will include profit sharing (set at 10% of pretax earnings) and bonuses based on newly registered accounts.

Board of Directors: Members of the Board of Directors have been selected for their ability to bring specialized skills and experience to the company. In addition to the three principals involved in daily operations, these Directors will include Frank White, whose expertise lies in the area of small business law; Stan Novak, who works extensively with several community organizations in Newton in a fund-raising capacity; and Bill Miles, who is the Chairman of the Newton Community Gardeners organization. These nonmanagement Directors will not be compensated for their participation.

Organizational Structure

Our organizational structure is informal, without written descriptions of specific areas of responsibilities. This is primarily because the three key members of the management team work closely across many aspects of the company's operations. As a matter of practice, however, here is who takes the primary role in each of the major functional areas:

Finance: Jack Duffy
Marketing and Sales: Janice Kendall
Operations/Office: Ed Davis

Being a very small company, our selection and use of outside contractors and service providers is an important part of our operation. Here is a breakout of the key outsiders who will be supporting our business:

Accounting: Arnold Financial Services, taxes and strategic planning
Legal: White and Associates, review and prepare legal documents
Graphics and Design: Desktop Graphics, Inc., brochures and other collateral

Human Resources Plan

We recognize that human resources are an extremely important asset, especially in a service busi-

ness in which work is performed on customers' property. Our competitors do not generally recognize this fact, and in general, the personnel standards in the lawn maintenance industry are low. Often, unskilled, unqualified individuals are hired, paid minimum wage, and worked hard until they leave. Field staff of this sort obviously do not reflect well on the company.

At Lawn Masters of Newton, we have decided that although all of our field staff are seasonal workers, we will nevertheless only hire people who are qualified or who can be trained to do the work as required, and who can interact with customers in a friendly and professional manner. Thus, we screen new applicants carefully, including in-person interviews and reference checks. We will strive to hire people who have a solid work ethic and work well with others. Working well with others is especially important in our system of 3-person work crews, each having a consistent set of scheduled assignments and a crew leader.

We will recruit employees by newspaper help-wanted advertising, and offering referral bonuses to current employees. We will review each employee's performance regularly, and when possible promote from within.

The company's salary structure will be higher than market rates, and an extremely competitive benefit package will be offered (most of our competitors offer no benefits at all to seasonal workers), not only to help the recruitment effort but to increase the chance of retaining employees for the entire lawn maintenance season. We hope bring them back each year. Benefits offered will include paid vacation days after the season (accrued at a rate of 1.25 days/month of employment), and a comprehensive health plan (employer pays 50%).

Training

Building a sense of teamwork among all personnel is an essential component for the success of the business. By allocating significant time and resources to staff training, we expect to increase every employee's ability to provide valuable services for our customers, and to feel that he or she is an important, contributing part of the organization. Responsibility for training will come under Operations (Ed Davis), but all three members of the management team have taken part in developing or reviewing training materials or in actually delivering training sessions as appropriate.

Due to the short, seasonal nature of the business, all employees need feedback on their performance with a much greater frequency than the normal annual review process. Lawn Masters of Newton uses a standard form, completed on a weekly basis by the crew leader. This form contains specific feedback on job performance and also makes summary recommendations as to areas for improvement.

Service Delivery

Here are some of the standards we have adopted to help ensure that we provide high quality service:

1. We will answer our phones within 3 rings.
2. We will provide a free, written estimate within 48 hours.
3. We will begin work within 3 days of receiving a signed agreement.
4. We will not interrupt work for any reason until we finish a job.
5. We will use the highest quality equipment and supplies available.
6. We will leave the property clean and neat at the end of each day.
7. We will follow up after every job to be sure the customer is satisfied.
8. We will guarantee satisfaction for all of our work.

Our strategy is built around offering highly personalized service to our customers. Integral to this approach is the careful selection of field staff, in-depth training so that they may respond quickly to customer requests, and in-depth backup support for more difficult requests.

Quality control changes: Overall responsibility for control is handled by Ed Davis. After a major review of our current procedures, which included soliciting input from customers, we have redesigned certain aspects of the process. In particular, we will institute new incentive programs and emphasize training and rewards to help motivate employees to ensure that our high-quality standards are being met.

Customer Service/Support

We intend to prioritize customer service and make it a key component of our marketing programs. We believe that providing our customers with what they want in the area of lawn maintenance, when and how they want it, is the key to repeat business and to word-of-mouth advertising. Not only will we train our employees to deliver excellent service, we will give them the flexibility to respond creatively to client requests. In addition, we will continually monitor our clients' level of satisfaction with our service through surveys and convenient feedback opportunities.

We plan on using the World Wide Web for a significant portion of our service/support effort. On the Web we can offer support 24 hours a day, 365 days a year. And on the Web, customers don't have to wait for the next available service representative. Once the service area of our Web site is up, the cost to maintain it will be minimal. On our Web site we plan on offering a choice of text options explaining basic service issues, lists of frequently asked questions and answers about lawn maintenance, and the ability to e-mail for help with highly specific questions and any requested changes in the scheduled maintenance plan.

Facilities

The company's current facility is not large enough to accommodate the new size and scope of the business. We are utilizing approximately 2,000 square feet at the present time, located on Wells Avenue in an industrial section of Newton, for equipment storage and maintenance as well as office space. We plan to move to a new facility, within the same industrial park development, offering at least twice the space (c. 4,000 square feet), which will meet current and anticipated needs for the foreseeable future. The move is scheduled to take place in January 2000.

Appendix 3:
Plan for a Consulting Business

Capital City Consulting

**FINANCIAL & BUSINESS MANAGEMENT
CONSULTING SERVICES
1999**

Table of Contents

CAPITAL CITY CONSULTING
January 1, 1999
Mr. Don Biggs, Loan Officer
Bank of Arizona
1234 W. El Camino Avenue
Phoenix, Arizona 85058

Dear Mr. Biggs:

The main purpose of Capital City Consulting is to make a reasonable profit and to serve the small business community's need for our services. We provide financial services to the small business owner. The enclosed business plan outlines these services and the potential for growth and profit.

We have currently invested a combined total of $25,000 of personal assets. We are currently seeking a loan for $8,500 for operating cash. This loan will be secured by the company's assets. We are asking for a 24-month term at 12% interest.

This company is owned and operated by two partners, Albert Johnson and Robert Brown. Albert Johnson is a graduate of business school with a major in small business management and has five years experience as the manager of a large retail firm. Robert Brown has earned an M.B.A. in financial management and is a Certified Public Accountant. In addition, he has been recognized by the Internal Revenue Service as a qualified income tax professional and is authorized to represent clients in formal IRS actions. For more background on the owners, please refer to the resumes included in the appendix of the business plan.

Thank you for your consideration.

Sincerely,

Albert Johnson, CEO

SECTION II: EXECUTIVE SUMMARY

Capital City Consulting is a sound investment for the following reasons:

- The personnel are highly skilled and experienced in the field.
- The gross profit margin of the company is projected to be 30% plus.
- The growth of the company is expected to exceed 3.6% annually.
- The marketing of this company is highly diversified.
- Owner investment is 80% of the cash investment.
- Company assets exceed the cash requested in this proposal.

In conclusion, Capital City Consulting is a very sound investment. The company is expected to grow continuously over its life. The government has projected that companies providing similar services will grow at a rate of nearly 20% or better annually nationwide.

SECTION III: BUSINESS DESCRIPTION

Capital City Consulting is a small business management services provider. We at Capital City Consulting service the small-business person to help them become more profitable and effective. Capital City Consulting provides the following services: general accounting, payroll accounting, business plan development, income tax preparation, auditing, information system setup, computerized bookkeeping system setup, and other general consulting services as requested by our clients.

Capital City Consulting is a California corporation that has received authority from the Internal Revenue Service to operate as an S Corporation. We are a for-profit organization. The principal shareholders provide personal services to the business on a full-time basis. As needed, temporary and part-time employees are hired.

The success of our business is directly related to the degree that we advertise and promote our services. We continually advertise through a variety of means. This includes an aggressive direct mail campaign, Yellow Pages advertising, and periodic newspaper advertising. We also use a method of referral for continued growth of our client base. Through these advertising programs we will reach a large market for our services. This market is estimated to be approximately 1.25 million individuals and approximately 9,000 businesses within the area served by Capital City Consulting.

This business is unique in that it offers a service that is vital to all small businesses. Customer surveys have shown that they are looking for service at a higher quality level than is currently available. We provide that to our clients over our competition, and our services are affordable for even the smallest of businesses.

Capital City Consulting has currently contracted eighteen accounts for bookkeeping-related services, which brings in an estimated $1975 in revenue per month. We have an additional four accounts for payroll services, which generates an additional $450 in monthly revenue. Billings for other services during a typical month are:

General Consulting	20 hours
Information System Set-Up	10 hours
Auditing	5 hours
Total:	35 @ $75/hour = $2,625

During the income tax season, January through April, revenues increase significantly due to the large number of individual tax returns that we prepare. It is not unusual for open accounts receivable to exceed $10,000 during this period.

Our estimated revenue is expected to grow at an average of 15% to 20% each year over the next five to seven years. We anticipate a profit margin of 23% of gross revenue.

Owners are paid a salary, which is included in the cash flow analysis. Both principals commit an estimated 50+ hours each week to the business and, in addition, complete annual requirements for continuing education by attending a minimum of 40 hours per year of professional skills training.

SECTION IV: MARKETING

Service fees are figured on the common market rate. We took an independent survey of local businesses that provide similar services. This survey is how we have based our service fees. The prices we have set for our services are very competitive with the local market.

The services provided by Capital City Consulting are not generally subject to sale pricing. However, the services provided are competitive with other local companies that provide similar services. For example, the tax preparation services that are provided is competitive in pricing with other firms that advertise these services. Tax services are also subject to seasonal increase in sales.

Pricing is very important in our overall strategy. The services are priced at the middle of the scale of market value. However, the quality of the services provided are more important to the overall market strategy. Capital City Consulting provides an exceptionally high quality of services. Hence, our marketing approach is to stress value.

The period of December through April will be the heaviest sale period of our sales for tax services. However, we will experience a continued income throughout the year due to extensions. This continued income is not reflected in our projections, due to the lack of reliable research to make reasonable projections.

Capital City Consulting has a full fee schedule. In the fee schedule is the discount and relative charges for services. Please refer to fee schedule included in the appendix. The services provided are not discounted.

Promotional strategy will include a wide variety of advertising media. Direct mail will be 20% of budget, 10% will be for online Internet advertising and 10% will be in local sponsorship. Direct mail will be done on a once-a-month basis. Once a year Capital City Consulting will sponsor a local youth group sporting-associated team, for example, Little League, Pop Warner, etc. Print advertising will run continuous Yellow Page ads, and during the tax season, ads will run two times a month in the local paper. Online advertising will be maintained year-round.

Capital City Consulting provides professional services to the small business owner and general public. Services provided include bookkeeping, tax preparation, financial planning, business plans, payroll accounting, auditing, information systems setup, consulting services, and business analysis that are customized to the needs of the client.

Payments acceptable include cash, check, MasterCard, Visa, and American Express. We will also set up charge accounts for ongoing clients who have established an outstanding credit rating and have shown to be credit-worthy to Capital City Consulting.

Capital City Consulting is a member of the local Chamber of Commerce. We are also registered with the Better Business Bureau. The primary market for Capital City Consulting is small business start-ups. We will use lists provided by the Chamber of Commerce of new business start-ups as part of our direct mail strategy.

The Better Business Bureau has recently published its yearly figures for new business start-ups. The study showed that in the metropolitan area alone there were nearly 15,000 new businesses started last year. Next year is expected to have a 3.6% increase due to the expanding growth in the economy. We expect to reach approximately 10% of this market. With the 3.6% increase we expect to bring in about 1,554 new clients next year alone. That figure is based on the 10% market share and the 3.6% growth in the market. The current market shows that the average company that provides a similar service has on the average 2,000 clients and an annual growth rate of 10% or more.

In conclusion, Capital City Consulting has demonstrated that it has a healthy market and an outstanding growth potential. We feel we have demonstrated that our market strategy is well within the local economy, and we will have an outstanding profitability level.

SECTION V: OPERATIONS

Office hours will be: Monday–Friday 8 A.M. till 6 P.M. Appointments will be scheduled for Saturdays and evenings.

Operations will be computerized. Tax services will be electronically filed and we will also offer Refund Anticipation Loans (RALs). Loans are provided by the bank of Arizona in Phoenix, Arizona. Clients will have the ability to inquire online about our services through our Internet Web page. However, our clients will not be able to access client files, reports, etc. due to the inability to provide competent security at this time. We will have electronic mail available for clients who wish to receive information during normal business hours.

The key operational position for the company is the Chief Executive Officer (CEO). Responsibilities will include overview of daily operations and the provision of primary services such as Auditing, Consulting, Financial Planning, and Corporate Income Tax Preparation. This is a function carried out by Albert Johnson. Robert Brown possesses a Master's in Business Administration (MBA) in financial management. He is the Chief Financial Officer for the corporation and carries out key responsibilities in the making of operational policy and the financial management of the business. In addition, he provides services to clients in income tax consulting and preparation and other consulting responsibilities.

Capital City Consulting will hire on part-time and seasonal employees as necessary. We will utilize an employment agency to assist in the initial screening of potential employees to help ensure that only quality employees are retained. All employees will be required to meet minimum requirements for hire.

SECTION VI: APPENDIX

Sources For Marketing Analysis
Small Business Administration
112 Cobalt Drive, San Francisco, CA

Better Business Bureau
3421 Sweet Street, Phoenix, AZ

TRW Market Research Inc.
45632 Professional Drive, Sacramento, CA

U.S. Department of Labor
10067 15th Avenue, Washington D.C.

The figures and schedules used in this business plan are taken from the abovementioned institutions. Actual case studies can be produced upon request.

FEE STRUCTURE

Income Tax Services:

Electronic Filing of Form 1040	$ 40
Refund Anticipation Loan Fees	$ 35
Basic Short Form Income Tax Preparation	$ 50
Basic Long Form Income Tax Preparation	$ 100
Business Income Tax Return	$ 350
Audit Representation	$ 100/hr

Bookkeeping Services:

Full-Service Bookkeeping	$ 200/mo.
Part-Time Service	$ 25/hr

Payroll Services

Setup Fees	$ 225
10 employees or less	$75/mo
Over 10 employees	$200/mo

Other Services

Information System Set Up	$ 75/hr
Consulting	$ 85/hr
Comprehensive Business Plan	$2,500
Auditing	$ 150/hr

Appendix 4:
Plan for a Restaurant

Ling Garden Restaurant

112 Main Street, Milford CT 06340

(203) 555-1234

Ling's Investment Group, Inc.

Principles: Samuel Liang

Lin Tang

November 15, 1998

Table of Contents

*Titles in boldface included as examples for financial data.

Summary

On September 30, Samuel Liang signed a lease agreement to rent the premises located at 112 Main Street, Milford, Connecticut, from New England Savings Bank to open the Ling Garden Restaurant with an option to purchase for $500,000.

Due to the collapse of New England Savings Bank in July, the Federal Deposit Insurance Corporation now holds the property and has offered it for sale to Samuel Liang for $280,000.

Statement of Purchase

Samuel Liang is seeking a loan of $224,000 to purchase the land and building located at 112 Main Street, Milford, Connecticut, where he presently leases an existing, fully equipped restaurant named Ling Garden Restaurant.

The funds sought will result in a great increase in fixed assets. Most important of all is to ensure Ling Garden Restaurant can continue to provide a unique upscale cuisine in a pleasant atmosphere.

I. THE BUSINESS

A. Description

The Ling Garden Restaurant is an upscale restaurant featuring Chinese and Japanese cuisine. The restaurant seats 100 in the dining room. An etched glass wall encloses a second dining area of 120 seats, which is used as an alternate dining room or as a banquet room.

Dining tables are strategically placed to give each group privacy, but allow for maximum seating in the space available. The dining area is aesthetically appealing due to its newness, spaciousness, and cleanliness. It is attractively decorated with Chinese screens and decorations. Extensive lighting is provided from a bank of windows along the dining room wall. Tables, chairs, and benches appear new. The cleanliness of the restaurant is also evident in the restrooms.

In addition, there is a bar and lounge, which seats 120. It is furnished with a 20-ft. bar, several tables, chairs, and bar stools. Future plans include developing this area as a distinctly separate American pub.

Takeout service and catering are also available.

The restaurant is owned and operated by Ling's Investment Group, Inc. The principals are Samuel Liang and Lin Tang. The Ling Garden Restaurant has been operational since January 1993. The building was renovated by the owners in order to create a more upscale environment.

In a restaurant review in *The Day* in February 1993, the Ling Garden Restaurant was awarded three stars out of four with praises of ". . . absolutely delicious . . . positively wonderful . . . perfectly cooked . . ."

B. Customer Base

The Ling Garden attracts a variety of customers, including luncheon clientele from the surrounding offices and businesses, families, couples, parties, and banquets. Customers reside or work in Milford, New London, Mystic, Waterford, and North Stonington. Commuters pick up dinner on the way home. The dinner clientele include guests from the four area motels, U.S. Navy submarine base families and individuals, couples, families, parties, and banquets.

C. Location

The Ling Garden Restaurant is located at 112 Main Street between Milford and Mystic. The site, located approximately one mile northeast of the intersection with Route 16, is surrounded by the New City Office Park complex, an open grass lot.

The building has been utilized as a restaurant since its construction in 1955. A paved parking lot and concrete sidewalks are located on the north, west, and south sides of the building. The well-lit parking lot allows convenient, unobstructed access from the street.

The average daily traffic count for this particular section of Route 184 is 17,300 cars and is expected to increase by at least 3% next year. Several factors contribute to the traffic count. Route 184 is an alternate route to Foxwood's Casino and Resort (approximately 20,000–40,000 visitors per day). A new Wal-Mart store opened within one half-mile in October 1994. Route 184 is a main commuter feeder to/from Milford, New London, Ledyard, N. Stonington, and parts of Mystic.

The town of Milford is currently spending over one million dollars to expand the water and sewer systems along Route 184. The town is working with business owners to minimize construction impact on the affected businesses.

D. Operations

The Ling Garden is open seven days a week from 11:00 A.M. to 10:00 P.M. Monday through Thursday, 11:00 A.M. to 11:00 P.M. Friday and Saturday,

and noon through 10:00 P.M. on Sunday. The restaurant is closed for Thanksgiving.

E. Market

All of the present clientele have been attracted by either word-of-mouth advertising or the location. Due to the uncertainty of the building ownership and the potential to be evicted with only 30 days' notice by any new landlord, the owners were reluctant to conduct extensive marketing efforts. However, if the sale occurs according to plan, the owners will launch a wide-reaching marketing campaign. National statistics show that the top five chain restaurants spend an average of 2.8% of sales on advertising. The anticipated expenditures of the owners for this area are 2% over the next year.

Additional advertising will be achieved in *The Weekly* and *The Tuna* newspapers, more informative Yellow Pages ads, direct mail coupons, menus distributed to four nearby motels, and promotion by a local radio auction (WSUB). It is expected that this approach will target local families, tourists, banquet patrons, and business travelers.

The marketing campaign will emphasize the availability of sushi and sashimi. These menu items are so unique that one must otherwise travel to Providence or Hartford to obtain them. The menu also offers healthy steamed selections that have a lower fat content. The menu will also be Asian in character, featuring Thai, Vietnamese, and Indonesian, as well as Chinese and Japanese.

With their ownership, Ling's Investment Group, Inc., is interested in making some additional enhancements to the property. Development of the present bar and lounge into a new American-style pub will attract a different type of clientele from the restaurant. It is anticipated that the casual atmosphere of the pub will draw more business travelers, tourists, and upscale couples.

National expenditure trends show that items most affected by increased household income include foods prepared away from home. Households with incomes between $20,000 and $30,000 spend just 2% less than average on food away from home. Households with incomes of $30,000 to $40,000 spend 25% more than average on food during out-of-town trips, at restaurants and carry-outs. Forty-six percent above average is spent for food away from home in households with incomes between $40,000 and $50,000. Households with incomes greater than $50,000 spend 96% more than the average household on food eaten away from home. Married couples account for 55% of all households and those without children at home devote 44 percent of their food dollars to restaurants, take-outs, and other food prepared away from home. Married

couples with children spend 41% on restaurants, take-outs, and food prepared away from home.

National spending patterns are important when evaluating the local demographics of the surrounding towns that frequent the Ling Garden. Table 1 displays incomes and ages of households from the neighboring towns. Assuming that national trends are applicable to this area, then it is apparent that households in the surrounding towns will mature into age groups that spend higher than average amounts on food away from home. In addition, household incomes in the surrounding neighborhood are also above average in amounts spent on food away from home.

With a planned marketing campaign, increased tourist trade, neighboring residential areas representing groups (age, income) that spend higher percentages of income on food away from home, the prognosis for steadily increasing revenues is very promising.

TABLE 1.
INCOME AND AGES IN NEIGHBORING TOWNS

TOWN	Present	Under 25	25–44	45–64	65+	<$10K	$10–25K	$25–50K	>$50K
East Lyme	13,488	34.4	30.5	23.5	11.5	6.6	16.4	35.2	41.9
Milford	30,478	42.4	34.6	14.2	8.8	8.7	37.9	41.3	22.1
Ledyard	12,110	40.4	31.0	21.4	5.2	3.2	14.4	40.0	42.4
Gales Ferry	2,558	43.8	30.4	20.1	5.7	4.3	12.6	36.4	46.7
New London	23,943	38.2	33.1	15.0	13.9	19.4	29.2	34.6	19.8
Mystic	8,027	32.4	31.3	22.0	14.4	5.7	19.3	37.7	37.2
Old Mystic	259	31.4	25.2	23.0	17.3	3.8	20.2	34.6	41.3
N. Stonington	4,271	37.8	30.0	23.3	8.8	6.7	18.3	46.3	38.7
Stonington	10,771	31.5	29.5	22.1	16.9	8.6	21.7	37.7	31.8
Waterford	19,576	30.9	29.9	22.1	16.2	8.7	19.3	38.9	33.1
Quaker Hill	4,052	41.5	26.5	19.0	13.1	8.2	22.1	33.2	36.7

F. Competitors

There are several direct competitors. Geographically, the closest Chinese restaurant is the Asian Kitchen. It is located approximately one mile away on Route 16. This restaurant appears small since most of the parking area is in front of the building and it is placed back from the roadway. Inside the restaurant are two dining areas divided into smoking and non-smoking sections. The smoking section has five tables, which seat 25 people, while the non-smoking section seats 20 people at four tables. The exterior of the building is plain. The interior decor is red and black with lanterns, fans, framed tapestries, and Chinese wall hangings. The two dining rooms are narrow and not as bright. Also open 7 days a week, the hours are shorter than the Ling Garden hours.

An analysis of the menu prices for similar items at both restaurants reveals that neither restaurant is consistently higher or lower. The prices vary up to $1.25 depending on the menu item.

A second direct competitor of a Chinese restaurant with table service is Polynesian Paradise, located five miles southeast from the Ling Garden. The one-story building is surrounded on three sides by its parking lot. The restaurant is sectioned into three areas: the bar and lounge, and two dining areas. The dining areas have 16 booths and six tables, which seat approximately 100 patrons. A metal serving table on which Sunday brunches are displayed is in the center of the first dining area. It sits empty in the dining room when not in use. The decor is black, red, and green with mirrors and other Chinese ornaments. There are no windows except those in the front door.

A comparison of the menu shows that the prices are less than at the Ling Garden. An additional difference between the two restaurants is the Sunday brunch for $7.99 for adults/$4.50 for children.

Indirect competitors include G. Willikers, the Golden Cup Restaurant, Rosie's Diner, India Mahal, Linda's Spa, and the fast-food chains on Route 16.

G. Management/Personnel

Ling's Investment Group, Inc., is the owner and operator of the Ling Garden Restaurant. The principals are Samuel Liang as President and Treasurer, and Lin Tang as Vice President and Secretary.

The professional support team includes George Mason (accountant), Peter Mitchell (attorney), Robert Gray (banker), Jeff Baker (insurance agent), and Wallace Long (restaurant business consultant).

The personnel at the restaurant include Samuel Liang as owner/manager, Lin Tang as assistant manager, five serving and kitchen staff, and several part-time workers.

It should be noted that Ling's Investment Group, Inc., is committed to its business. Throughout the uncertainty of the ownership during the transition from New England Savings Bank to FDIC they continued to pay rent even though this is not always done by other companies in similar situations. It should also be noted that the discussed mortgage payment is even less than the rent presently being paid.

II. FINANCIAL PLAN

A. Application and Expected Effect of Loan

The $224,000 will be used solely to purchase the land and building at 112 Main Street, Milford, CT, where the applicant's business is presently located.

As this business plan indicates, sales will start to increase significantly after the acquisition of the subject real estate. Due to the precarious nature of the applicant's tenancy during the period of F.D.I.C. ownership, the applicant has recently done little to aggressively promote his business. The specifics of the advertising and promotion campaign are contained elsewhere in this business plan; however, it should be noted that approximately $60,000 has been budgeted for the advertising and promotional campaign during the first year of property ownership. An additional $600 has been budgeted for the acquisition of a fax machine, permitting menus to be faxed out and orders faxed in. Both of these cost items will be financed from cash flow.

B. SOURCES OF DOWN PAYMENT TO PURCHASE PROPERTY

Down Payment Held by F.D.I.C.	$14,000.00
Source: Personal Funds	
Rental Security Deposit Held by F.D.I.C.	$ 5,000.00
Sale of 50% Interest of Business Known as Ling Garden of Mystic (see copy of of purchase intent letter attached)	$50,000.00
To Be Contributed from Personal Funds	$ 400.00
TOTAL = 25% of Acquisition Price	$70,000.00

C. Sales Projections

The following assumptions were used to build the financial projections: An average gross profit percentage of 68.5% was utilized throughout the sales projections. This is a conservative percentage based on statistical data as provided by the National Restaurant Association (NRA) for the category "full menu, table service-ethnic." Although it is slightly more than that based on actual operating results since opening, it is nonetheless realistic in light of other assumptions that support an increased sales volume. Robert Morris Associates competitive historical data was also consulted; however, its category "Retailers-Restaurants" was for all types of restaurants, not the specific category data as provided by NRA.

It was assumed that a mortgage commitment would be given in December, and that a closing on the property would occur by no later than next February.

The applicant/business owner will commence an aggressive advertising campaign upon receipt of the mortgage commitment. As otherwise noted, advertisements promoting the healthy benefits of the sushi menu will be run. Additionally, advertising and promotion will be done on a continual basis to promote the usage of the restaurant banquet and party facilities as well as to promote the projected increased bar business.

Finally, the ability of customers to utilize the restaurant's fax machine to be acquired to send menus and receive orders will be extensively promoted as well.

D. Operating Expenses

The advertising and promotion budget reflects both the start of an immediate aggressive advertising and promotional campaign as well as the assumption that Yellow Pages advertising will increase in July, upon the issuance of the latest telephone directory.

Gross wages, exclusive of officer's salaries, is assumed to be in line with NRA statistical data in this category.

Total payroll tax expense is assumed to be 15% of gross wages paid.

Advertising and promotion expense is budgeted at $1,000 per month for the first 6 months; it is assumed a $500 per month increase would occur in July, due to the increased Yellow Pages advertising at that time.

Rent expense assumes a late February closing on the property acquisition, after which the corporation would commence leasing the real estate from the applicant at a fair market rental of $2,200 per month.

Connecticut corporation income tax is calculated at an assumed rate of 11.5% of net taxable income.

I. SOURCES AND APPLICATIONS OF FUNDING

Source
Bank Mortgage Loan $224,000
Application
Purchase Land and Building $224,000

To be secured by real estate being purchased
Signatures of the principals
Samuel Liang
Jody (Muoi Thi) Cheung
SBA Guarantee

K. BREAK-EVEN ANALYSIS

	9 Months Ended 9/30/98	1st Year 1999	2nd Year 2000	3rd Year 2001
Sales	$221,718	$438,000	$500,000	$575,000
Cost of Sales	85,480	137,970	157,500	181,125
Gross Profit	136,238	300,030	342,500	393,875
Fixed Expenses	61,100	97,634	100,000	110,000
Net Profit (Loss)	18,234	40,593	45,500	52,325
Gross Profit Percent	61.4%	68.5%	68.5%	68.5%

We Have
EVERYTHING!

Everything® **After College Book**
$12.95, 1-55850-847-3

Everything® **American History Book**
$12.95, 1-58062-531-2

Everything® **Angels Book**
$12.95, 1-58062-398-0

Everything® **Anti-Aging Book**
$12.95, 1-58062-565-7

Everything® **Astrology Book**
$12.95, 1-58062-062-0

Everything® **Baby Names Book**
$12.95, 1-55850-655-1

Everything® **Baby Shower Book**
$12.95, 1-58062-305-0

Everything® **Baby's First Food Book**
$12.95, 1-58062-512-6

Everything® **Baby's First Year Book**
$12.95, 1-58062-581-9

Everything® **Barbeque Cookbook**
$12.95, 1-58062-316-6

Everything® **Bartender's Book**
$9.95, 1-55850-536-9

Everything® **Bedtime Story Book**
$12.95, 1-58062-147-3

Everything® **Bicycle Book**
$12.00, 1-55850-706-X

Everything® **Build Your Own Home Page**
$12.95, 1-58062-339-5

Everything® **Business Planning Book**
$12.95, 1-58062-491-X

Everything® **Casino Gambling Book**
$12.95, 1-55850-762-0

Everything® **Cat Book**
$12.95, 1-55850-710-8

Everything® **Chocolate Cookbook**
$12.95, 1-58062-405-7

Everything® **Christmas Book**
$15.00, 1-55850-697-7

Everything® **Civil War Book**
$12.95, 1-58062-366-2

Everything® **College Survival Book**
$12.95, 1-55850-720-5

Everything® **Computer Book**
$12.95, 1-58062-401-4

Everything® **Cookbook**
$14.95, 1-58062-400-6

Everything® **Cover Letter Book**
$12.95, 1-58062-312-3

Everything® **Crossword and Puzzle Book**
$12.95, 1-55850-764-7

Everything® **Dating Book**
$12.95, 1-58062-185-6

Everything® **Dessert Book**
$12.95, 1-55850-717-5

Everything® **Digital Photography Book**
$12.95, 1-58062-574-6

Everything® **Dog Book**
$12.95, 1-58062-144-9

Everything® **Dreams Book**
$12.95, 1-55850-806-6

Everything® **Etiquette Book**
$12.95, 1-55850-807-4

Everything® **Fairy Tales Book**
$12.95, 1-58062-546-0

Everything® **Family Tree Book**
$12.95, 1-55850-763-9

Everything® **Fly-Fishing Book**
$12.95, 1-58062-148-1

Everything® **Games Book**
$12.95, 1-55850-643-8

Everything® **Get-A-Job Book**
$12.95, 1-58062-223-2

Everything® **Get Published Book**
$12.95, 1-58062-315-8

Everything® **Get Ready for Baby Book**
$12.95, 1-55850-844-9

Everything® **Ghost Book**
$12.95, 1-58062-533-9

Everything® **Golf Book**
$12.95, 1-55850-814-7

Everything® **Grammar and Style Book**
$12.95, 1-58062-573-8

Everything® **Guide to Las Vegas**
$12.95, 1-58062-438-3

Everything® **Guide to New York City**
$12.95, 1-58062-314-X

Everything® **Guide to Walt Disney World®,
Universal Studios®, and
Greater Orlando, 2nd Edition**
$12.95, 1-58062-404-9

Everything® **Guide to Washington D.C.**
$12.95, 1-58062-313-1

Everything® **Guitar Book**
$12.95, 1-58062-555-X

Everything® **Herbal Remedies Book**
$12.95, 1-58062-331-X

Everything® **Home-Based Business Book**
$12.95, 1-58062-364-6

Everything® **Homebuying Book**
$12.95, 1-58062-074-4

Everything® **Homeselling Book**
$12.95, 1-58062-304-2

**For more information, or to order, call 800-872-5627
or visit everything.com**
Adams Media Corporation, 57 Littlefield Street, Avon, MA 02322

Visit us at everything.com

Everything® **Home Improvement Book**
$12.95, 1-55850-718-3

Everything® **Horse Book**
$12.95, 1-58062-564-9

Everything® **Hot Careers Book**
$12.95, 1-58062-486-3

Everything® **Internet Book**
$12.95, 1-58062-073-6

Everything® **Investing Book**
$12.95, 1-58062-149-X

Everything® **Jewish Wedding Book**
$12.95, 1-55850-801-5

Everything® **Job Interviews Book**
$12.95, 1-58062-493-6

Everything® **Lawn Care Book**
$12.95, 1-58062-487-1

Everything® **Leadership Book**
$12.95, 1-58062-513-4

Everything® **Learning Spanish Book**
$12.95, 1-58062-575-4

Everything® **Low-Fat High-Flavor
    Cookbook**
$12.95, 1-55850-802-3

Everything® **Magic Book**
$12.95, 1-58062-418-9

Everything® **Managing People Book**
$12.95, 1-58062-577-0

Everything® **Microsoft® Word 2000 Book**
$12.95, 1-58062-306-9

Everything® **Money Book**
$12.95, 1-58062-145-7

Everything® **Mother Goose Book**
$12.95, 1-58062-490-1

Everything® **Mutual Funds Book**
$12.95, 1-58062-419-7

Everything® **One-Pot Cookbook**
$12.95, 1-58062-186-4

Everything® **Online Business Book**
$12.95, 1-58062-320-4

Everything® **Online Genealogy Book**
$12.95, 1-58062-402-2

Everything® **Online Investing Book**
$12.95, 1-58062-338-7

Everything® **Online Job Search Book**
$12.95, 1-58062-365-4

Everything® **Pasta Book**
$12.95, 1-55850-719-1

Everything® **Pregnancy Book**
$12.95, 1-58062-146-5

Everything® **Pregnancy Organizer**
$15.00, 1-58062-336-0

Everything® **Project Management Book**
$12.95, 1-58062-583-5

Everything® **Puppy Book**
$12.95, 1-58062-576-2

Everything® **Quick Meals Cookbook**
$12.95, 1-58062-488-X

Everything® **Resume Book**
$12.95, 1-58062-311-5

Everything® **Romance Book**
$12.95, 1-58062-566-5

Everything® **Sailing Book**
$12.95, 1-58062-187-2

Everything® **Saints Book**
$12.95, 1-58062-534-7

Everything® **Selling Book**
$12.95, 1-58062-319-0

Everything® **Spells and Charms Book**
$12.95, 1-58062-532-0

Everything® **Stress Management Book**
$12.95, 1-58062-578-9

Everything® **Study Book**
$12.95, 1-55850-615-2

Everything® **Tall Tales, Legends, and
    Outrageous Lies Book**
$12.95, 1-58062-514-2

Everything® **Tarot Book**
$12.95, 1-58062-191-0

Everything® **Time Management Book**
$12.95, 1-58062-492-8

Everything® **Toasts Book**
$12.95, 1-58062-189-9

Everything® **Total Fitness Book**
$12.95, 1-58062-318-2

Everything® **Trivia Book**
$12.95, 1-58062-143-0

Everything® **Tropical Fish Book**
$12.95, 1-58062-343-3

Everything® **Vitamins, Minerals, and
    Nutritional Supplements
    Book**
$12.95, 1-58062-496-0

Everything® **Wedding Book, 2nd Edition**
$12.95, 1-58062-190-2

Everything® **Wedding Checklist**
$7.95, 1-58062-456-1

Everything® **Wedding Etiquette Book**
$7.95, 1-58062-454-5

Everything® **Wedding Organizer**
$15.00, 1-55850-828-7

Everything® **Wedding Shower Book**
$7.95, 1-58062-188-0

Everything® **Wedding Vows Book**
$7.95, 1-58062-455-3

Everything® **Wine Book**
$12.95, 1-55850-808-2

Everything® **World War II Book**
$12.95, 1-58062-572-X

Everything® is a registered trademark of Adams Media Corporation.

**For more information, or to order, call 800-872-5627
or visit everything.com**
Adams Media Corporation, 57 Littlefield Street, Avon, MA 02322

We Have

EVERYTHING KIDS'

Everything® Kids' Baseball Book
$6.95, 1-58062-688-2

Everything® Kids' Joke Book
$6.95, 1-58062-686-6

Everything® Kids' Mazes Book
$6.95, 1-58062-558-4

Everything® Kids' Money Book
$6.95, 1-58062-685-8

Everything® Kids' Nature Book
$6.95, 1-58062-684-X

Everything® Kids' Online Book
$9.95, 1-58062-394-8

Everything® Kids' Puzzle Book
$6.95, 1-58062-687-4

Everything® Kids' Science Experiments Book
$6.95, 1-58062-557-6

Everything® Kids' Space Book
$9.95, 1-58062-395-6

Everything® Kids' Witches and Wizards Book
$9.95, 1-58062-396-4

Available wherever books are sold!

For more information, or to order,
call 800-872-5627 or visit everything.com

Adams Media Corporation, 57 Littlefield Street, Avon, MA 02322

Everything® is a registered trademark of Adams Media Corporation.